Wood Whimsies

Making Bead & Dowel Toys

▲

Lee Lindeman & Patricia Harste

Sterling Publishing Co., Inc.   New York

We would like to thank George Ross for the beautiful color photographs. Stephen Donelian for the picture-perfect black and white photos, Woman's World for permission to reprint U.S.S. Playtime, Tumbleweed Junction, and Down on the Farm. Plaid Enterprises for supplying Folk Art Acrylic Color, and WesTrim Crafts for beads, trims, and notions.

Metric Equivalents

INCHES TO MILLIMETRES AND CENTIMETRES

MM—millimetres   CM—centimetres

Inches	MM	CM	Inches	CM	Inches	CM
⅛	3	0.3	9	22.9	30	76.2
¼	6	0.6	10	25.4	31	78.7
⅜	10	1.0	11	27.9	32	81.3
½	13	1.3	12	30.5	33	83.8
⅝	16	1.6	13	33.0	34	86.4
¾	19	1.9	14	35.6	35	88.9
⅞	22	2.2	15	38.1	36	91.4
1	25	2.5	16	40.6	37	94.0
1¼	32	3.2	17	43.2	38	96.5
1½	38	3.8	18	45.7	39	99.1
1¾	44	4.4	19	48.3	40	101.6
2	51	5.1	20	50.8	41	104.1
2½	64	6.4	21	53.3	42	106.7
2	76	7.6	22	55.9	43	109.2
3½	89	8.9	23	58.4	44	111.8
4	102	10.2	24	61.0	45	114.3
4½	114	11.4	25	63.5	46	116.8
5	127	12.7	26	66.0	47	119.4
6	152	15.2	27	68.6	48	121.9
7	178	17.8	28	71.1	49	124.5
8	203	20.3	29	73.7	50	127.0

Library of Congress Cataloging-in-Publication Data

Lindeman, Lee.
    Wood whimsies : making bead & dowel toys / Lee Lindeman and Patricia Harste.
        p.   cm.
    Includes index.
    1. Wooden toy making.   I. Harste, Patricia.   II. Title.
TT174.5.W6L56   1992
745.592—dc20   91-39589
                                                                                CIP

10 9 8 7 6 5 4 3 2 1

Published in 1992 by Sterling Publishing Company, Inc.
387 Park Avenue South, New York, N.Y. 10016
© 1992 by Lee LIndeman and Patricia Harste
Distributed in Canada by Sterling Publishing
℅ Canadian Manda Group, P.O. Box 920, Station U
Toronto, Ontario, Canada M8Z 5P9
Distributed in Great Britain and Europe by Cassell PLC
Villiers House, 41/47 Strand, London WC2N 5JE, England
Distributed in Australia by Capricorn Link Ltd.
P.O. Box 665, Lane Cove, NSW 2066
Manufactured in the United States of America

Sterling ISBN 0-8069-8390-6

Contents

Color section follows page 32.

Introduction

BEFORE YOU BEGIN

To save time, read through the project directions to familiarize yourself with them and to enable you to gather all the necessary materials, tools, and equipment you will need. The General Directions illustrate the techniques used to create a Wood Whimsy project.

MATERIALS

The materials list for each project is always presented in the same order making it an easy reference when gathering or shopping for the materials. Beads are listed from the largest to the smallest. We used Wes-Trim beads (as well as nailheads, sequins, rhinestones, and pompons); however, to help you in your selection of these items, we have included a Bead Comparison Chart.

Dowels are listed from the smallest diameter to the largest and lumber from the thinnest to the thickest. The remaining items listed under the wood heading (axle pegs, ice-cream sticks, toothpicks, etc.) follow the lumber and are always presented in the same order. If you have dowels but are unsure of their size, refer to the Bead Comparison Chart.

Itemized under the hardware heading are wire brads, wood screws, and nails. These are listed from the smallest size to the largest.

Paint colors are listed in the order in which they were used.

Fabrics and trims, plus the items listed under the miscellaneous heading, are also presented in the order in which they are used. Fabrics and trims are commonly found in craft and fabric stores. Miscellaneous items can be purchased at art, hardware, and grocery stores, but you probably have most of these items on hand already.

Synthetic suede was used for ears, manes, tails, robes, and the like, because of its rich color and texture. Bags of suede scraps containing assorted sizes and colors are available by mail order, but you can substitute felt or some other synthetic suede.

As with synthetic suede, feel free to substitute when using embellishments. If you have blue ribbon on hand, use it instead of pink. If you want to change paint colors to match embellishments or to suit your own taste, please do so.

DOWEL ESTIMATES

Dowel lengths were calculated by adding $1/8''$ waste for each cut plus another $2''$ added to the overall length as a safety margin for handling. The total was then rounded off to the next full inch.

WOOD

Lattice and plywood estimates allow for waste. The thickness and width dimensions of lumber are nominal. For example, $1/4 \times 5 1/4$ clear pine lattice actually measures $7/32'' \times 5 3/16''$.

TOOLS AND EQUIPMENT

Here are the tools and equipment you will need to make the Wood Whimsy projects. The list of additional tools and equipment includes items that are used less frequently.

For All Projects

small, sharp scissors: for cutting tagboard circles and other small items

white tagboard: for covering bead holes

tacky glue: for adhering paper, fabric, trims, and painted wood

wood glue: for adhering raw wood to raw wood

small dish: for holding glues

toothpicks: for applying glue to small areas

ice-cream sticks: for applying glue to large areas

pen with cap or pencil: for holding bead head while painting

tall glass: for holding pen or pencil with painted bead head

no. 000 round watercolor brush: for painting small details

no. 1 flat brush: for painting bodies and medium-size areas

1/2'' flat brush: for painting large areas

paint palette or small ceramic dish: for holding paint

jar and water: for washing brushes

4

paper towelling: for drying brushes

flexible ruler: for accurate measuring around and across dowels.

We recommend the Schaedler Precision Ruler. It is available in commercial art departments of art supply stores.

straightedge ruler: for measuring flat items and as a guide when drawing straight lines

pencil: for marking measurements and tracing patterns

safety glasses: for eye protection

wood vise: for holding pieces securely while sawing or drilling

coping saw: for cutting lengths and angles of dowels

scroll saw: for cutting lengths of dowels and patterns from lumber

medium and fine-grit sandpapers: for sanding edges and surfaces smooth

whittling knife: for whittling areas to flatten, routing grooves, and cutting beads in half

hand drill: for drilling holes. An adjustable-speed power drill can be used

drill bits: 1/16", 3/32", 1/8", 3/16", and 1/4"

tracing paper: for tracing patterns

dressmaker's carbon: for transferring patterns onto fabric

carbon paper: for transferring patterns onto wood

masking tape: for holding patterns in place while they are being transferred

waterbase varnish: for protecting painted finishes

Additional Tools and Equipment

hammer: for driving brads and nails, and cutting beads in half

ice pick: for piercing holes and making indentations in wood

needle-nose pliers: for cutting and bending wire

medium-size scissors: for cutting large items from paper or fabric

pencil compass: for describing circles

pinking shears: for making decorative edging

screwdrivers: for driving screws (use a screwdriver that matches the screw head type)

art knife: for cutting small areas from pattern pieces and for making slits in dowels

SAFETY PRECAUTIONS

- Wood whimsies are intended for age 7 and up.
- To protect your eyes, always wear safety glasses when sawing, drilling, whittling, or sanding.
- Always wear short sleeves when using tools.
- Never wear rings, bracelets, or a watch when using tools.
- Always keep long hair tied back and out of the way when using tools.
- To prevent interruptions when using power tools, take the phone off the hook and make sure small children and pets are safely out of the way.
- Read the General Directions before you begin.

LEFT AND RIGHT

Unless otherwise stated, left and right always refer to the Wood Whimsy character's left and right side. The left and right of all other items is how you view them on your work surface.

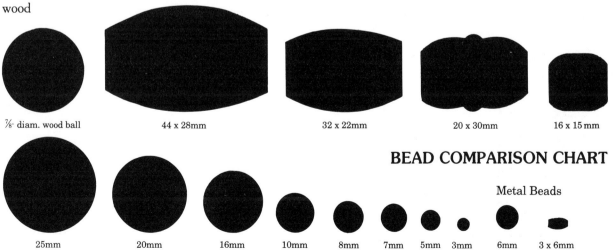

| ⅞" diam. wood ball | 44 x 28mm | 32 x 22mm | 20 x 30mm | 16 x 15 mm |

BEAD COMPARISON CHART

Metal Beads

| 25mm | 20mm | 16mm | 10mm | 8mm | 7mm | 5mm | 3mm | 6mm | 3 x 6mm |

5

General Directions

COVERING BEAD HOLES

1. To cover the bead hole of a bead head or body, use small, sharp scissors to cut a circle from white tagboard that is slightly larger than the size of the bead hole. (See 1.)

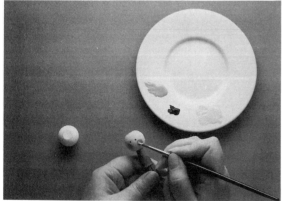

1

2. Using a toothpick, apply a narrow bead of tacky glue around the rim of the bead hole.
3. Adhere tagboard circle to bead hole.
4. Always allow glue to dry thoroughly before proceeding to the next step.

PAINTING

1. To paint features, place bead head snugly onto the end of a pen cap or pencil. (See 2.)
2. Stand pen, or pencil, in a tall glass until paint is dry.
3. Always allow paint to dry thoroughly before proceeding to the next paint color or the next step.
4. When assembling and painting is completed, apply one or two coats of waterbase varnish to all painted

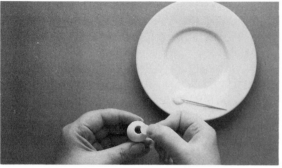

2

areas before applying hair and trims. This will protect the paint and prevent chipping.

MEASURING ARM AND LEG POSITIONS

1. Draw a line down the length of the body to indicate center front. (See 3.)
2. To determine arm or leg positions, measure and mark from each side of the center line.

3

DRILLING ARM, TAIL, AND LEG HOLES

1. To drill an arm or a tail hole into a dowel body, place body in the wood vise so the marked position is facing up and is centered from left to right in the vise.
2. Unless otherwise directed, drill the hole with the bit perpendicular to the body.
3. To drill leg holes into a dowel body, place body in the wood vise so all of the marked positions are facing up and are centered from left to right in the vise.
4. Drill each hole at the angle indicated in the directions, making sure the bit is parallel with the flat (front and rear) ends of the body.
5. To drill a tail hole into a bead body, place body in the wood vise so the marked position is facing up and is centered from left to right in the vise. (See 4.)
6. Drill the hole with the bit perpendicular to the body.

SANDING

For best results, after cutting dowels or lumber, sand all surfaces, first with medium- and then with fine-grit sandpaper.

WHITTLING

After measuring and marking the arm, leg, neck, or head positions on a dowel or bead body, you must

4

whittle to flatten the area specified in the directions so the part that will be adhered to it (arms, legs, neck, or head) will lie close to the body. Whittling also increases the size of the area glued, making a much stronger bond.

Depending on the pose of a Wood Whimsy character, the directions for other parts cut from dowelling, such as arms, legs, air tanks, also specify whittling so they can lie close together, flat to the work surface, or close to the body. There are also instances where the directions specify whittling to flatten areas of beads or wooden eggs.

1. To flatten arm, leg, neck, or head positions on a body, hold the body securely on the work surface with one hand. (See 5.)
2. Using a whittling knife, and working away from you, carefully whittle off wood, using firm, short strokes.

5

3. To flatten area of upper arm, hold completed arm securely on the work surface with one hand. (See 6.)

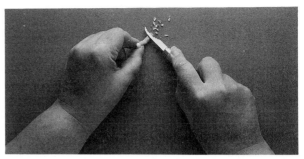

6

4. Using a whittling knife, and working away from you, carefully whittle off wood, using firm, short strokes.

KEEPING TRACK OF PARTS

Each Wood Whimsy is made of several small parts. To prevent confusion, after a part is cut, use a pencil to make an identifying mark. Use R for right, L for left, A for arm, LG for leg, U for upper, LW for lower, H for hip cut, AK for ankle cut, E for elbow cut, and N for neck cut. When the Wood Whimsy is painted, the marks will be covered over.

MEASURING AND SAWING ANGLE CUTS

1. To indicate angle of an elbow, knee, or combination (shoulder/elbow for example) cut, measure and mark from right end of dowel and tick with a pencil.
2. Rotate dowelling so pencil mark is away from you, then measure and mark from left end. (See 7.)
3. To saw an elbow, knee, or combination angle cut, place marked dowel in the wood vise so end of dowel is angled up and both marks are parallel with the front of the vise. (See 8.)
4. Using the coping saw, saw from mark to mark with the blade level and parallel with the front of the vise.
5. To indicate angle of a single shoulder, ankle, knee, or hip cut, place arm or leg on work surface so the previously cut angled end is at top. (See 9.)

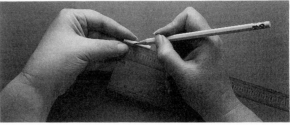

7

7

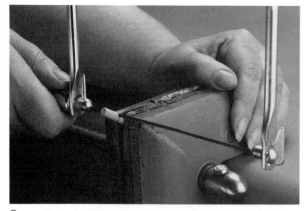

8

9

10

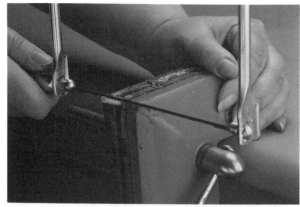

11

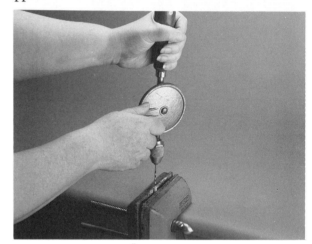

12

6. Rotate arm or leg so the face of the cut (shown darkened) is facing up. At opposite end, measure and mark from flat end.

7. Using a coping saw, cut angle. (See 11.) The face of each cut will be facing in opposite directions.

11. To saw a single shoulder, ankle, knee, or hip cut, place arm or leg in the wood vise so end of dowel is angled up, mark is at the bottom and is parallel with the front of the vise. (See 11.)

12. Using the coping saw, saw from edge of dowel to mark with the blade level and parallel with the front of the vise.

DRILLING HAND HOLES AND ATTACHING BEAD HANDS

1. To drill a hand hole in the lower end of an arm to accommodate a bead hand, place arm in the wood vise

so the end specified in the directions is facing up. (See 12.)

2. Using a ³⁄₃₂″ bit, drill a ⅛″-deep hole into the center of the arm with the bit perpendicular to the dowel.

3. For hands, cut ³⁄₈″ off each end of a round toothpick, then cut the toothpick in half. Wood-glue the tapered end of each toothpick into the bead size specified.

4. Trim toothpick ends so only ⅛″ extends beyond hole. Wood-glue ends into holes at flat ends of arms.

CUTTING BEADS IN HALF

1. To cut a bead in half, place bead, hole side up, on work surface. (See 13.)

2. Place center of whittling knife blade over center of hole (unless otherwise directed).

3. Using a hammer, firmly tap center top of blade.

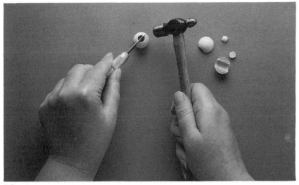

13

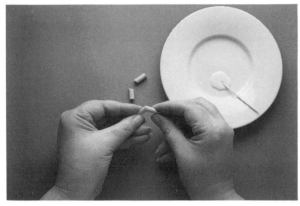

14

GLUING JOINTS TOGETHER

1. To complete an arm or a leg where you reverse the cuts so the joint forms a right angle, use a toothpick to apply a small amount of wood glue to the angled end of the upper arm or leg. (See 14.)

2. Adhere the angled end of a lower arm or leg to the angled end of the upper part, making sure the joint is crooked.

3. Always allow glue to dry thoroughly before painting or proceeding to next step.

1. To complete an arm or a leg where you do not reverse the cuts so the joint forms a more open angle, use a toothpick to apply a small amount of wood glue to the flat end of the upper arm or leg. (See 15.)

2. Adhere the angled end of a lower arm or leg to the flat end of the upper part making sure the joint is crooked.

3. Always allow glue to dry thoroughly before painting or proceeding to next step.

BALANCING

Some Wood Whimsy characters require precise bal-

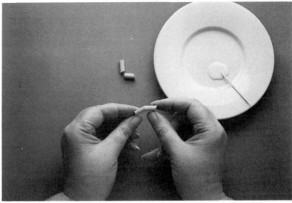

15

ancing in order to stand up unaided. If one of the characters you've made needs balancing, very thin wedges cut from an ice-cream stick can be tacky-glued to the bottom of one or both feet until the character stands unaided. Repaint, using appropriate color.

MAKING PATTERNS

All patterns in this book are actual-size. Use tracing paper and pencil to trace outlines as well as designs, positioning dots, etc. Most patterns in the book are complete.

To complete a half-pattern, trace the one half of the half-pattern shown in the book onto tracing paper. Flop tracing over to reverse it, align dashed line of tracing with dashed line of pattern in book, and trace half-pattern again to complete the pattern.

To complete a two-part pattern, trace both pattern halves onto separate sheets of tracing paper, then tape the two halves together, matching the dotted lines.

For patterns with long straight edges (such as the tepee in Project 6) use a straightedge ruler as a guide to ensure uniform lines.

TRANSFERRING PATTERNS

To transfer a pattern onto fabric, tape the fabric onto your work surface. Place dressmaker's carbon (carbon side down) over the fabric and tape it in place. Place pattern tracing over the dressmaker's carbon and tape it in place. Retrace lines and marks with a pencil to transfer the pattern.

To transfer a pattern onto lumber, place carbon paper (carbon side down) over the lumber and tape it in place. Place tracing over the carbon and tape it in place. Retrace lines and positioning dots with a pencil.

9

1 · Men on the Moon!

MATERIALS

Beads

one white 44mm × 28mm large-hole wood bead
five white 20mm large-hole wood beads
two white 10mm regular-hole wood beads
eight white 8mm regular-hole wood beads

Wood

28″ length of ¼″ dowelling
8″ length of ⅝″ dowelling
5⅜″ length of 1¼″ dowelling
48″ length of ¼ × 5¼ clear pine lattice
twelve ice-cream sticks
eight round toothpicks

Paints (Acrylic)

Pale blue-grey, white, flesh, black, dark pink, light
yellow, pale grey, medium taupe

Miscellaneous

small amount of white tagboard
1⅜″-diameter × 3″-long cardboard tube from paper
towels
small amount of blue, chrome, and red decorative
adhesive vinyl
¼″ blue Helvetica self-adhesive vinyl letters
⅛″-diameter × ⅞″-long gold-tone spring

CAPTAIN BUCK

1. For head, cover one hole of a 20mm bead with a
tagboard circle.

2. To indicate position of earphones, draw a horizontal line around the equator, parallel with the bead
holes, and a vertical line around the meridian. Where
lines cross, whittle a ¼″ × ¼″ area flat to accommodate earphones.

3. For earphones, cut two ⅛″ lengths of ¼″ dowelling.

4. Wood-glue earphones to each side of head.

5. Paint earphones pale blue-grey.

6. Paint head white.

7. Referring to 1–2, paint face flesh, eyes black, and
cheeks dark pink.

1–1.

8. For body, cut a ⅞″ length of ⅝″ dowelling.

9. Draw a line down length of body to indicate
center front.

10. Measure and mark position of left and right arms
⅛″ from top of body and 9/16″ from center line. At
each mark, whittle a ¼″ × ¼″ area flat.

11. Sand bottom edge of head to expose raw wood.

12. Wood-glue head to body so head faces forward.

13. For legs, cut a 2½″ length of ¼″ dowelling.

14. To indicate angle of ankle cut, measure and mark
1 3/16″ from right end. Rotate dowelling so mark is
away from you, then measure and mark 1 3/16″ from
left end. Cut angle.

15. To indicate angle of each hip cut, place leg on
work surface so the ankle end is at top. Rotate leg so
the face of the ankle angle cut is facing down. At
opposite end, measure and mark ⅛″ from flat end.
Cut angle.

16. With side of left leg flush with side of body and
centered from front to back, wood-glue left hip to
bottom of body so ankle juts forward.

17. With side of right leg flush with side of body and centered from front to back, wood-glue right hip to bottom of body so ankle juts back and is slightly behind left leg.

18. For boots, cut two $1\frac{1}{16}''$ lengths from the rounded ends of an ice-cream stick. Sand corners to round them.

19. Wood-glue boots to bottom of legs so heels are flush with back of ankles, left toe points forward, right toe points slightly to the right, and Captain Buck stands upright.

20. For arms, cut two 1″ lengths of ¼″ dowelling.

21. To indicate angle of each elbow cut, measure and mark $\frac{7}{16}''$ from right end. Rotate dowelling so mark is away from you, then measure and mark $\frac{7}{16}''$ from left end. Cut angle.

22. At flat end of two arm halves, attach 8mm-bead hands.

23. To complete the arms, reverse the elbow cuts and wood-glue upper and lower arms together so elbow joints are crooked.

24. For each arm, whittle inside area of upper arm flat.

25. With shoulders even with top of body, wood-glue arms to body so hands are at cheek level.

26. Paint body white.

27. Following 1–3, cut star from blue decorative adhesive vinyl. Adhere to center of back.

1–2. Captain Buck.

1–3. Pattern for small star.

1–4. Science Officer Stephens.

1–5. Communications Officer Smith.

SCIENCE OFFICER STEPHENS

1. Repeat steps 1 to 6 of Captain Buck.

2. Referring to 1–4, paint face flesh, eyes black, and cheeks dark pink.

3. For body, cut a $\frac{7}{8}''$ length of $\frac{5}{8}''$ dowelling.

4. Draw a line down length of body to indicate center front on one side and center back on opposite side.

5. Measure and mark position of left and right arms $\frac{1}{8}''$ from top of body and $1\frac{1}{16}''$ from center front line. At each mark, whittle a $\frac{1}{4}'' \times \frac{1}{4}''$ area flat.

6. Measure and mark position of left and right air tanks $\frac{1}{4}''$ from center back line. Between each mark, whittle a $\frac{1}{2}'' \times \frac{7}{8}''$ area flat.

7. Sand bottom edge of head to expose raw wood.

8. Wood-glue head to body so head is forward.

9. For legs, cut two $1\frac{3}{16}''$ lengths of ¼″ dowelling.

10. With sides of legs flush with sides of body and centered from front to back, wood-glue legs to bottom of body.

11. For boots, cut two $1\frac{1}{16}''$ lengths from the rounded ends of an ice-cream stick. Sand corners to round them.

12. Wood-glue boots to bottom of legs so heels extend $\frac{1}{8}''$ behind ankles, toes point slightly out, and Officer Stephens stands upright.

13. For arms, cut two $1\frac{1}{4}''$ lengths of ¼″ dowelling.

14. To indicate angle of each elbow cut, measure and mark $\frac{9}{16}''$ from right end. Rotate dowelling so mark is away from you, then measure and mark $\frac{9}{16}''$ from left end. Cut angle.

15. At flat end of two arm halves, attach 8mm-bead hands.

16. To complete the arms, reverse the elbow cuts and wood-glue upper and lower arms together so elbow joints are crooked.

17. Whittle inside area of each upper arm flat.

18. With shoulders even with top of body, wood-glue arms to body so hands are at cheek level.

19. Paint body white.

20. For air tanks, cut two $\frac{7}{8}''$ lengths of ¼″ dowelling. Sand cut edges of each tank to round them.

21. Whittle length of one side of each tank flat.

22. Paint tanks pale blue-grey.

23. With top edge of tanks extending $\frac{1}{8}''$ above top edge of body, tacky-glue tanks side by side to back.

COMMUNICATIONS OFFICER SMITH

1. For head, cover one hole of a 20mm bead with a tagboard circle. Paint head white.

2. Referring to 1–5, paint face flesh, eyes black, and cheeks dark pink.

3. For body, cut a $13/16''$ length of $5/8''$ dowelling.

4. Draw a line down length of body to indicate center front on one side and center back on opposite side.

5. Measure and mark position of left and right arms $1/8''$ from top of body and $5/8''$ from center front line. At each mark, whittle a $1/4'' \times 1/4''$ area flat.

6. Measure and mark position of left and right air tanks $1/4''$ from center back line. Between each mark, whittle a $1/2'' \times 7/8''$ area flat.

7. Sand bottom edge of head to expose raw wood.

8. Wood-glue head to body so head is forward.

9. For legs, cut a $2 1/4''$ length of $1/4''$ dowelling.

10. To indicate angle of ankle cut, measure and mark $1 1/16''$ from right end. Rotate dowelling so mark is away from you, then measure and mark $1 1/16''$ from left end. Cut angle.

11. To indicate angle of each hip cut, place leg on work surface so the ankle end is at top. Rotate leg so the face on the ankle angle cut is facing down. At opposite end, measure and mark $1/8''$ from flat end. Cut angle.

12. With side of left leg flush with side of body and centered from front to back, wood-glue left hip to bottom of body so ankle juts forward.

13. With side of right leg flush with side of body and centered from front to back, wood-glue right hip to bottom of body so ankle juts back.

14. For boots, cut two $5/8''$ lengths from the rounded ends of an ice-cream stick. Sand corners to round them.

15. Wood-glue boots to bottom of legs so heels extend $1/16''$ behind ankles, toes point slightly out, and Officer Smith stands upright.

16. For arms, cut two $15/16''$ lengths of $1/4''$ dowelling.

17. To indicate angle of each elbow cut, measure and mark $3/8''$ from right end. Rotate dowelling so mark is away from you, then measure and mark $1/2''$ from left end. Cut angle.

18. At flat end of two lower (shorter) arms, attach 8mm-bead hands.

19. To complete the arms, reverse the elbow cuts and wood-glue upper and lower arms together so elbow joints are crooked.

20. Whittle inside area of each upper arm flat.

21. With shoulders even with top of body, wood-glue arms to body so left hand is down at side and right hand is at mouth level.

22. Paint body white.

23. Repeat steps 25 to 28 of Science Officer Stephens.

SPACECRAFT

1. Use the $1 5/8'' \times 3''$ cardboard tube for the third stage of the spacecraft.

2. Using a pencil compass, describe two $1 5/8''$-diameter circles onto $1/4 \times 5 1/4$ lattice. Cut out circles.

3. Sand edge of one circle to round. (This is now the top of the third stage.)

4. Tacky-glue circles to each end of cardboard tube.

5. Following 1–6, cut four landing gears from $1/4 \times 5 1/4$ lattice.

6. Tacky-glue landing gears to bottom of third stage, spacing them evenly around.

7. Use the $5 3/8''$ length of $1 1/4''$ dowelling for the second stage of the spacecraft.

8. Sand edge of one end of second stage to round. (This is now the top of the second stage.)

9. Wood-glue bottom of second stage to center top of third stage.

10. For first stage of spacecraft, cut the 44mm $\times$ 28mm-bead in half along the equator. Discard one half.

11. For top of first stage, cut a $1/8''$ length of $5/8''$ dowelling.

12. Sand bead hole of first stage to expose raw wood.

13. Wood-glue top to bead hole of first stage.

14. To indicate position of needle-nose hole, locate center top of first stage.

15. Using a $3/32''$ bit, drill a hole for needle-nose through center.

16. For needle-nose, cut a $1 3/4''$ length from the pointed end of a toothpick.

17. Wood-glue cut end of needle-nose into needle-nose hole.

18. Wood-glue bottom of first stage to center top of second stage.

19. Paint spacecraft white.

20. For vertical stripes on third stage, cut four $5/8'' \times$

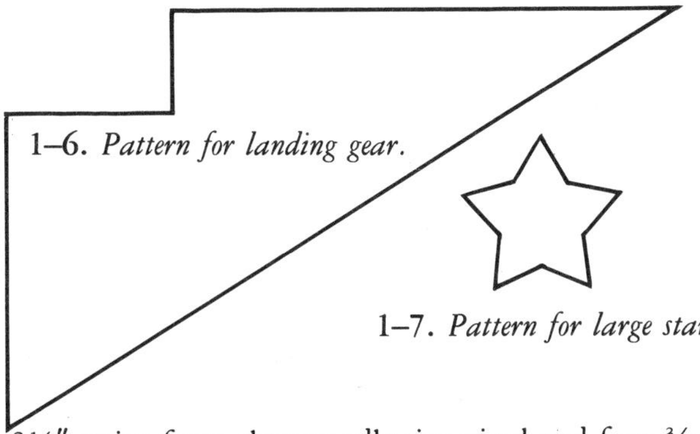

1–6. *Pattern for landing gear.*

1–7. *Pattern for large star.*

3 1/8″ strips from chrome adhesive vinyl and four 3/16″ × 3 1/8″ strips from red adhesive vinyl.

21. With one short edge flush with bottom edge of third stage, adhere chrome stripes to third stage, centering them between landing gear. Adhere red stripes to center of chrome stripes.
22. For horizontal stripe on third stage, cut a 3/16″ × 6″ strip from blue adhesive vinyl.
23. Butting bottom edge of blue stripe to top edge of chrome and red stripes, adhere around top of third stage, overlapping short edges.
24. For horizontal stripes on second stage, cut two 1 9/16″ × 4 1/2″ strips from chrome adhesive vinyl and four 3/16″ × 4 1/2″ strips from blue adhesive vinyl.
25. Adhere a chrome stripe around second stage, butting bottom edge with top of third stage and overlapping short edges.
26. Adhere a chrome stripe around second stage, with top edge of stripe flush with top edge of second stage.
27. Adhere two blue stripes over each chrome stripe, positioning them 1/8″ from top and bottom edges of chrome stripes and overlapping short edges.
28. For horizontal stripe around first stage, cut a 1/8″ × 2 1/2″ strip of red adhesive vinyl. Adhere around top of first stage, overlapping short edges.
29. Adhere vinyl letters of your choice vertically on one side of second stage.
30. Following 1–7, cut three stars from blue adhesive vinyl. Adhere to center of second stage, spacing them evenly around.

LADDER

1. For sides, use two ice-cream sticks.
2. To indicate position of the five ladder rungs, measure and mark from one end (bottom) of each ladder side. Mark first rung 3/4″ from bottom, second 1 9/16″ from bottom, third 2 3/16″ from bottom, fourth 2 15/16″ from bottom, and fifth 3 5/8″ from bottom.
3. At each mark, rout out a 1/16″ wide × 3/8″ long × 1/32″-deep groove to accommodate sides of rungs.
4. Trim bottom end of each ladder side to a 30° angle.
5. Referring to 1–1, place angled (bottom) end of each ladder side on work surface and rounded end against spacecraft. Sand inside of rounded ends to flatten so ladder will lean close to spacecraft.
6. For rungs, cut five 1 3/16″ lengths of ice-cream sticks.
7. Wood-glue rungs to ladder sides.
8. Paint ladder black.

ENGINEER ALLEN

1. For head, cover one hole of a 20mm bead with a tagboard circle. Paint head white.
2. Referring to 1–8, paint face flesh, eyes black, and cheeks dark pink.
3. For body, cut a 13/16″ length of 5/8″ dowelling.
4. Draw a line down length of body to indicate center front.
5. Measure and mark position of left and right arms 1/8″ from top of body and 9/16″ from center line. At each mark, whittle a 1/4″ × 1/4″ area flat.
6. Measure and mark position of left leg 1/8″ from bottom of body and 1/8″ from each side of center line. Whittle a 1/4″ × 1/4″ area flat.
7. Sand bottom edge of head to expose raw wood.
8. Wood-glue head to top of body so head faces slightly towards left.
9. For left leg, cut a 1″ length of 1/4″ dowelling.
10. To indicate angle of knee cut, measure and mark 7/16″ from right end. Rotate dowelling so mark is away from you, then measure and mark 7/16″ from left end. Cut angle.
11. At underside of angled end of one leg half (upper), whittle a 1/8″-deep × 1/4″-long notch so angled end of lower leg will lie close to upper leg and form a right angle (knee bend). Wood-glue lower leg to notch of upper leg.
12. With underside of left leg flush with bottom of body, wood-glue hip to center front of body.
13. For right leg, cut a 1 1/8″ length of 1/4″ dowelling.
14. Wood-glue right leg to bottom of body, flush with side of body, and centered from front to back.
15. For boots, cut two 11/16″ lengths from the rounded ends of an ice-cream stick. Sand corners to round them.

16. Wood-glue boots to bottom of legs so heels are flush with back of ankles and toes point forward.

17. For arms, cut two $^{15}/_{16}''$ lengths of $^1/_4''$ dowelling.

18. To indicate angle of each elbow cut, measure and mark $^3/_8''$ from right end. Rotate dowelling so mark is away from you, then measure and mark $^7/_{16}''$ from left end. Cut angle.

19. At flat end of two lower (shorter) arms, attach 8mm-bead hands.

20. To complete the arms, reverse the elbow cuts and wood-glue upper and lower arms together so elbow joints are crooked.

21. For each arm, whittle inside area of upper arm flat.

22. With shoulders even with top of body, wood-glue arms to body so right hand touches the fourth ladder rung and left hand reaches up towards the fifth ladder rung.

23. Paint body white.

24. Following 1–3, cut star from blue adhesive vinyl. Adhere to center of back.

25. Tacky-glue bottom of right boot to first ladder rung and bottom of left boot to second ladder rung.

ROCK-E THE MOON CREATURE

1. For head, cover one bead hole of a 20mm bead with a tagboard circle.

2. To indicate position of nose, draw a horizontal line around the equator, parallel with the bead holes, and a vertical line around the meridian. Where lines cross, mark for nose hole.

3. For left and right antennae holes, measure and mark $^1/_{16}''$ from edge of covered bead hole and $^3/_8''$ from the meridian.

4. Using a $^3/_{32}''$ bit, drill $^1/_8''$-deep nose and antennae holes.

5. For nose, cut a $^3/_8''$ length from the thickest part of a toothpick.

6. Wood-glue nose into nose hole.

7. For antennae, cut two $1^1/_8''$ lengths from the pointed ends of a toothpick.

8. Wood-glue cut ends into antennae holes.

9. Paint head, nose, and antennae light yellow.

10. Referring to 1–9, paint eyes black and cheeks dark pink.

11. For body, cut a $^{13}/_{16}''$ length of $^5/_8''$ dowelling.

12. Draw a line down length of body to indicate center front.

13. Measure and mark position of left and right arms $^1/_8''$ from top of body and $^9/_{16}''$ from center line. At each mark, whittle a $^1/_4'' \times ^1/_4''$ area flat

14. Sand bottom edge of head to expose raw wood.

15. Wood-glue head to top of body so head faces forward.

16. For legs, cut two $1''$ lengths of $^1/_4''$ dowelling.

17. With sides of legs flush with sides of body and centered from front to back, wood-glue legs to bottom of body.

18. For feet, cut two $^1/_8''$ lengths of $^5/_8''$ dowelling.

19. Wood-glue feet to bottom of legs so heels are flush with back of ankles, toes point out, and Rock-E stands upright.

20. For arms, cut two $1''$ lengths of $^1/_4''$ dowelling.

21. To indicate angle of each shoulder/elbow cut, measure and mark $^7/_{16}''$ from right end. Rotate dowelling so mark is away from you, then measure and mark $^7/_{16}''$ from left end. Cut angle.

22. At flat end of two arm halves, attach 10mm-bead hands.

23. To complete each arm, wood-glue angled end of lower arm to flat end of upper arm, making sure the elbow is crooked and the shoulder angle of the upper arm is parallel with the angled end of the lower arm.

24. With shoulders even with top of body, wood-glue tops of arms to body so hands are raised up.

25. Paint body light yellow.

26. Stretch wire spring to measure same length as distance between antennae. Wrap ends over each antenna and tacky-glue in place.

SMALL MOON ROCK

1. Following 1–10, cut small moon rock from $^1/_4 \times 5^1/_4$ lattice.

2. For easel stand, cut a triangle with $1^1/_8'' \times 1^1/_2''$ right-angle sides from $^1/_4 \times 5^1/_4$ lattice.

3. Locate and mark center back of rock. Hold rock upright with bottom edge flat against work surface. With $1^1/_8''$ edge of easel stand flat against work surface, wood-glue the $1^1/_2''$ edge vertically to center back of rock.

4. Paint rock pale grey.

MEDIUM MOON ROCK

1. Following 1–11, cut medium moon rock from $^1/_4 \times 5^1/_4$ lattice.

1–8. Engineer Allen.   *1–9. Rock-E the Moon Creature.*

2. For easel stand, cut a triangle with 1½″ × 1¾″ right-angle sides from ¼ × 5¼ lattice.

3. Locate and mark center back of rock. Hold rock upright with bottom edge flat against work surface. With 1½″ edge of easel stand flat against work surface, wood-glue the 1¾″ edge vertically to center back of rock.

4. Paint rock pale blue-grey.

LARGE MOON ROCK

1. Following 1–12, cut large moon rock from ¼ × 5¼ lattice.

2. For easel stand, cut a triangle with 1½″ × 2½″ right-angle sides from ¼ × 5¼ lattice.

3. Locate and mark center back of rock. Hold rock upright with bottom edge flat against work surface. With 1½″ edge of easel stand flat against work surface, wood-glue the 2½″ edge vertically to center back of rock.

4. Paint rock medium taupe.

LUNAR LANDSCAPE

1. Following 1–13, cut lunar landscape from ¼ × 5¼ lattice.

2. For easel stand, cut a triangle with 2″ × 3¼″ right-angle sides from ¼ × 5¼ lattice.

3. Locate and mark center back of landscape. Hold landscape upright with bottom edge flat against work surface. With 2″ edge of easel stand flat against work surface, wood-glue the 3¼″ edge vertically to center back of landscape.

4. Paint lunar landscape pale blue-grey.

1–12. Pattern for large moon rock.

1–11. Pattern for medium moon rock.

1–10. Pattern for small moon rock.

15

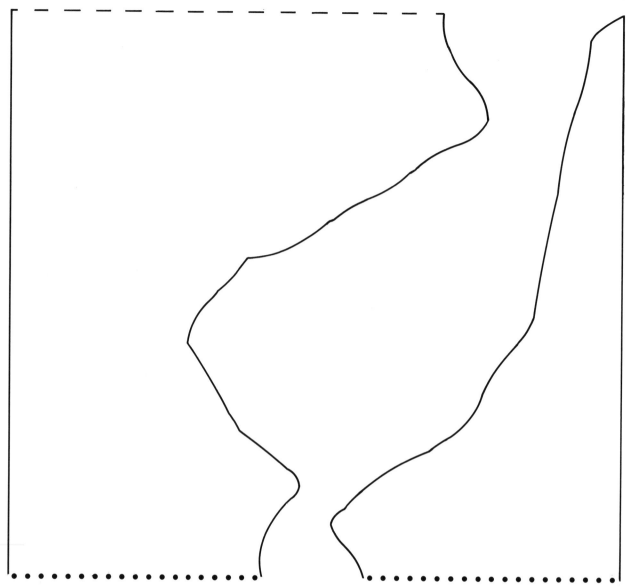

1–13. *Two-part pattern for lunar landscape.*

2 · U.S.S. Playtime

MATERIALS

Beads

four white 20mm large-hole wood beads

Wood

10″ length of ⁵⁄₁₆″ dowelling
10″ length of ⅝″ dowelling

2¼″ length of 1″ dowelling
9″ length of 1¼″ dowelling
36″ length of ¼ × 5¼ clear pine lattice
three 5½″ × 16″ rectangles of ¾″ plywood
9″ length of clear pine 2 × 4
twenty 1¼″ long × ¼″ diameter axle pegs

Wheels

three 1½″ diameter wooden spoked wheels

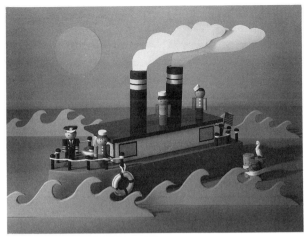

2–1.

Paints (Acrylic)

Flesh, black, dark brown, white, medium yellow, medium ultramarine, medium blue-grey, light grey, and light blue

Metallic Acrylic Color: Silver enamel: red high-gloss

Hardware

eight 6 × 2 flathead wood screws

Miscellaneous

small amount of white tagboard

small amount of yellow, black, and red decorative adhesive vinyl

one pair 40″-long round nylon shoelaces

7/8″ × 1 3/8″ paper American flag on toothpick

three wine-bottle corks

small sitting plastic shore bird, about 1 1/4″ tall

Please refer to Introduction for Safety Precautions. Before proceeding, see General Directions for whittling and marking.

CAPTAIN MONSEES

1. For head, cover one hole of a 20mm bead with a tagboard circle. Paint head flesh.

2. Referring to 2–2, paint eyes black and hair dark brown.

3. For body, cut a 1 1/2″ length of 5/8″ dowelling.

4. Draw a line down length of body to indicate center front.

5. Sand bottom edge of head to expose raw wood.

6. Wood-glue head to top of body so head faces forward.

7. For arms, cut two 7/8″ lengths of 5/16″ dowelling.

Along the length of each arm, whittle one side flat.

8. With shoulders even with top edge of body, wood-glue arms to body so left arm is parallel with body and right arm angles slightly forward.

9. For hands, paint bottom 3/16″ of arms flesh.

10. Paint body and sleeves black.

11. For shirt and necktie, measure and mark for a 3/8″ × 1/2″ triangle at center front of body. Paint triangle white. Paint necktie black.

12. Paint four buttons medium yellow. Paint first row 3/8″ from top of body and spaced 3/8″ apart horizontally. Paint last row 1/4″ below first row.

13. For sleeve stripes, cut four 1/16″ × 13/16″ strips from yellow adhesive vinyl. Beginning 1/16″ above sleeve cuff, adhere two rows of stripes to each sleeve, spacing them 1/16″ apart.

14. For cap, cut a slice of 1″ dowelling that angles 3/16″ to 1/16″ thick. (Angled side is top of cap.)

15. Cut a 1″ circle from tagboard. Tacky-glue to top of cap.

16. Paint top and sides of cap black.

17. Following 2–3, cut cap visor from tagboard. Tacky-glue to bottom of cap.

18. Paint bottom of cap black.

19. Tacky-glue cap to top of head.

20. For cap badge, cut a 3/16″-high × 1/4″-long oval from yellow adhesive vinyl. Adhere to cap above visor.

FIRST MATE MATTHEWS

1. For head, cover one hole of a 20mm bead with a tagboard circle. Paint head flesh.

2. Referring to 2–4, paint eyes black and hair dark brown.

3. For body, cut a 1 1/2″ length of 5/8″ dowelling.

4. Draw a line down length of body to indicate center front.

5. Sand bottom edge of head to expose raw wood.

2–2. Captain Monsees.

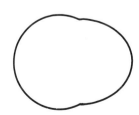

2–3. Pattern for Captain Monsees's cap visor.

6. Wood-glue head to top of body so head faces forward.

7. For arms, cut two $^{13}/_{16}''$ lengths of $^5/_{16}''$ dowelling. Along the length of each arm, whittle one side flat.

8. With shoulders even with top edge of body, wood-glue arms to body so arms are angled slightly towards the back.

9. For hands, paint bottom $^3/_{16}''$ of arms flesh.

10. For pants, paint bottom $^7/_8''$ of body medium ultramarine.

11. For shirt, paint sleeves and top of body medium blue-grey.

12. Using white, paint three shirt buttons, evenly spaced and centered on shirt front.

13. For hat, cut a $^1/_4''$ length of $^5/_8''$ dowelling. Paint white. Tacky-glue hat to top of head.

MACHINIST FIRST CLASS SWABBY

1. For head, cover one hole of a 20mm bead with a tagboard circle. Paint head flesh.

2. Referring to 2–5, paint eyes and hair black.

3. For body, cut a $1^1/_2''$ length of $^5/_8''$ dowelling.

4. Draw a line down length of body to indicate center front.

5. Sand bottom edge of head to expose raw wood.

6. Wood-glue head to top of body so head faces forward.

7. For arms, cut two $^7/_8''$ lengths of $^5/_{16}''$ dowelling. Along the length of each arm, whittle one side flat.

8. With shoulders even with top edge of body, wood-glue arms parallel with body.

9. Paint top $1^1/_{16}''$ of body and arms flesh.

10. For pants, paint bottom $^{13}/_{16}''$ of body medium ultramarine.

11. Using white, paint a button each side of pants top.

12. Add chest details, using dark brown. Using a fairly dry brush, paint chest hair dark brown.

13. For hat, cut a $^1/_4''$ length of $^5/_8''$ dowelling. Paint white. Tacky-glue hat to top of head.

SECOND MATE MICHAELS

1. For head, cover one hole of a 20mm bead with a tagboard circle. Paint head flesh.

2. Referring to 2–6, paint eyes and hair black.

3. For body, cut a $1^1/_2''$ length of $^5/_8''$ dowelling.

4. Draw a line down length of body to indicate center front.

5. Sand bottom edge of head to expose raw wood.

6. Wood-glue head to top of body so head faces forward.

7. For arms, cut two $^7/_8''$ lengths of $^5/_{16}''$ dowelling. Along the length of each arm, whittle one side flat.

8. With shoulders even with top edge of body, wood-glue arms parallel with body.

9. For hands and arms, paint bottom $^9/_{16}''$ of arms flesh.

10. For pants, paint bottom $^{13}/_{16}''$ of body medium ultramarine.

11. For shirt, paint sleeves and top of body medium blue-grey.

12. Using white, paint three shirt buttons, evenly spaced and centered on shirt front.

13. For hat, cut a $^1/_4''$ length of $^5/_8''$ dowelling. Paint white.

14. Position hat on head so it tilts towards Michael's right and slightly towards the front. Using very short strokes and firm, even pressure, scrape hat against head to transfer white paint to black hair. Sand the white spot on the head flat. Tacky-glue hat to head.

U.S.S. PLAYTIME

1. Following 2–7, transfer bow of hull pattern to each of three pieces of $^3/_4''$ plywood, butting bow with center of one short side. Cut out hulls.

2. On one hull piece (upper deck), trim off $^3/_8''$ from stern for transom.

3. With upper deck on top, wood-glue hulls together.

4. To reinforce hull, measure and mark for three

2–4. First Mate Matthews. *2–5. Machinist First Class Swabby.* *2–6. Second Mate Michaels.*

pilot holes centered down length of upper deck. Mark the first 6″ from bow, the second 9½″ from bow, and the third 13″ from bow.

5. Using a ³⁄₃₂″ bit, drill 1⅜″-deep pilot holes. Insert screws.

6. Paint hull light grey.

7. For railing posts at bow, measure and mark for postholes. Measuring ⅜″ from edge, mark for first hole at center of bow. Working towards the right, mark for second hole 1⅜″ from center hole, third hole 1⅜″ from second, fourth hole 1⅜″ from third, and fifth hole 1¼″ from fourth. Repeat for left side.

8. Using a ¼″ bit, drill ¼″- deep postholes.

9. For railing posts at stern, measure and mark for postholes. Measuring ⅜″ from edge, mark for first hole at the right corner. Working along right edge towards bow, mark second hole 1″ from first, and third hole 1″ from second. Repeat for left corner and left edge towards bow. Starting at the right corner and working towards center back, measure and mark

for holes ⅞″ from corner and 1⅞″ from corner. Repeat for left side starting at left corner and working towards center back.

10. Using a ¼″ bit, drill ¼″-deep postholes.

11. For steering-wheel column hole, measure and mark 3⅜″ from tip of bow and centered from side to side.

12. Using a ¼″ bit, drill a ¼″-deep hole for column.

13. For flagpole hole at stern, locate center bottom of transom.

14. Using a ³⁄₃₂″ bit, drill a ¼″-deep flagpole hole at a 45° angle towards bow.

15. For cabin, using white, paint sides and a 1″ band around top and bottom of the 9″ length of 2 × 4.

16. On each short side, measure and mark for a 3″ × 1″ window centered vertically and horizontally.

17. On each long side, measure and mark for two 1⅝″ × 1″ windows centered vertically and with each window ¼″ from a corner edge of cabin.

18. Paint windows light blue. Using white and a

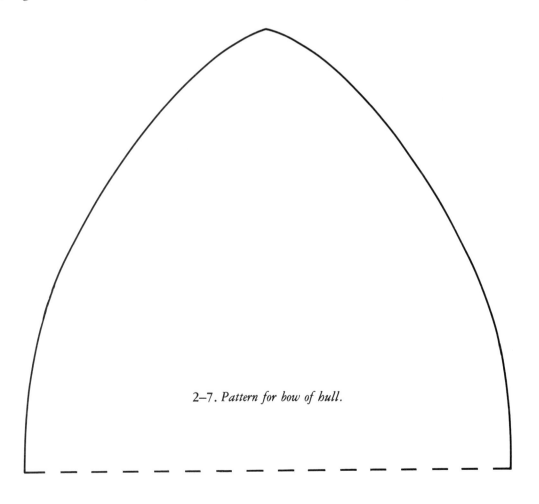

2–7. *Pattern for bow of hull.*

2–8. Two-part pattern for waves.

fairly dry brush, paint angled streaks on windows to highlight.

19. To outline each large window, cut two $\frac{1}{8}'' \times 3''$ and two $\frac{1}{8}'' \times 1''$ strips from black adhesive vinyl. Adhere strips around window.

20. To outline small windows, cut two $\frac{1}{8}'' \times 1\frac{5}{8}''$ and two $\frac{1}{8}'' \times 1''$ strips from black adhesive vinyl. Adhere strips around window.

21. Tacky-glue cabin to hull, with back edge of cabin $2''$ from back edge of upper deck and centered side to side.

22. To reinforce cabin to the hull, measure and mark for three pilot holes centered down the length of cabin. Mark for the first hole $1\frac{1}{2}''$ from front edge of cabin, the second $4\frac{1}{2}''$ from front edge of cabin, and the third $1\frac{1}{2}''$ from back edge of cabin.

23. Using a $\frac{3}{32}''$ bit, drill $1\frac{3}{8}''$-deep pilot holes. Insert screws.

24. For roof, cut a $4\frac{1}{4}'' \times 10\frac{1}{2}''$ rectangle from $\frac{1}{4} \times 5\frac{1}{4}$ lattice.

25. Using red high-gloss enamel, paint top, sides, and a $2''$ band around the perimeter of the underside.

26. With wrong side facing you, measure and mark for two smokestack pilot holes centered down the length of the roof. Mark the first $3\frac{5}{8}''$ from front edge and the second $3\frac{3}{8}''$ from back edge.

27. Using a $\frac{3}{32}''$ bit, drill pilot holes through roof.

28. For smokestacks, cut the $1\frac{1}{4}''$ dowelling in half to make two $4\frac{1}{4}''$ lengths. Paint sides and tops black.

29. Using a $\frac{3}{32}''$ bit, drill a $1\frac{3}{8}''$-deep pilot hole into center bottom of each smokestack.

30. Apply wood glue and insert screws through roof and into smokestacks.

31. Cut four $\frac{5}{16}'' \times 1\frac{3}{4}''$ strips from yellow adhesive vinyl. For each stack, adhere first stripe $\frac{1}{2}''$ from top and second stripe $\frac{1}{16}''$ below first.

32. Wood-glue roof to center top of cabin.

33. For steering-wheel column and railing posts, paint all axle pegs black.

34. For steering wheel, paint one spoked wheel silver.

35. Insert axle peg into steering wheel and tacky-glue peg into column hole.

36. Tacky-glue railing posts into postholes.

37. For life preservers, use a knife to cut away spokes from the two remaining spoked wheels. Paint white.

38. Marking lightly, divide the preserver into quarters around the outer edge.

39. For each life preserver, cut an 8″ length of shoelace. Referring to 2–1 and with right side of preserver facing you, tacky-glue one end of shoelace at a tick mark so loose end of shoelace is at your right. The tick mark where the shoelace end was glued is now at 12 o'clock.

40. For each life preserver, cut four ³⁄₁₆″ × 1¾″ strips of red adhesive vinyl. Starting at 3 o'clock, loosely wrap shoelace around outer edge of preserver and secure with a red strip. Repeat at 6, 9, and 12 o'clock. To end, form a ¾″ loop at 12 o'clock, trim off excess and tacky-glue end to wrong side.

41. Place one life preserver loop over last bow-rail post at right and left sides of ship.

42. Cut a 23″ length of shoelace for rope along bow-rail posts. Beginning at last rail at right side of ship, and working around the bow, wrap shoelace once around each post from front to back to front. Trim ends and secure in place with tacky glue.

43. Cut a 24″ length of shoelace for rope along stern-rail posts. Beginning at first rail at right side of ship, and working around the stern, wrap shoelace once around each post from front to back to front. Trim ends and secure in place with tacky glue.

44. Tacky-glue flag into flagpole hole.

PILINGS

1. Using a knife, cut two corks so they are ⅛″ and ¼″ shorter than the third cork. With bottom edges even, tacky-glue corks together.

2. Cut a 24″ length of white shoelace. Wrap it four times around corks. Tacky-glue ends in place.

3. Tacky-glue bird to top of pilings.

WAVES (MAKE 4)

1. Following 2–8, cut out wave from ¼ × 5¼ lattice.

2. Paint wave light blue.

3 · Tumbleweed Ranch

MATERIALS

Beads

nine white 32mm × 22mm large-hole wood beads
one white 25mm large-hole wood bead
eight white 10mm regular-hole wood beads

Wood

9″ length of ⅛″ dowelling
11″ length of ³⁄₁₆″ dowelling
77″ length of ¼″ dowelling
5″ length of ⅜″ dowelling
9″ length of ½″ dowelling
3″ length of ¾″ dowelling
10″ length of ⅞″ dowelling

3–1.

16″ length of 1″ dowelling
30″ length of ¼ × 5¼ clear pine lattice
14″ × 14″ square of ¾″ plywood
one ⅞″-diameter ready-to-finish wood ball
twelve ice-cream sticks
seven round toothpicks

Wheels

Four 2¼″-diameter metal wheels with fasteners

Paints (Acrylic)

Flesh, black, medium pink, dark ultramarine, bright red, beige, dark red-brown, white, light pink, dark blue-grey, off-white, dark brown, light red-brown, light yellow-green, and light grey.

Fabric and Trims

9″ × 12″ piece of beige felt
black, white, yellow, and orange curly chenille hair
one yard of ⅛″ wide black satin ribbon
one yard of brown leatherette lacing or sportweight cotton yarn stiffened by coating with a thin coat of tacky glue worked into fibres
small amount of tan leather
small amount of beige, black, and grey synthetic suede

Hardware

seven ⅝ × 18 wire brads
six ⅞ × 17 wire brads

Miscellaneous

small amount of white tagboard
paper towelling
small amount of 22-gauge galvanized wire
natural-color raffia
9½″ length of waxed-ribbon dental floss
weathered-wood patterned self-stick vinyl adhesive
3″ × 2½″ rectangle of stiff cardboard
Spanish moss

BUCKBOARD BILL

1. For head, cover one hole of a 32mm × 22mm bead with a tagboard circle. Paint head flesh.
2. Referring to 3–2, paint eyes black and cheeks medium pink.
3. For body, cut a 1⁵⁄₁₆″ length of ⅞″ dowelling.
4. Draw a line down length of body to indicate center front.

5. Measure and mark position of left and right armholes ⁵⁄₁₆″ from top of body and ⁵⁄₁₆″ from center line.
6. Using a ¼″ bit, drill ¼″-deep armholes, angling the bit slightly towards back of body.
7. Measure and mark position of left and right leg holes ¼″ from bottom of body and ⁵⁄₁₆″ from center line.
8. Using a ¼″ bit, drill ¼″-deep leg holes, angling the bit slightly towards back of body.
9. Sand bottom edge of head to expose raw wood.
10. Wood-glue head to top of body so head faces forward.
11. For arms, cut two 1⅛″ lengths of ¼″ dowelling.
12. At one end of each arm, attach a 10mm-bead hand.
13. Wood-glue arms into armholes.
14. For upper legs, cut two ⅞″ lengths of ¼″ dowelling.
15. Wood-glue upper legs into leg holes.
16. For lower legs, cut two ¹³⁄₁₆″ lengths of ¼″ dowelling.
17. For each knee joint, whittle a ¹⁄₁₆″ deep × ¼″ long notch at top of each lower leg. Wood-glue ends of upper legs to notches of lower legs.
18. For boots, cut two ⅜″ lengths of ¼″ dowelling.
19. For each ankle joint, whittle a ¹⁄₁₆″ deep × ³⁄₁₆″ long notch at top of each boot. Wood-glue ends of lower legs to notches of boots.
20. Paint hands and bottom ⅛″ of arms flesh.
21. Paint boots black.
22. For pants, paint legs and bottom ¾″ of body dark ultramarine.

3–2. Buckboard Bill.

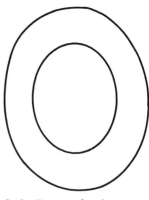

3–3. Pattern for the cowpokes' hats.

23. For shirt, paint top of body and rest of arms bright red.

24. Following 3–3, cut hat brim from beige felt.

25. To indicate hat crown, pull hat brim down over head so front brim is ½″ from edge of bead and back brim is ⅝″ from edge of bead. Trace a line around head underneath hat brim. Remove brim.

26. Using line as a guide, paint top of head beige.

27. Tacky-glue hat brim to head.

28. Cut five ¼″ lengths of black hair. Tacky-glue one to center forehead, just beneath hat brim. Tacky-glue remaining hair around back neck, just beneath brim.

29. For necktie, cut a 6″ length of black satin ribbon and tie around neck. Tacky-glue knot to secure. Trim ends at an angle.

30. Following 3–4, cut two spurs from beige felt. Tacky-glue long straight edge of each spur to outside of each boot.

31. For reins, cut a 17½″ length of leatherette lacing. Tacky-glue ends into bead holes of hands.

BUCKBOARD

1. For floorboards, cut two 1⅝″ × 6½″ rectangles from ¼ × 5¼ lattice.

2. Wood-glue long edges of floorboards together.

3. For axles, cut two ⅝″ × 3¼″ rectangles from ¾″ plywood.

4. Placing the ⅝″ face of axles against the floorboards, wood-glue axles ½″ from ends of floorboards.

5. Turn assembly over and nail floorboards to axles, using two ⅝ × 18 wire brads for each axle.

6. At end of each axle, measure and mark for the center. Using a ⅛″ bit, drill ⅝″-deep pilot holes for wheel fasteners.

7. For back rail, cut a 2⁷⁄₁₆″ length of ¼″ dowelling.

8. Along one side of length, measure and mark ⅛″ from one end, then make five marks at ⁷⁄₁₆″ increments. Using a ⅛″ bit, drill six ⅛″-deep postholes.

9. For posts, cut six ¾″ lengths of ⅛″ dowelling. Wood-glue posts into postholes.

10. To attach back rail to buckboard, draw a line ⁵⁄₁₆″ from back edge of floorboards. Measure and mark ½″ from one side of floorboards, then make five marks at ⁷⁄₁₆″ increments.

 3–4. Pattern for spurs.

11. Using a ⅛″ bit, drill six ⅛″ deep postholes. Wood-glue posts of back rail into postholes.

12. For footrest, cut a ¾″ × 2⅞″ rectangle from ¼ × 5¼ lattice.

13. Whittle one long edge so footrest will tilt at a 45° angle.

14. Wood-glue footrest to front of buckboard so it is ¾″ from front edge, tilted forward, and centered side to side.

15. To stain the buckboard, mix a small amount of dark red-brown with an equal amount of water. Brush on, then wipe off excess with paper towelling.

16. For bench, cut one ⅞″ × 2¾″ (seat) and one ⅝″ × 2¾″ (back) rectangles from ¼ × 5¼ lattice. On one long edge of each piece, sand corners to round them.

17. For bench platform, cut two ¾″ × 2″ rectangles from ¼ × 5¼ lattice. Wood-glue faces together.

18. Using two ⅝ × 18 wire brads evenly spaced, wood-glue and nail bench seat to platform, placing back of bench flush with back of platform and centered side to side.

19. With bottom edge of bench back flush with bottom of seat, wood-glue back to seat.

20. Stain platform dark red-brown.

21. Paint bench dark red-brown.

22. Tacky-glue bench platform to floorboards with back edge of platform 2″ from back edge of buckboard and centered side to side.

23. For rigging, cut two 4⅜″ lengths from ³⁄₁₆″ dowelling. Stain dark red-brown.

24. Using needle-nose pliers, fashion four small eye screws from wire. Use the pliers to embed the straight end of each eye screw into one end of each rig. Dot with tacky glue.

25. On front side of front axle, measure and mark 1″ from each end centered on height of axle. Use an icepick to make shallow pilot holes. Embed the straight end of the two remaining eye screws into front axle. Dot with tacky glue.

26. Attach wheels by hammering fasteners into pilot holes.

27. Hook eye screws on rigging to eye screws on front axle.

28. For hay, cut sufficient raffia into 2½″ lengths to make a 1″ diameter bundle. Wrap a 12″ length of raffia around the center and tie with a knot to secure. Place bundle behind bench.

BUCKBOARD BRONCO

1. For body, cut a 2¹⁄₁₆″ length of 1″ dowelling.

2. To indicate position of first two leg holes, measure and mark ⁵⁄₁₆″ from each end of body. To indicate position of last two leg holes, measure ⁵⁄₁₆″ from each end of body and ⅝″ from first two leg holes.

3. Using a ¼″ bit, drill ¼″-deep leg holes, angling the bit slightly towards the center top of body.

4. To indicate position of tail hole, turn body so leg holes face down. At center back, measure and mark ³⁄₁₆″ from end.

5. Using a ³⁄₃₂″ bit, drill a ⅛″-deep tail hole.

6. To indicate position of neck, turn body so leg holes face down. At center front, measure and mark ¼″ from each side of center and ⅝″ from end. Whittle area flat.

7. For neck, cut a 1³⁄₁₆″ length of ½″ dowelling.

8. For neck/body angle, measure and mark ¼″ from one cut end. Cut angle.

9. Wood-glue angled end of neck to body so neck juts forward.

10. For head, whittle a ½″ × ½″ area at a hole end of a 32mm × 22mm bead to flatten. Test-fit flat end of neck with whittled end of head to make sure head is approximately parallel with body. Wood-glue head to neck so head faces forward.

11. Cover both holes with tagboard circles.

12. For legs, cut four 1¾″ lengths of ¼″ dowelling.

13. Wood-glue legs into leg holes.

14. Paint entire body beige.

15. For hooves, paint bottom ⅛″ of each leg dark red-brown.

16. Referring to 3–5, use black to paint eyes, nostrils, and mouth.

17. Following 3–6, cut mane, ears, and tail from beige synthetic suede.

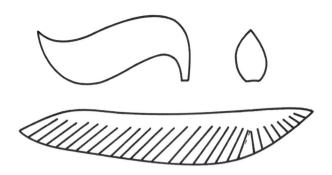

3–6. Patterns for manes, ears, and tails.

18. Tacky-glue straight edge of mane to center top of head and down back of neck.

19. On right side of ears, dot straight edge with tacky glue. Fold over and pinch to secure. Tacky-glue ears to each side of head.

20. Tacky-glue end of tail into tail hole.

21. Referring to 3–5 for bridle, wrap leatherette lacing around head from back to front, overlap ends, cut, and tacky-glue to secure. Wrap lacing around muzzle, overlap ends, cut, and tacky-glue to secure. Wrap lacing over forehead, cut, and tacky-glue ends to bridle.

22. Referring to 3–1 for harness, wrap leatherette lacing around body from back to front, overlap ends, cut, and tacky-glue to secure. Wrap lacing around rear body, overlap ends, cut, and tacky-glue to secure. Wrap lacing over front body behind neck, cut, and tacky-glue ends to harness. For loops, cut two 1″ lengths of lacing. Loop one around each side of harness at front overlap ends and tacky-glue to secure. Insert rigging into loops and tacky-glue to secure.

DANDY DAWG

1. For body, cut a 1¼″ length of ¾″ dowelling.

2. To indicate position of first two leg holes, measure and mark ¼″ from each end of body. To indicate position of last two leg holes, measure ¼″ from each end of body and ⅜″ from the first two leg holes.

3. Using a ⅛″ bit, drill ¼″-deep leg holes, angling the bit slightly towards the center top of body.

4. To indicate position of tail hole, turn body so leg holes face down. At center back, measure and mark ⅛″ from end.

5. Using a ³⁄₃₂″ bit, drill a ⅛″-deep tail hole.

6. To indicate position of neck hole, turn body so

3–5. Buckboard Bronco.

leg holes face down. At center front, measure and mark ⅛″ from end.

7. Using a ³⁄₃₂″ bit, drill a ³⁄₁₆″-deep neck hole.

8. For legs, cut four 1⅛″ lengths of ⅛″ dowelling.

9. Wood-glue legs into leg holes.

10. Make one paw at a time. Using a ⅛″ bit, drill a ¹⁄₁₆″-deep hole (slightly off-centered) into ⅜″ dowelling. Cut a ³⁄₁₆″ length from drilled end of dowelling. Make four paws.

11. With the widest part of each paw facing forward, wood-glue bottom of legs into holes in paws.

12. For head, use a ³⁄₃₂″ bit to drill a ³⁄₁₆″-deep hole into the ⅞″ ready-to-finish wood ball.

13. Cut a ⅜″ length from the thickest part of a toothpick. Wood-glue one end into head hole and other end into neck hole.

14. For nose hole at top of muzzle, use a ³⁄₃₂″ bit to drill a ¹⁄₁₆″-deep perpendicular hole into side and close to cut edge of ⅜″ dowelling. Cut a ¼″ length from drilled end of dowelling.

15. For nose, cut a ³⁄₁₆″ length from the thickest part of a toothpick. Wood-glue nose into nose hole. Trim so only ³⁄₃₂″ extends from muzzle.

16. With nose pointed up, position muzzle on front of head so it is centered from top to bottom, but slightly off-centered towards Dandy's right. Trace outline of muzzle position. Sand muzzle area flat.

17. Wood-glue muzzle to head.

18. For tail, cut a 1″ length from the pointed end of a toothpick.

19. Wood-glue cut end of tail into tail hole.

20. Paint body, legs, head, and muzzle white. Paint nose, paws, and tail black.

21. Referring to 3–7, use black to paint eyes, nose, mouth, and chest ruff.

3–8. Pattern for Dandy Dawg's ears.

3–7. Dandy Dawg.

22. Following 3–8, cut two ears from black synthetic suede. On wrong side of ears, apply a dot of tacky glue to each short straight edge. Glue ears to each side of head.

CACTUS PETE

1. For head, cover one hole of a 32mm × 22mm bead with a tagboard circle. Paint head flesh.

2. Referring to 3–9, paint eyes black and cheeks light pink.

3. For body, cut a 3″ length of ⅞″ dowelling.

4. Draw a line down length of body to indicate center front.

5. Measure and mark position of left and right armholes ¼″ from top of body and ⅝″ from center line.

6. Using a ¼″ bit, drill ¼″-deep armholes, angling the bit slightly towards back of body.

7. Sand bottom edge of head to expose raw wood.

8. Wood-glue head to top of body so head faces slightly towards right.

9. For arms, cut two 1¼″ lengths of ¼″ dowelling.

10. At one end of each arm, attach a 10mm-bead hand.

11. Wood-glue arms into armholes.

12. Paint hands flesh.

13. For boots, paint bottom ⁷⁄₁₆″ of body dark red-brown.

14. For pants, paint 1⅝″ above boots dark blue-grey.

15. Paint shirt and sleeves off-white.

16. For bandana, paint top edge of body around neck bright red. Referring to 3–9, paint knot and tie ends at front and a ¾″ × ½″ triangle at center back.

17. Repeat steps 24 to 27 of Buckboard Bill.

18. Cut a ¼″ length of white hair and tacky-glue to center forehead, just beneath hat brim.

19. For belt, cut a ¼″ × 3″ strip from tan leather. Tacky-glue around waist, butting short ends at center back.

20. Following 3–4, cut two spurs from beige felt. Tacky-glue long straight edge of each spur to each side of boots.

SAGEBRUSH SAL

1. For head, cover one hole of the 25mm bead with a tagboard circle. Paint head flesh.

2. Referring to 3–10, paint eyes black and cheeks light pink.

3. For body, cut a 2¾" length of 1" dowelling.

4. Draw a line down length of body to indicate center front.

5. Measure and mark position of left and right armholes ¼" from top of body and ⅝" from center line.

6. Using a ¼" bit, drill ¼"-deep armholes, angling the bit slightly towards back of body.

7. Sand bottom edge of head to expose raw wood.

8. Wood-glue head to top of body so head faces forward.

9. For arms, cut two 1¼" lengths of ¼" dowelling.

10. At one end of each arm, attach a 10mm-bead hand.

11. Wood-glue arms into armholes.

12. Paint hands flesh.

13. For boots, paint bottom ½" of body dark brown.

14. For legs, paint 11/16" above boots flesh.

15. For bloomers, paint ⅝" above legs white.

16. For blouse, paint rest of body and arms bright red.

17. Following 3–3, cut hat brim from beige felt.

18. To indicate hat crown, pull hat brim down over head so front brim is ¼" from edge of bead and back brim is 13/16" from edge of bead. Trace a line around head underneath hat brim. Remove brim.

19. Using line as a guide, paint top of head beige.

20. Tacky-glue hat brim in place.

21. Cut a ¼" length of yellow hair and tacky-glue it horizontally to center forehead, just beneath hat brim. Cut a 1" length of hair and glue it vertically to center back of head. Allow end to hang loosely. Cut two 2" lengths of hair and tacky-glue to each side of head, just beneath hat brim, beginning at forehead curl and ending at back of head. Allow ends to hang loosely.

22. Following 3–11, cut skirt from beige felt, using pinking shears to cut hem. Tacky-glue around waist, overlapping short edges at center back.

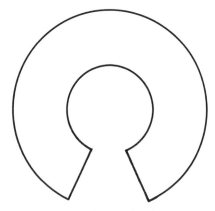

3–11. *Pattern for Sagebrush Sal's skirt.*

23. Tie black satin ribbon around waist, making a knot at center back. Tacky-glue knot to secure. Trim ends at an angle.

24. Make a small bow from ⅛"-wide black satin. Tacky-glue knot to secure bow. Trim ends at an angle. Tacky-glue to center front of neck.

25. Following 3–4, cut two spurs from beige felt. Tacky-glue long straight edge of each spur to each side of boots.

LASSO JOE

1. For head, cover one hole of a 32mm × 22mm bead with a tagboard circle. Paint head flesh.

2. Referring to 3–12, paint eyes black and cheeks light pink.

3. For body, cut a 3" length of ⅞" dowelling.

4. Draw a line down length of body to indicate center front.

5. Measure and mark position of left and right armholes ⅜" from top of body and ⅝" from center line.

6. Using a ¼" bit, drill a ¼"-deep right armhole, angling the bit slightly towards bottom of body. Drill a ¼"-deep left armhole, angling bit slightly towards top of body.

7. Sand bottom edge of head to expose raw wood.

8. Wood-glue head to top of body so head faces forward.

9. For arms, cut two 1⅜" lengths of ¼" dowelling.

10. At one end of each arm, attach a 10mm-bead hand.

11. Using a 3/32" bit, drill a hole in the top center of the left hand for lasso.

12. Wood-glue arms into armholes, so drilled hole in left hand faces up.

3–9. *Cactus Pete.*

3–10. *Sagebrush Sal.*

13. Paint hands and bottom ¼″ of arms flesh.

14. For pants, paint bottom 2⅛″ of body dark red-brown.

15. For shirt, paint top of body and rest of arms dark ultramarine.

16. For bandana, paint top edge of body bright red. Referring to 3–12, paint knot and tie ends at front and a ¾″ × ½″ triangle at center back.

17. Repeat steps 24 to 27 of Buckboard Bill.

18. Fold front brim up and tacky-glue in place.

19. Cut a ¼″ length of orange hair and tacky-glue to center forehead, just beneath hat brim.

20. Following 3–13, cut chaps from tan leather. Tacky-glue around waist, butting short edges at center back.

21. For lasso, make a 2¼″-diameter loop at one end of the dental floss. Tacky-glue opposite end into bead hole in left hand.

WILDFIRE

1. For body, cut a 2¹⁄₁₆″ length of 1″ dowelling.

2. To indicate position of first two leg holes, measure and mark ⁵⁄₁₆″ from each end of body. To indicate position of last two leg holes, measure ⁵⁄₁₆″ from each end of body and ⅝″ from first two leg holes.

3. Using a ¼″ bit, drill ¼″-deep right and left back leg holes and left front leg hole, angling the bit slightly towards the center top of body.

4. To indicate position of tail hole, turn body so leg holes face down. At center back, measure and mark ³⁄₁₆″ from end.

5. Using a ³⁄₃₂″ bit, drill a ⅛″-deep tail hole.

6. To indicate position of neck, turn body so leg holes face down. At center front, measure and mark ¼″ from each side of center and ½″ from end. Whittle area flat.

7. For neck, cut a 1⅛″ length of ½″ dowelling.

3–12. Lasso Joe.

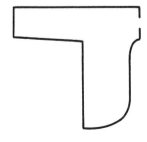

3–13. Half-pattern for Lasso Joe's chaps.

3–14. Wildfire.

3–15. Half-pattern for saddles.

8. For neck/head angle, measure and mark ¼″ from one cut end. Cut angle.

9. For head, whittle a ½″ × ½″ area at a hole end of a 32mm × 22mm bead to flatten. Test-fit angled end of neck with whittled end of head to make sure they form a right angle. Wood-glue head to neck.

10. Wood-glue flat end of neck to body so head is turned slightly towards left.

11. Cover both holes with tagboard circles.

12. For straight legs, cut two 1⅞″ (back legs) and one 2⅛″ (left front leg) lengths of ¼″ dowelling.

13. Wood-glue legs into leg holes.

14. For right front leg, cut a ⅞″ (upper leg), a ¹⁵⁄₁₆″ (lower leg), and a ⁵⁄₁₆″ (hoof) lengths from ¼″ dowelling.

15. At one end of upper leg, whittle a ⅛″-deep × ⅜″-long notch so upper leg will lie close to body.

16. At each end of lower leg, and on same side, whittle a ⅛″-deep × ¼″-long notch for knee and ankle bend. With notched side of upper leg facing up, wood-glue opposite end to a lower leg notch. Wood-glue hoof to other lower leg notch. Wood-glue upper leg notch to body at mark.

17. Paint entire body dark red-brown.

18. For hooves, paint bottom ⅛″ of each leg black.

19. Referring to 3–14, use black to paint eyes, nostrils, and mouth.

20. Following 3–6, cut mane, ears, and tail from beige synthetic suede.

21. Tacky-glue straight edge of mane to center top of head and down back of neck.

22. On right side of ears, dot straight edge with tacky glue. Fold over and pinch to secure. Tacky-glue ears to each side of head.

23. Tacky-glue end of tail into tail hole.

24. Following 3–15, cut saddle from tan leather. Tacky-glue to body.

HAPPY

1. For body, cut a 2″ length of 1″ dowelling.

2. To indicate position of first two leg holes, measure ⁵⁄₁₆″ from each end of body and mark with a pencil. To indicate position of last two leg holes, measure ⁵⁄₁₆″ from each end of body and ⅝″ from first two leg holes.

3. Using a ¼″ bit, drill ¼″-deep leg holes, angling the bit slightly towards the center top of body.

4. Repeat steps 4 to 6 of Wildfire.

5. For neck, cut a 1″ length of ½″ dowelling.

6. Repeat steps 8 to 10 of Wildfire.

7. Wood-glue flat end of neck to body so head is turned towards left.

8. Cover both holes with tagboard circles.

9. For legs, cut four 2¹⁄₁₆″ lengths of ¼″ dowelling.

10. Wood-glue legs into leg holes.

11. Paint entire body light red-brown.

12. For hooves, paint bottom ⅛″ of each leg black.

13. Referring to 3–16, use black to paint eyes, nostrils, and mouth.

14. Following 3–6, cut mane, ears, and tail from black synthetic suede.

15. Repeat steps 20 to 24 of Wildfire. Substitute grey synthetic suede for tan leather.

SLOWPOKE

1. Repeat steps 1 to 5 of Buckboard Bronco.

2. For neck, cut a 1¼″ length of ½″ dowelling.

3. For neck/body angle, measure and mark ¼″ from one cut end. Cut angle.

4. With back/neck edge flush with top of body, wood-glue angled end of neck to front of body so neck hangs down.

5. For head, whittle a ½″ × ½″ area at a hole end of a 32mm × 22mm bead to flatten. Test-fit flat end of neck with whittled end of head to make sure head is approximately parallel with front of body. Wood-glue head to neck so head faces down.

6. Cover both holes with tagboard circles.

7. For legs, cut four 2¹⁄₁₆″ lengths of ¼″ dowelling.

8. Wood-glue legs into leg holes.

9. Paint entire body dark red-brown.

3–16. *Happy*.

3–17. *Slowpoke*.

10. For hooves, paint bottom ⅛″ of each leg black.

11. Referring to 3–17, use black to paint eyelashes and nostrils.

12. Following 3–6, cut mane, ears, and tail from black synthetic suede.

13. Repeat steps 21 to 24 of Wildfire.

THUNDER

1. Repeat steps 1 to 11 of Buckboard Bronco. Make sure head faces forward.

2. For legs, cut four 2¹⁄₁₆″ lengths of ¼″ dowelling.

3. Wood-glue legs into leg holes.

4. Paint entire body light red-brown.

5. For hooves, paint bottom ⅛″ of each leg black.

6. Referring to 3–18, use black to paint eyes, nostrils, and mouth.

7. Following 3–6, cut mane, ears, and tail from black synthetic suede.

8. Repeat steps 21 to 24 of Wildfire. Substitute grey synthetic suede for tan leather.

STABLE

1. For facade, cut a 7¼″-wide × 6⅞″-tall rectangle from ¾″ plywood.

2. For base and roof, cut two 1⅝″ × 8⅜″ rectangles from ¼ × 5¼ lattice.

3. Center base on facade. Wood-glue and nail with three evenly spaced ⅞ × 17 wire brads.

4. Place roof on facade with one long edge aligned with back of facade and centered side to side. Wood-glue and nail with three evenly spaced ⅞ × 17 wire brads.

5. Paint base light yellow-green.

6. Paint roof black.

7. With grain pattern running vertically, cover front, sides, and back of facade with self-stick vinyl.

28

3–18. *Thunder.*　　3–19. *Stormy.*

3–20. *Corner post of corral.*

8. For window opening, make a 3″-wide × 2½″-tall cardboard template.

9. Position template so one short side is ¾″ from left edge and one long side is 2⅜″ above base.

10. Using an art knife, cut around template. Remove vinyl rectangle.

11. Paint opening black.

12. For window frame, cut two 3¼″ (top and bottom) and two 2″ (sides) lengths of ice-cream stick.

13. Paint frame pieces light grey.

14. Referring to 3–1, tacky-glue frame pieces around opening.

15. For Stormy's neck, cut a 1″ length of ½″ dowelling.

16. For neck/body angle, measure and mark ¼″ from one cut end. Cut angle.

17. For head, whittle a ½″ × ½″ area at a hole end of a 32mm × 22mm bead to flatten. Test-fit flat end of neck with whittled end of head to make sure Stormy's head hangs down slightly. Wood-glue head to neck.

18. Cover both holes with tagboard circles.

19. Paint head and neck off-white.

20. Referring to 3–19, use black to paint eyes, nostrils, and mouth.

21. Following 3–6, cut mane and ears from beige synthetic suede.

22. Tacky-glue straight edge of mane to center top of head and down back of neck.

23. On right side of ears, dot straight edge with tacky glue. Fold over and pinch to secure. Tacky-glue ears to each side of head.

24. Position Stormy at center bottom of window so his neck juts upward. Lightly trace around neck onto the window opening. Sand the traced area to expose raw wood. Wood-glue Stormy to opening.

CORRAL

1. For base, cut a ⅝″ × 6″ and a ⅝″ × 7⅛″ length of ¼ × 5¼ lattice.

2. To make right-angle lap joint, whittle a ⅛″-deep × ⅝″-long notch at one end of each base. Wood-glue joint.

3. For posts, cut five 2⅝″ lengths of ¼″ dowelling.

4. Measure and mark 1⅛″ from each end of post. Whittle a ⅛″-deep × ⅜″-wide notch between marks on one side of four posts. For corner post, whittle two notches ⅛″ deep × ⅜″ wide at right angles to each other.

5. Draw a line down the center of both the short and long bases. Mark the intersection of the lines at the right-angle corner for the corner post. Across short base, measure and mark 2¾″ from corner post, then 2¾″ from second mark. Across long base, measure and mark 3¼″ from corner post, then 3⅜″ from second mark.

6. Using a ¼″ bit, drill ⅛″-deep postholes.

7. Refer to 3–20. With notched sides of the posts facing out and the notched side of the corner post facing the outside corner, wood-glue posts into postholes.

8. For lower railings on short side, cut two 2¾″ square-edged lengths of ice-cream stick. Butting short edges, wood-glue railings to notches.

9. For lower railings on long side, cut a 3⅜″ and a 3½″ square-edged length of ice-cream stick. Wood-glue shorter railing to notches at corner (overlapping railing of short side) and center on post notch. Butting short edges, wood-glue longer railing to notches.

10. For upper railings on short side, cut a 2¾″ squared-edged length of ice-cream stick and a 3½″ length of ice-cream stick, leaving one end rounded.

Cut one end of shorter railing at a 45° angle. Butting the short straight edges on top of center post, wood-glue railings so angled end is at corner.

11. For upper railings on long side, cut one 3¼″ square-edged length of ice-cream stick and one 4⅛″ length of ice-cream stick, leaving one end rounded. Cut one end of short railing at a 45° angle. Butting the short straight edges on top of center post, wood-glue railings so angled end is at corner.

12. Paint railings and posts white.

13. Paint base light yellow-green.

14. Following 3–15, cut saddle from beige synthetic suede. Tacky-glue onto long railing 1⅛″ from rounded end.

TUMBLEWEED (MAKE 5)

1. Gather one or two strands of Spanish moss and wind around index finger until a 1″ diameter bundle is formed.

2. Trim loose ends.

CACTUS

1. Following 3–21, cut cactus from ¼ × 5¼ lattice.

2. For base, cut a 1″ × 1⅛″ rectangle from ¼ × 5¼ lattice.

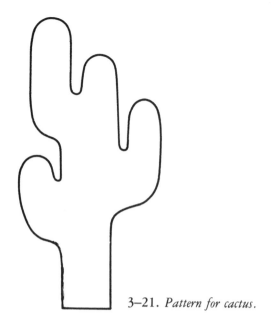

3–21. *Pattern for cactus.*

3. Wood-glue and nail cactus to base using a ⅝ × 18 wire brad.

4. Paint cactus light yellow-green, dots dark blue-grey and base beige.

4 · Buddy and Rover

MATERIALS

Beads

one white 25mm large-hole wood bead
one white 20mm large-hole wood bead
one white 10mm regular-hole wood bead
six white 8mm regular-hole wood beads

Wood

8″ length of ¼″ dowelling
1″ length of ⅝″ dowelling
¹⁵⁄₁₆″ length of ¾″ dowelling
one ice-cream stick
seven round toothpicks

4–1.

Paints (Acrylic)

Flesh, black, dark pink, dark brown, medium yellow, bright red, khaki, dark blue-grey, white, light blue-grey, light red-brown and dark green.

Fabric and Trims

small amount of brown and black synthetic suede
3¼″ length of black sportweight cotton yarn

Miscellaneous

small amount of white tagboard
paste wood filler
two 1½″ × 2¼″ rectangles of small type from a magazine

BUDDY

1. For head, cover one hole of the 25mm bead with a tagboard circle. Paint head flesh.

2. Referring to 4–2, paint eyes black, cheeks dark pink, and hair dark brown. Paint freckles black.

3. For cap's buttonhole, use an ice pick to pierce a tiny hole in center top of tagboard circle.

4. For button, cut a ¼″ length from the thickest part of a toothpick.

5. Tacky-glue button into buttonhole, allowing ¹⁄₁₆″ of toothpick to extend beyond hole at top.

6. To indicate crown of cap, measure and mark around head ⁹⁄₁₆″ from button.

7. Paint button medium yellow.

8. Paint crown bright red.

9. Following 4–3, cut cap peak from tagboard.

10. Fold back tabs on peak.

11. Paint peak bright red.

12. With tabs facing down, tacky-glue peak to center front of forehead, butting peak with bottom edge of crown.

13. Paint tabs dark brown.

14. For body, use the ¹⁵⁄₁₆″ length of ¾″ dowelling.

4–2. Buddy.

4–3. Pattern for Buddy's cap peak. Clip lines to form tabs.

15. Draw a line down length of body to indicate center front.

16. Measure and mark position of left arm ⅛″ from top of body and ⁷⁄₁₆″ from center line. Measure and mark position of right arm ⅛″ from top of body and ⁹⁄₁₆″ from center line. At each mark, whittle a ¼″ × ¼″ area flat.

17. Sand bottom edge of head to expose raw wood.

18. Wood-glue head to top of body so head is slightly to right of center and faces forward.

19. For left leg, cut a 1⁵⁄₁₆″ length of ¼″ dowelling.

20. To indicate angle of left knee cut, measure and mark ⅝″ from right end. Rotate dowelling so mark is away from you, then measure and mark ⅝″ from left end. Cut angle.

21. To indicate angle of left hip cut, place one leg half on work surface so the knee end is at top. Rotate leg so the face of the knee angle cut is facing up. At opposite end, measure and mark ⅛″ from flat end. Cut angle.

22. To complete the left leg, reverse the knee cuts and wood-glue upper and lower legs together so knee joint is crooked.

23. With side of left leg ¹⁄₁₆″ from side of body, and centered from front to back, wood-glue left hip to bottom of body so ankle juts straight back.

24. For right leg, cut a 1⁷⁄₁₆″ length of ¼″ dowelling.

25. To indicate angle of right hip/knee cut, measure and mark ¹¹⁄₁₆″ from right end. Rotate dowelling so mark is away from you, then measure and mark ⅝″ from left end. Cut angle.

26. With side of right upper (longer) leg ¹⁄₁₆″ from side of body, and centered from front to back, wood-glue right hip to bottom of body so flat end juts straight forward.

27. Wood-glue knee angle of right lower (shorter) leg to flat end of right upper leg so point of knee angle is at front of leg.

28. For shoes, cut two ⅝″ lengths from the rounded ends of the ice-cream stick. Sand corners to round them.

29. Wood-glue left shoe to bottom of left leg so heel extends ⅛″ behind ankle and toe points down. Wood-glue right shoe to bottom of right leg so heel extends ⅛″ behind ankle, side of ankle is flush with outside edge of shoe, toe points forward, and Buddy stands upright.

30. For arms, cut two 1³⁄₁₆″ lengths of ¼″ dowelling.

31. To indicate angle of each elbow cut, measure and mark ⁹⁄₁₆″ from right end. Rotate dowelling so mark is away from you, then measure and mark ⁹⁄₁₆″ from left end. Cut angle.

32. At flat end of two arm halves, attach 8mm-bead hands.

33. To complete the arms, reverse the elbow cuts and wood-glue upper and lower arms together so elbow joints are crooked.

34. For each arm, whittle inside area of upper arm to flatten.

35. With shoulders even with top of body, wood-glue arms to body so left hand is down at side and right hand is at neck level.

36. Paint hands flesh.

37. For jacket, paint arms, torso, and top edge of torso khaki.

38. Referring to 4–1, use black to define right and left jacket fronts and curved bottom edges. Paint triangle at bottom edge of center front dark blue-grey.

39. Use black to paint five buttons evenly spaced down right side of center front of jacket. Paint a single button at outside of each cuff black.

40. Paint horizontal slash pockets black.

41. Use black to define a small triangular vent at bottom edge of center back. Paint vent dark blue-grey.

42. For socks, paint bottom ³⁄₁₆″ of legs white.

43. For cuffs, paint ⅛″ above socks light blue-grey.

44. For jeans, paint legs and bottom edge of torso dark blue-grey.

45. For shoes, paint top of shoes dark brown and soles black.

46. For shoelaces, use black to paint three ⅛″-wide horizontal stripes across instep and lace ties at base of ankles.

47. For newspaper, fold a 1½″ × 2¼″ rectangle of magazine print in half vertically. Fold short end over ¼″ and continue to fold at ¼″ intervals to the end. Tacky-glue last fold to secure.

48. Tacky-glue newspaper under Buddy's left arm.

ROVER

1. For body, use the 1″ length of ⅝″ dowelling. (Mark one end front and the other end rear.)

2. To indicate position of first two leg holes, mea-sure and mark ³⁄₁₆″ from each end of body. To indicate position of last two leg holes, measure ³⁄₁₆″ from each end of body and ⁵⁄₁₆″ from first two leg holes.

3. Using a ³⁄₃₂″ bit, drill ⅛″-deep right front and left back leg holes, pointing the drill bit towards the rear of body. For left front and right back leg holes, point drill bit towards the front of body.

4. To indicate position of tail hole, turn body so leg holes face down. At center back, measure and mark ³⁄₁₆″ from rear.

5. Using a ³⁄₃₂″ bit, drill a ⅛″-deep tail hole.

6. To indicate area where the head will be glued, turn body so leg holes face down. At center front, measure and mark ³⁄₁₆″ from each side of center and ¼″ from end. Whittle area flat.

7. For legs, cut one 1″ (right front leg) and three ⅞″ lengths from the thickest part of four toothpicks.

8. Wood-glue legs into leg holes.

9. For each paw, wood-glue leg into an 8mm bead with bottom of leg flush with bottom of paw.

10. For head, cover one hole of the 20mm bead with a tagboard circle. Sand edge of opposite hole to expose raw wood.

11. To indicate area where head will be glued to body, draw a line around the equator parallel with the covered bead hole. Measure and mark ³⁄₁₆″ from equator towards covered bead hole. Between equator and mark, whittle a ³⁄₁₆″ × ³⁄₁₆″ area flat.

12. Wood-glue head to body so covered bead hole is at back of head and open bead hole faces forward.

13. For muzzle, cut a 10mm bead in half. Discard one half.

14. To indicate position of nose hole, measure and mark ⅛″ from the center of one half-hole.

15. Using a ³⁄₃₂″ bit, drill a ⅛″-deep nose hole.

16. For nose, cut a ¼″ length from the thickest part of a toothpick. Wood-glue end into nose hole.

17. For mouth, measure and mark ⅛″ from the other half-hole.

4–4. *Rover.*

4–5. *Pattern for Rover's ears.*

The Claus family and some helpful
elves can be seen above, hard at work.
Instructions start on p. 119.

A

Below is Tumbleweed Ranch. Instructions start on p. 21.

Instructions for the beach scene on the facing page start on p. 89.

Instructions for making the African safari on the facing page, start on p. 53.

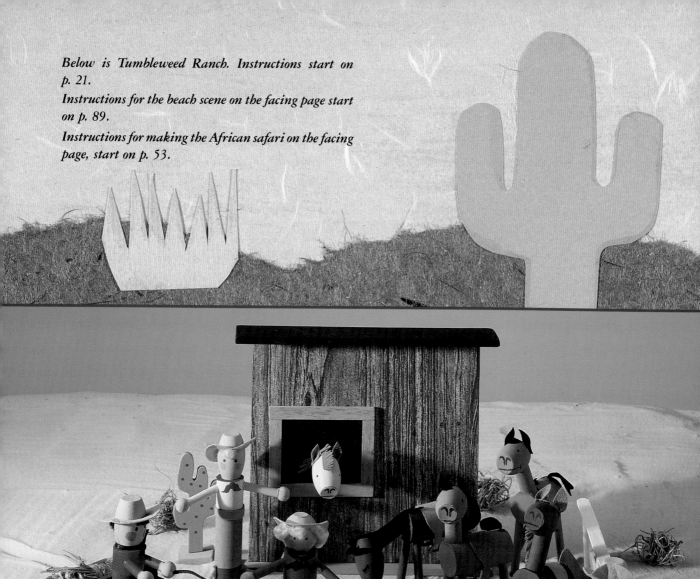

B

Instructions for the ballet scene start on p. 111.

D *Instructions for the Indian village start on p. 44.*

Instructions for making this space scene start on p. 10.

Instructions for the farm scene on this page start on p. 80.

On facing page: Instructions for the girl and her cat start on p. 97 and instructions for the boy and his dog start on p. 30.

F

At left, the U.S.S. Play-time. Instructions start on p. 16.
Below are to be seen the residents of a medieval castle along with a trusty steed and the traditional dragon. Instructions start on p. 33.

H

18. Whittle a ¹⁄₁₆″-deep × ⁵⁄₁₆″-wide horizontal groove for mouth.

19. Wood-glue muzzle to head so nose points up.

20. Fill half-holes with paste wood filler. Allow to dry and sand smooth.

21. For tail, cut a ¹⁵⁄₁₆″ length from the pointed end of a toothpick.

22. Wood-glue cut end of tail into tail hole.

23. Paint body, legs, tail, head, and muzzle light red-brown.

24. Paint top ⁵⁄₁₆″ of tail white. Paint bottom of paws black.

25. Referring to 4–4, paint front of muzzle and chest ruff white. Paint eyes, nose, and mouth black.

26. Following 4–5, cut two ears from brown synthetic suede.

27. On wrong side of ears, apply a dot of tacky glue to narrow end. Glue ears to each side of head so bottom of ears points slightly towards back.

28. For collar, cut a ¹⁄₈″ × 1⅝″ strip of black synthetic suede. Tacky-glue collar around neck, overlapping short edges at center back of neck.

29. For leash, tacky-glue one end of yarn along center of back, butting end with collar. To stiffen leash, apply a thin coat of tacky glue and work into fibres with your fingertips.

30. Repeat step 47 of Buddy.

31. Tacky-glue center of newspaper to Rover's mouth.

32. Tacky-glue end of leash into Buddy's right-hand hole.

5 · In Days of Olde When Knights Were Bold!

MATERIALS

Beads

one 44mm × 28mm large-hole wood bead
two white 32mm × 22mm large-hole wood beads
six white 25mm large-hole wood beads
fourteen white 10mm regular-hole wood beads
four white 8mm regular-hole wood beads
seven 6mm gold-plated beads

Wood

10″ length of ³⁄₁₆″ dowelling
15″ length of ¼″ dowelling
9″ length of ⅜″ dowelling
⅞″ length of ½″ dowelling
1″ length of ⅝″ dowelling
11″ length of ¾″ dowelling
2″ length of 1″ dowelling
58″ length of ¼ × 5¼ clear pine lattice
9¾″ length of ½ × 5½ clear pine lattice
fourteen ice-cream sticks
two flat wooden ice-cream spoons
seventeen round toothpicks

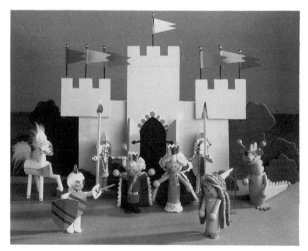

5–1.

Paints (Acrylic)

Flesh, black, dark pink, dark ultramarine, bright red, medium purple, medium yellow, white, light yellow-green, pale grey, dark green, medium grey-green, dark grey, very dark green, and metallic gold

Paint (Enamel)

Silver metallic aerosol spray paint

Fabric and Trims

2″ × 4″ piece of navy synthetic suede
3″ × 4¼″ piece of purple synthetic suede
small amount of white and black synthetic suede
9″ × 12″ piece of white felt
white, yellow, and orange curly chenille hair
small amount of white fake fur
36″ length of medium gold tubular cording
2¾″ length of ½″-wide ecru lace
2¾″ length of medium gold rickrack
3½″ length of green metallic ribbon

Hardware

thirteen ¾ × 18 wire brads

Miscellaneous

small amount of white tagboard
small amount of brass, chrome, red, blue, black, and
yellow decorative adhesive vinyl
small amount of gold iridescent wrapping paper
two 9mm gold nailheads

KING RICHARD

1. For head, cover one hole of a 25mm bead with a
tagboard circle. Paint head flesh.

2. Referring to 5–2, paint eyes black and cheeks
dark pink.

3. For body, cut a 2″ length of ¾″ dowelling.

4. Draw a line down length of body to indicate
center front.

5. Measure and mark position of left and right arms
³⁄₁₆″ from top of body and ⁹⁄₁₆″ from center line. At
each mark, whittle a ¼″ × ¼″ area flat.

6. Sand bottom edge of head to expose raw wood.

7. Wood-glue head to top of body so head faces
forward.

8. For shoe portion of boots, cut two ⅝″ lengths
from the rounded ends of an ice-cream stick. Sand
corners to round them.

9. Wood-glue shoes to bottom of body so heels are
flush with back of body, toes are pointed slightly out,
and King Richard stands upright.

5–2, 5–3. *King Richard.*

10. For arms, cut a 1⅝″ length of ¼″ dowelling.

11. To indicate angle of shoulder cut, measure and
mark ¾″ from right end. Rotate dowelling so mark is
away from you, then measure and mark ¾″ from left
end. Cut angle.

12. At flat end of each arm, attach a 10mm-bead
hand.

13. Wood-glue arms to body, making sure they are
raised up and slightly forward.

14. Paint hands flesh.

15. For boots, paint shoe portion and bottom ½″ of
body black.

16. For pants, paint ½″ above boots dark ultramarine.

17. For jacket, paint remaining body and arms bright
red.

18. For front sash, cut a ³⁄₁₆″ × 1⁵⁄₁₆″ strip of brass
adhesive vinyl. Starting at left shoulder, adhere to
body at an angle, ending at right side of waist. Trim
bottom end at an angle parallel with waistline. Repeat
for back sash.

19. For belt, cut a ³⁄₁₆″ × 2¾″ strip of brass adhesive
vinyl. Adhere around waist, overlapping short edges
at center back.

20. For cuff braids, cut two ¹⁄₁₆″ × ½″ strips of brass
adhesive vinyl. Adhere around arms ¹⁄₁₆″ above hands.
Secure overlapping ends with tacky glue.

21. For boot buckles, cut two ⅛″ × ³⁄₁₆″ rectangles
from chrome adhesive vinyl. Adhere to boot insteps.

22. For crown, adhere a ⅝″ × 2½″ strip of brass
adhesive vinyl to a ⅝″ × 2½″ strip of tagboard. Trim

5–4. *Half-pattern for King Richard's robe.*

one long edge with pinking shears. Overlap short edges ¼" and tacky-glue to secure. Tacky-glue crown to top of head.

23. Cut a ¼" length of white hair and tacky-glue to center forehead, just below crown. Cut a 2½" length of hair. Referring to 5–3, tacky-glue top row of hair to head. For bottom row, cut a 1½" length of hair and tacky-glue it centered below top row.

24. Following 5–4, cut robe from dark blue synthetic suede.

25. For trim, use pinking shears to cut a ⅜"-wide (measured from pinked point to pinked point) × 10" strip from white felt. On right side of robe, tacky-glue trim around edge, easing it around curves. Trim off excess.

26. Tacky-glue neck edge of robe to neck and shoulders.

27. Tie gold cording around neck, making a knot at center back. Trim ends close to knot.

QUEEN ELEANORA

1. For head, cover one hole of a 25mm bead with a tagboard circle. Paint head flesh.

2. Referring to 5–5, paint eyes black and cheeks dark pink.

3. For body, cut a 2" length of ¾" dowelling.

4. Draw a line down length of body to indicate center front.

5–5, 5–6. *Queen Eleanora.*

5. Measure and mark position of left and right arms ³⁄₁₆" from top of body and ⁹⁄₁₆" from center line. At each mark, whittle a ¼" × ¼" area flat.

6. Sand bottom edge of head to expose raw wood.

7. Wood-glue head to top of body so head faces forward.

8. For shoes, cut two ⅝" lengths from the rounded ends of an ice-cream stick. Sand corners to round them.

9. Wood-glue shoes to bottom of body so heels are flush with back of body, toes are pointed slightly out, and Queen Eleanora stands upright.

10. For arms, cut a 1⅜" length of ¼" dowelling.

11. To indicate angle of shoulder cut, measure and mark ⅝" from right end. Rotate dowelling so mark is away from you, then measure and mark ⅝" from left end. Cut angle.

12. At flat end of each arm, attach a 10mm-bead hand.

13. Wood-glue arms to body, making sure they are pointing down and slightly forward.

14. Paint hands flesh.

15. Paint shoes metallic gold.

16. For gown, paint body and arms medium purple.

17. For ruffle, tacky-glue the ecru lace around bottom edge of body, overlapping short edges at center back.

18. For sash, cut a ⅛" × 1⅜" strip of brass adhesive vinyl. Starting at left shoulder, adhere to body at an angle and ending at right side of waist. Trim end into an inverted V.

19. For belt, cut a ³⁄₁₆" × 2¾" strip of brass adhesive vinyl. Adhere around waist, overlapping short edges at center back, and allowing notched end of sash to extend below belt.

20. Referring to 5–5, cut a ½" length of yellow hair

5–7. *Half-pattern for Queen Eleanora's robe.*

and tacky-glue it vertically to center forehead, beginning at center top head and ending ¼″ above eyes. Cut two 1¾″ lengths of hair and fold in half. With cut ends pointed down, tacky-glue one length to each side of head, butting their folds against center front curl and framing the face. Referring to 5–6, cut two 1″ lengths of hair. Beginning at center top and working towards back of head, tacky glue one length at each side of previously glued hair. Cut a 1″ length of hair and fold in half. With fold at top and butted against previously glued hair, tacky-glue it to back of head, making sure its cut ends are even with rest of hair. Cut a ⅜″ length of hair. Tacky-glue it vertically to center back of head to fill empty space, making sure its cut ends are even with rest of hair.

21. Following 5–7, cut robe from purple synthetic suede.

22. For trim, use pinking shears to cut a ⅜″-wide (measured from pinked point to pinked point) × 14″ strip from white felt. On right side of robe, tacky-glue trim around edge, easing it around curves. Trim off excess to allow ends to butt.

23. Referring to 5–6, gather robe across back of neck. Tie gold cording around neck, making a knot at center back. Trim ends close to knot.

24. For crown, adhere an 11⁄16″ × 2½″ strip of brass adhesive vinyl to an 11⁄16″ × 2½″ strip of tagboard. Trim one long edge with pinking shears. Overlap short edges ¼″ and tacky-glue to secure. Tacky-glue crown to top of head.

LADY ANN

1. For head, cover one hole of a 25mm bead with a tagboard circle. Paint head flesh.

2. Referring to 5–8, paint eyes black and cheeks dark pink.

5–8, 5–9. *Lady Ann.*

36

3. For body, cut a 2″ length of ¾″ dowelling.

4. Draw a line down length of body to indicate center front.

5. Measure and mark position of left and right arms 3⁄16″ from top of body and ⅝″ from center line. At each mark, whittle a ¼″ × ¼″ area flat.

6. Sand bottom edge of head to expose raw wood.

7. Wood-glue head to top of body so head faces forward.

8. For shoes, cut two ⅝″ lengths from the rounded ends of an ice-cream stick. Sand corners to round them.

9. Wood-glue shoes to bottom of body so heels are flush with back of body, toes are pointed slightly out, and Lady Ann stands upright.

10. For arms, cut two ¾″ lengths of ¼″ dowelling. Along the length of each arm, whittle one side flat.

11. At one end of each arm, attach a 10mm-bead hand.

12. With shoulders even with top edge of body, wood-glue arms to body so hands extend slightly forward.

13. Paint hands flesh.

14. Paint shoes gold metallic.

15. For gown, paint body and arms medium yellow.

16. For hem ruffle, tacky-glue the gold rickrack around bottom edge of body, overlapping short edges at center back.

17. Use metallic gold to paint beads around neck.

18. Referring to 5–8, for bangs, cut a ¾″ length of orange hair and tacky-glue it horizontally across center forehead, about ⅛″ above eyes. Referring to 5–9, cut three 5½″ lengths of hair. Placing them side by side, tacky-glue first length from top of head, butting bangs and framing face. Tacky-glue second and third lengths in the same manner. (The space at the center back of head will be filled after the conical hat is glued in place.)

19. For conical hat, use a pencil compass to describe a 3″-diameter circle onto iridescent wrapping vinyl. Cut circle in half and discard one half. Roll half-circle into a tight cone with a ½″-diameter bottom opening. Tacky-glue overlap.

20. For streamers, cut six 1⁄16″-wide strips from metallic ribbon. Gather strips together with edges even. Dip gathered ends into tacky glue and insert into opening at top of hat.

21. Referring to 5–9, tacky-glue hat to head.

22. Cut two 2″ lengths of hair. Tacky-glue them vertically side by side to back of head to fill the remaining space.

23. Tie gold cording around head just above bangs and knot at center back of head. Trim ends close to knot.

SIR GALLANT

1. For body, cut a 1¼″ length of ¾″ dowelling.

2. Draw a line down length of body to indicate center front.

3. Measure and mark position of left and right armholes ³⁄₁₆″ from top of body and ⅝″ from center line.

4. Using a ¼″ bit, drill ¼″-deep armholes.

5. For head, cover one hole of a 25mm bead with a tagboard circle. Wood-glue head to top of body.

6. For legs, cut two 1″ lengths of ⅜″ dowelling.

7. Wood-glue legs side by side to bottom of body and centered from front to back.

8. For shoe armor, cut two ⅝″ lengths from the rounded ends of an ice-cream stick. Sand corners to round them.

9. Wood-glue shoes to bottom of legs so heels are flush with back of ankles, toes are pointed slightly out, and Sir Gallant stands upright.

10. For arms, cut two 1⅛″ lengths of ¼″ dowelling.

11. To indicate angle of each elbow cut, measure and mark ⁷⁄₁₆″ from right end. Rotate dowelling so mark is away from you, then measure and mark ⅝″ from left end. Cut angle.

12. At flat end of two lower (shorter) arms, attach 10mm-bead hands.

13. To complete the arms, reverse the elbow cuts and wood-glue upper and lower arms together so elbow joints are crooked.

14. Wood-glue arms into arm holes so right hand is slightly above waist and left hand is at mouth level.

15. Paint entire body white.

16. Following 5–10, cut breastplate from brass adhesive vinyl. Adhere to tagboard and cut out again.

17. For decorative stripes cut one ³⁄₃₂″ × 1½″ strip from blue adhesive vinyl and two ³⁄₁₆″ × 1½″ strips from red adhesive vinyl. With front of breastplate facing you, adhere first red stripe at an angle, beginning at upper left corner and ending at center of right side. Adhere blue stripe ¹⁄₁₆″ below it. Adhere the second red stripe ¹⁄₁₆″ below the blue stripe.

18. With pointed side down, tacky-glue breastplate to center of chest so rounded side is slightly above top of body.

19. Following 5–11, cut visor from brass adhesive vinyl. Adhere to tagboard and cut out again. Using an art knife, cut vents out of the tagboard. Fold visor in half. With pointed side down, tacky-glue sides of visor to head, allowing fold to extend ⅛″ from face.

20. Following 5–12, cut a helmet plume from brass adhesive vinyl. Flop pattern over to reverse it and cut one more.

21. Following 5–12, and omitting the half-round tab, cut a helmet plume lining from tagboard. Keeping the protective vinyl over the tabs at the bottom of each brass plume intact, adhere plumes to both sides of lining.

22. Spread tabs out, remove protective vinyl, and tacky-glue tabs to top of head.

23. For sword, cut the tip off a toothpick. Tacky-glue cut end into hole in left hand.

24. Paint sword white.

25. Following 5–13, cut sword hilt from brass adhesive vinyl. Adhere to tagboard and cut out again. Working from wrong side to right, use an ice pick to pierce a hole through center of hilt. Insert sword through hole. Tacky-glue hilt to hand.

26. Following 5–14, cut two shields (front and back) from brass adhesive vinyl. Adhere front to tagboard and cut out again. On right side of back shield, measure and mark for a hand hole ½″ below top edge. Cut out a ¼″ × ¼″ square at mark. Adhere back shield to front shield.

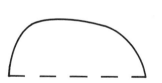

5–10. *Half-pattern for the knights' breastplates.*

5–11. *Half-pattern for the knights' visors.*

5–12. *Pattern for the knights' helmet plumes.*

5–13. *Pattern for sword hilt.*

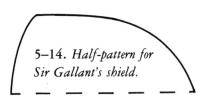

5–14. Half-pattern for Sir Gallant's shield.

27. For decorative stripes, cut one $3/32'' \times 2''$ strip from blue adhesive vinyl and two $3/16'' \times 2''$ strips from red adhesive vinyl. With front of shield facing you, adhere first red stripe at an angle, beginning at upper left corner and ending 1'' below upper right corner. Adhere blue stripe $3/32''$ below it. Adhere the second red stripe $3/32''$ below the blue stripe.

28. Bend shield along center to bow front.

29. Tacky-glue hand hole of shield to right hand.

KNIGHTS OF THE SILVER GUARD (MAKE 2)

1. Repeat steps 1 to 13 of Sir Gallant.

2. Wood-glue arms into armholes so right wrist is raised even with top of body and left wrist is $3/8''$ higher than right. (Reverse arm positions for second knight.)

3. Spray-paint entire body silver metallic.

4. Following 5–10, cut breastplate from chrome adhesive paper. Adhere to tagboard and cut out again. (Omit decorative stripes.)

5. Repeat steps 19 to 22 of Sir Gallant.

6. For lance, cut a 5'' length of $3/16''$ dowelling. Use an art knife to cut a $1/4''$-deep slit at one end for lance point.

7. Spray-paint lance silver metallic.

8. Following 5–15, cut two lance points from chrome adhesive vinyl. Adhere one point to tagboard and cut out again. Adhere second point to opposite side.

9. With point up, insert lance point into slit and tacky-glue in place.

10. Stand knight on work surface. Place lance at inside of left hand with bottom of lance flush with work surface and flat face of lance point facing forward. On lance, mark area where hand touches lance. Whittle area flat. (Place lance at inside of right hand for second knight.) Tacky-glue lance to left hand of first knight and right hand of second knight.

SIR STEED

1. For body, cut a $1 9/16''$ length of 1'' dowelling.

2. To indicate position of first two leg holes, measure and mark $5/16''$ from each end of body. To indicate position of last two leg holes, measure $5/16''$ from each end of body and $5/8''$ from first two leg holes.

3. Using a $1/4''$ bit, drill $1/4''$-deep right and left back leg holes and right front leg hole, angling the bit slightly towards the center top of body.

4. To indicate position of tail hole, turn body so leg holes face down. At center back, measure and mark $3/16''$ from rear end.

5. Using a $3/32''$ bit, drill a $1/8''$-deep tail hole.

6. To indicate position of neck, turn body so leg holes face down. At center front, measure and mark $1/4''$ from each side of center and $1/2''$ from end. Whittle area flat.

7. For neck, cut a $7/8''$ length of $1/2''$ dowelling.

8. For neck/head angle, measure and mark $1/4''$ from one cut end. Cut angle.

9. For head, whittle a $1/2'' \times 1/2''$ area at a hole end of a 32mm $\times$ 22mm bead to flatten. Test-fit angled end of neck with whittled end of head to make sure they form a right angle. Wood-glue head to neck.

10. Wood-glue flat end of neck to body so head is turned slightly towards Sir Steed's left.

11. Cover bead holes with tagboard circles.

12. For straight legs, cut three $1 3/4''$ lengths of $1/4''$ dowelling.

13. Wood-glue legs into leg holes.

14. For left front leg, cut one $1 3/16''$ (upper leg), one $15/16''$ (lower leg and hoof) length of $1/4''$ dowelling. To indicate angle of cut for lower leg and hoof, measure and mark $9/16''$ from right end. Rotate dowelling so mark is away from you, then measure and mark $5/16''$ from same end. Cut angle.

15. At one end of upper leg, whittle a $1/8''$-deep $\times$ $3/8''$-long notch so upper leg will lie close to body. On opposite end and opposite side of upper leg, whittle a $1/8''$-deep $\times$ $1/4''$-long notch so straight-cut end of lower leg will lie flat to upper leg and create a right angle (knee bend). Wood-glue upper leg to body.

16. Wood-glue straight-cut end of lower leg to upper leg.

17. Sand short side of hoof so it will lie close to ankle and form a right angle (ankle bend). Wood-glue hoof to bottom of lower leg with straight-cut end facing forward.

5–15. *Pattern for the Silver Guard's lance points.*

5–16. *Sir Steed.*

5–17. *Pattern for Sir Steed's ears.*

5–18. *Pattern for Sir Steed's tail.*

5–19. *Half-pattern for Sir Steed's breastplate.*

5–20. *Pattern for Sir Steed's visor.*

18. Paint Sir Steed white.

19. Referring to 5–16, use black to paint eyes, nostrils, and mouth.

20. For mane, cut a $\frac{1}{4}'' \times 2\frac{1}{4}''$ strip from white fake fur. Trim one end into a V. With V at center of forehead, tacky-glue mane to top of head and back of neck.

21. Following 5–17, cut ears from white synthetic suede.

22. On right side of ears, dot straight edge with tacky glue. Fold over and pinch to secure. Tacky-glue ears to each side of head.

23. Following 5–18, cut tail from white fake fur. Flop pattern over and cut another tail from fake fur. Tacky-glue tails together.

24. Tacky-glue end of tail into tail hole.

25. For hoof decoration, cut four $\frac{1}{8}'' \times \frac{1}{2}''$ strips of chrome adhesive vinyl. Adhere around ankle $\frac{1}{16}''$ from bottom of leg. Secure overlapping ends with tacky glue.

26. For chest armor strap, cut a $\frac{1}{8}'' \times 3\frac{1}{4}''$ strip of chrome adhesive vinyl and adhere it horizontally around body, beginning and ending $\frac{1}{4}''$ from chest.

27. Following 5–19, cut the breastplate from chrome adhesive vinyl. Adhere to tagboard and cut out again. Fold breastplate in half. Tacky-glue sides of breastplate to body, allowing fold to extend $\frac{1}{2}''$ from chest.

28. Following 5–20, cut visor from chrome adhesive vinyl. Adhere to tagboard and cut out again. Using an art knife, cut vents out of the tagboard. Fold visor in half. With pointed side down, tacky-glue sides of visor to head, allowing fold to extend $\frac{1}{4}''$ from face.

DRACO THE DRAGON

1. For body, cover one hole of the 44mm × 28mm bead with a tagboard circle (bottom).

2. Draw a line down length of body to indicate center front.

3. Measure and mark position of left and right arms $\frac{1}{16}''$ from top of body and $\frac{7}{8}''$ from center line. At each mark, whittle a $\frac{1}{4}'' \times \frac{1}{4}''$ area flat.

4. Draw a line down the center back of body. Rout out a $\frac{1}{8}''$-deep × $\frac{1}{16}''$-wide groove along line to accommodate tail and scales.

5. For neck, cut a 1'' length of $\frac{5}{8}''$ dowelling.

6. For neck/body angle, measure and mark $\frac{1}{8}''$ from one cut end. Cut angle.

7. With point of neck angle towards you and cut face of angle facing down, draw a line down center of neck. Rout out a $\frac{1}{8}''$-deep × $\frac{1}{16}''$-wide groove along line to accommodate scales.

8. For head, whittle a $\frac{1}{2}'' \times \frac{1}{2}''$ area at a hole end of 32mm × 22mm bead to flatten. Test-fit flat side of neck with whittled end of head to make sure they form a right angle.

9. With whittled side of head towards you and facing down, draw a line down center of head. Along this line, measure and mark $\frac{3}{4}''$ from end nearest you. Erase line above mark. Rout out a $\frac{1}{8}''$-deep × $\frac{1}{16}''$-wide × $\frac{3}{4}''$-long groove along line to accommodate scales.

10. With whittled side of head towards you and facing down, measure and mark for two horn holes $\frac{5}{8}''$ from end nearest you and $\frac{7}{16}''$ from each side of routed groove.

11. Using a $\frac{3}{32}''$ bit, drill $\frac{1}{8}''$-deep horn holes.

5–22. *Pattern for Draco's tail.*

5–23. *Pattern for Draco's ears.*

5–21. *Pattern for Draco's feet.*

12. Wood-glue angled end of neck to body so neck juts forward.

13. Wood-glue head to neck so head faces forward.

14. Cover bead holes with tagboard circles.

15. Following 5–21, cut two feet from wooden spoons. Flop one foot over to reverse it. Tacky-glue feet to bottom of body so toes point out and Draco stands upright.

16. For arms, cut two 1⁵⁄₁₆″ lengths of ¼″ dowelling.

17. To indicate angle of each elbow cut, measure and mark 1¹⁄₁₆″ from right end. Rotate dowelling so mark is away from you, then measure and mark ½″ from left end. Cut angle.

18. At flat end of two lower (shorter) arms, attach 10mm-bead hands.

19. To complete the arms, reverse the elbow cuts and wood-glue upper and lower arms together so elbow joints are crooked.

20. Test-fit arms to body so elbows point slightly out. Whittle inside of upper arms flat.

21. Wood-glue arms to body so left arm points slightly down and forearm of right arm is parallel with top of body.

22. Following 5–22, cut tail from ¼ × 5¼ lattice. Whittle the short edge so it fits snugly into groove at back of body.

23. Wood-glue tail to back of body so it is parallel with and ¹⁄₁₆″ above work surface.

24. For head scales, cut four ⅜″ lengths from the rounded ends of two ice-cream sticks. At top of head, wood-glue flat ends into groove. At back of head, tacky-glue to tagboard circle. (Second scale at back of head will extend onto back of neck.)

25. For neck scales, cut two ½″ lengths from the rounded ends of an ice-cream stick. At back of neck, wood-glue flat ends into groove.

26. For body scales, cut two ½″ lengths from the rounded ends of an ice-cream stick. Whittle flat end of one scale into a shallow V so it fits into corner between body and tail. Wood-glue both scales into groove.

27. For tail scales, cut one ⁷⁄₁₆″ and six ⁵⁄₁₆″ lengths from the rounded ends of four ice-cream sticks. Wood-glue the flat end of the larger scale next to scale at inside corner. Wood-glue remaining scales evenly spaced along the length of tail.

28. Wood-glue an 8mm bead to end of tail.

29. For each horn, wood-glue the pointed end of a toothpick into an 8mm bead. Trim tip that extends beyond hole. Sand to smooth. Trim so overall length is 1″. Wood-glue horns into horn holes.

30. Following 5–23, cut two ears from tagboard. Make a fold in each ear ⅛″ from flat end to form a tab. With tabs facing back of head and ears parallel to and just below horns, tacky-glue ears to each side of head.

31. Paint entire body light yellow-green.

32. For nose, cut an 8mm bead in half. Discard one half. Sand cut side of remaining bead half to eliminate bead-hole ridge as much as possible.

33. Paint nose black. With half-bead holes horizontal, tacky-glue nose to center top of head so bottom edge is flush with front of head.

34. Referring to 5–24, paint eyes and mouth black. Paint cheeks dark pink.

5–24. *Draco the Dragon.*

40

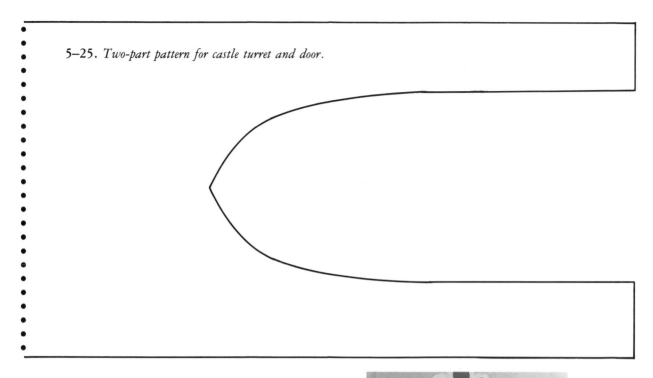

5–25. *Two-part pattern for castle turret and door.*

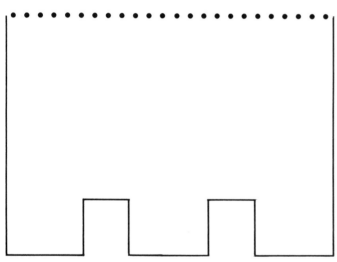

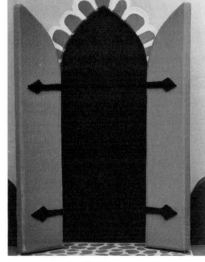

5–26. *Castle door.*

5–27. *Pattern for door hinges.*

CASTLE

1. For castle facade, use the 9¾″ × 5⅜″ rectangle of ½ × 5½ lattice.

2. For side walls of castle, cut two 1¼″ × 5⅜″ rectangles from ¼ × 5¼ lattice.

3. Wood-glue long edge of each side wall to back of facade. Position side walls flush with top, bottom, and side edges of facade.

4. To reinforce, nail facade to each side wall, using two wire brads spaced 1½″ from top and bottom and ³⁄₃₂″ from edge.

5. For base, cut a 3″ × 12½″ rectangle from ¼ × 5¼ lattice.

6. Wood-glue facade to base with back edge of side walls flush with back edge of base and centered side to side.

7. To reinforce, nail base to facade and each side wall, using seven wire brads. Draw a center line down

41

length of base bottom. Insert one wire brad at center of line and two spaced 2″ from ends of base. For side walls, measure and mark 1¼″ from short ends of base. At each side, insert wire brads ⅛″ and ⅞″ from back edge of base.

8. Following 5–25, cut center turret from ¼ × 5¼ lattice.

9. Cut out door from door opening.

10. Cut door in half lengthwise and set aside.

11. Using a ³⁄₃₂″ bit, drill a ¼″-deep flagpole hole at center top of middle turret.

12. Wood-glue center turret to facade, with bottom edge butted against base and centered side to side.

13. For side turrets, cut two 3¼″ × 2½″ rectangles from ¼ × 5¼ lattice.

14. Following 5–25, cut out side turrets.

15. Using a ³⁄₃₂″ bit, drill a ¼″-deep flagpole hole at center top of each turret.

16. Wood-glue side turrets to facade so they are 1⅛″ from center turret and extend 1½″ at top.

17. For stone step, draw a line from each side of center turret to front of base and continue down front edge of base.

18. Paint castle pale grey, base very dark green, and step medium grey-green.

19. Referring to 5–26, paint cobblestones dark grey.

20. Referring to 5–26, paint stonework around doorway dark grey. Outline stones using white.

21. Following 5–25, cut a door-opening shape from black adhesive paper. Adhere to back wall of doorway opening.

22. Paint door halves medium grey-green.

23. To indicate position of doorknobs, measure and mark 1⅞″ from bottom edge and ¼″ from long straight edge.

24. At each mark, hammer in a 9mm gold nailhead doorknob. (The side with the doorknob is now the outside of the door.)

25. Following 5–27, cut four door hinges from black synthetic suede.

26. With inside of left door facing you, tacky-glue one hinge ¾″ from bottom edge and the other 3⅛″ from bottom edge and spaced ⅛″ from long straight edge of door. Repeat for right door.

27. Fit door into opening and tacky-glue hinge ends to facade.

28. Position doors so they are three-quarters open.

On bottom of base, measure and mark for a pilot hole to secure each door with wire brads.

29. Using a ³⁄₃₂″ bit, drill pilot holes through base and into bottom edge of door. Nail in brads.

30. Following 5–28, cut two castle shrubs from ¼ × 5¼ lattice. Flop one shrub over to reverse it.

31. Paint shrubs dark green.

32. Tacky-glue shrubs to facade with straight edge butting center turret and bottom edges butting the base.

33. Make seven flags, one brass and two each of yellow, blue, and red. For each flagpole, paint a toothpick black. Tacky-glue one end of toothpick into a 6mm gold bead.

34. Following 5–29, cut flags from adhesive vinyl. To assemble each flag, remove protective paper, place flagpole (below bead) across center and adhere the two sides together. Trim off flagpole bottom so overall length is 2⅜″. Tacky-glue flags into flagpole holes.

SMALL SHRUB

1. Following 5–30, cut small shrub from ¼ × 5¼ lattice.

2. For easel stand, cut a triangle with ¾″ × ¾″ right-angle sides from ¼ × 5¼ lattice.

3. Locate and mark center back of shrub. Hold shrub upright with bottom edge flat against work surface. With one ¾″ edge of easel stand flat against work surface, wood-glue the other ¾″ edge vertically to center back of shrub.

4. Paint shrub dark green.

LARGE SHRUB (MAKE 2)

1. Following 5–31, cut two large shrubs from ¼ × 5¼ lattice. Flop one shrub over to reverse it.

2. For easel stand, cut a triangle with 2″ × 3½″ right-angle sides from ¼ × 5¼ lattice.

3. Locate and mark center back of shrub. Hold shrub upright with bottom edge flat against work surface. With 2″ edge of easel stand flat against work surface, wood-glue the 3½″ edge vertically to center back of shrub.

4. Paint shrub dark green.

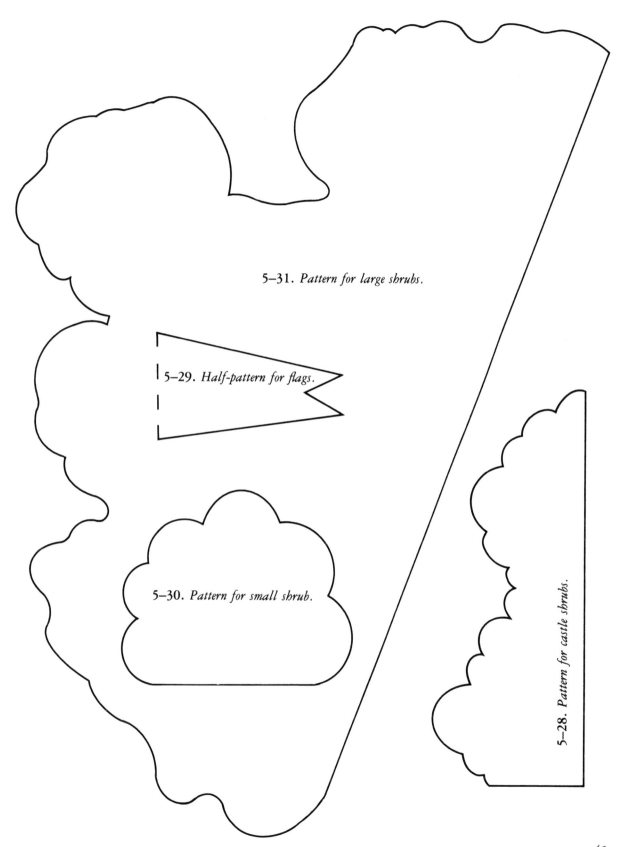

5-31. *Pattern for large shrubs.*

5-29. *Half-pattern for flags.*

5-30. *Pattern for small shrub.*

5-28. *Pattern for castle shrubs.*

43

6 · Shining Star Indian Village

MATERIALS

Beads

one white 32mm × 22mm large-hole wood bead
nine white 25mm large-hole wood beads
two white 20mm large-hole wood beads
one white 10mm regular-hole wood bead
sixteen white 8mm regular-hole wood beads

Wood

32″ length of ¼″ dowelling
12″ length of ⅜″ dowelling
16″ length of ¾″ dowelling
63″ length of ¼ × 5¼ clear pine lattice
six ice-cream sticks
eight round toothpicks
six square toothpicks
two 3″-long thin twigs (see 6–1)

Paints (Acrylic)

Light red-brown, black, dark pink, dark taupe, dark brown, medium yellow, bright red, medium green, and pale grey

Fabric and Trims

Seed beads, one ⁵⁄₁₆ oz. package each of: Red, Lt. Blue, and Yellow
small amount of beige synthetic suede
1″ × 8″ strip of dark red synthetic suede
¼″ × 5¼″ strip of white fake fur
five 1¼″-long brown-and-white striped feathers
one 1¼″-long yellow feather
one 1¼″-long blue feather
two skeins of black six-strand embroidery floss
small amount of orange felt

Miscellaneous

small amount of white tagboard
beading needle
beading thread
aluminum foil

44

6–1.

CHIEF STANDING TALL

1. For head, cover one hole of a 25mm bead with a tagboard circle. Paint head light red-brown.
2. Referring to 6–2, paint eyes black and cheeks dark pink. At center back of head, measure and mark ⅝″ from edge of top bead hole. Paint hair black, curving hairline from sides of head up to mark.
3. For body, cut a 2⅞″ length of ¾″ dowelling.
4. Draw a line down length of body to indicate center front.
5. Measure and mark position of left and right arms ⅛″ from top of body and ¾″ from center line. At each mark, whittle a ¼″ × ¼″ area flat.
6. Sand bottom edge of head to expose raw wood.
7. Wood-glue head to top of body so head faces forward.
8. For moccasins, cut two ¾″ lengths from the rounded ends of an ice-cream stick. Sand corners to round them.
9. Referring to 6–3, trim off one back corner of each moccasin so when moccasins are side by side the toes point slightly out.
10. Wood-glue moccasins to bottom of body, making sure the toes point slightly out and Chief Standing Tall stands upright.

11. For right arm, cut a 1⅛″ length of ¼″ dowelling.

12. To indicate angle of right elbow cut, measure and mark ⁹⁄₁₆″ from right end. Rotate dowelling so mark is away from you, then measure and mark ⁷⁄₁₆″ from left end. Cut angle.

13. For left arm, cut a 1⁵⁄₁₆″ length of ¼″ dowelling.

14. At flat end of one right lower (shorter) arm and one end of left arm, attach an 8mm-bead hand.

15. To complete the right arm, reverse the elbow cuts and wood-glue right upper and lower arms together so elbow joint is crooked.

16. For each arm, whittle inside area of upper arm flat.

17. With shoulders even with top of body, wood-glue arms to body so left hand is at nose level and right hand is at chest level.

18. Paint hands light red-brown.

19. Paint body, arms, and moccasins dark taupe.

20. To accent moccasins, tacky-glue three red seed beads, butted together and forming a triangle, to center top of instep.

21. For hem fringe, cut a ¼″ × 2½″ strip of beige synthetic suede. Trim one long edge with pinking shears. Tacky-glue fringe around bottom edge of body, butting short edges at center back.

22. For neck fringe, cut a ¼″ × 1¼″ strip of beige synthetic suede. Trim one long edge with pinking shears. Tacky-glue fringe to center front of body with long straight edge of fringe flush with top edge of body.

23. For sleeve fringe, cut two ¼″ × ⅝″ strips of beige synthetic suede. Trim one long edge of each with pinking shears. Tacky-glue long straight edge of one fringe to underside of right forearm so it hangs down and out and other fringe to left arm so it hangs straight down.

24. For headdress, use the ¼″ × 5¼″ strip of white fake fur.

25. Referring to 6–2, tacky-glue fake fur strip around head starting and ending at lower center back of head, allowing end to hang down back. Trim end at an angle.

26. With one striped feather positioned at center front of headdress and the remaining four striped feathers evenly spaced on each side of it, tacky-glue tips to underside of headdress.

27. For headband, cut a ¼″ × 1⅞″ strip of beige synthetic suede. Trim one long edge with pinking shears.

28. For decorative beaded loops, string two strands of twenty-four blue seed beads onto two 6″ lengths of beading thread. Knot ends securely. Trim ends ⅛″ from knots. Tacky-glue knotted ends of loops to wrong side of headband, ⅛″ from each side edge, so loops hang down from straight edge.

29. Tacky-glue headband to center front of headdress with bottom edge of headband ¹⁄₁₆″ above eyes.

30. For decorative beading on headband, string a strand of forty-two beads onto a 6″ length of beading thread as follows: four blue, * two red, six blue *, repeat between *'s four times, end with two red and four blue beads. Knot end, dot knot with tacky glue, and trim ends close to knot. Tacky-glue decorative beading across center of headband.

RUNNING DEER

1. For head, cover one hole of a 25mm bead with a tagboard circle.

2. To indicate position of braid holes, draw a line around the equator, parallel with the bead holes, and a line around the meridian. Where lines cross, measure and mark ¼″ below the equator towards the open hole side of the head.

3. Using a ³⁄₃₂″ bit, drill ⅛″-deep braid holes.

4. Paint head light red-brown.

5. Referring to 6–4, paint eyes black and cheeks

6–2. *Chief Standing Tall.*

6–3. *Chief Standing Tall's moccasins.*

6–4. *Running Deer.*

6–5. *Running Deer's papoose.*

dark pink. At center back of head, measure and mark ⅝″ from edge of top bead hole. Paint hair black, curving hairline from sides of head up to mark.

6. For body, cut a 2½″ length of ¾″ dowelling.

7. Draw a line down length of body to indicate center front on one side and center back on opposite side.

8. Measure and mark position of left and right arms ⅛″ from top of body and 1¹⁄₁₆″ from front center line. At each mark, whittle a ¼″ × ¼″ area flat.

9. Measure and mark position of papoose ¼″ on either side of back center line. Between each mark, whittle a ½″-wide × ⅞″-long area flat.

10. Sand bottom edge of head to expose raw wood.

11. Wood-glue head to top of body so head faces forward.

12. For moccasins, cut two ¹¹⁄₁₆″ lengths from the rounded ends of an ice-cream stick. Sand corners to round them.

13. Referring to 6–3, trim off one back corner of each moccasin so when moccasins are side by side the toes point slightly out.

14. Wood-glue moccasins to bottom of body, making sure the toes point slightly out and Running Deer stands upright.

15. For arms, cut two 1″ lengths of ¼″ dowelling.

16. To indicate angle of each elbow cut, measure and cut ⁷⁄₁₆″ from right end. Rotate dowelling so mark is away from you, then measure and mark ⁷⁄₁₆″ from left end. Cut angle.

17. At flat end of two arm halves, attach 8mm-bead hands.

18. To complete the arms, reverse the elbow cuts and wood-glue upper and lower arms together so elbow joints are crooked.

19. For each arm, whittle inside area of upper arm flat.

20. With shoulders even with top of body, wood-glue arms to body so left hand is at waist level and right hand is at chest level.

21. Paint hands light red-brown.

22. Paint body, arms, and moccasins dark taupe.

23. For hem fringe, cut a ¼″ × 2½″ strip of beige synthetic suede. Trim one long edge with pinking shears. Tacky-glue fringe around bottom edge of body, butting short edges at center back.

24. For sleeve fringe, cut two ¼″ × ¾″ strips of beige synthetic suede. Trim one long edge of each with pinking shears. Tacky-glue long straight edge of one fringe to outside of each arm.

25. For each braid, cut six 3″ lengths of black floss. Tacky-glue ends together at one end to secure.

26. Using two lengths for each section of braid, braid for 1⁷⁄₈″. Wrap a 6″ length of one strand of floss four times around bottom end of braid to secure. Tie ends in a knot and secure knot with tacky glue.

27. Trim braids so they measure 2⅛″ long.

28. Tacky-glue top ends of braids into braid holes.

29. For long necklace, string a strand of sixty-seven beads onto a 6″ length of beading thread as follows: two blue, * four red, two blue, one yellow *, two blue, repeat between *'s seven times, end with two blue beads.

30. Knot ends ¼″ from beads at each side so necklace will lie close to neck. Secure knot with tacky glue. Tacky-glue thread portion of necklace to center back of neck.

31. For short necklace, string a strand of forty red beads onto a 6″ length of beading thread.

32. Repeat step 30.

33. For papoose head, use the 10mm bead.

34. Paint head light red-brown.

35. Referring to 6–5, paint eyes black and cheeks dark pink.

36. For papoose body, cut a ⅞″ length of ⅜″ dowelling.

37. Sand bottom edge of body to round it.

38. Whittle one side of body (back) flat.

39. Sand bottom edge of head to expose raw wood.

40. Wood-glue head to body, making sure back of head is above whittled side of body.

41. Paint body dark taupe.

42. For bangs, cut four ¼″ lengths of black floss. With one end at center front of head, tacky-glue other end of each bang into bead hole at top of head. For hair, cut six 1⅛″ lengths of black floss. Placing them side by side, tacky-glue center of each length to center top of head.

43. For strap, cut a ⅛″ × 6½″ strip of beige synthetic suede.

44. Tacky-glue center of strap to lower center back of papoose body. Bring ends around to the front and crisscross at lower quarter of front. Bring straps around to back and crisscross at center of back. Bring straps around to front and crisscross at upper one-quarter of front. Bring straps around to back, trim

ends so they butt, and tacky-glue to secure.

45. Referring to 6–5, tacky-glue papoose at an angle to center back of Running Deer.

LITTLE DOVE

1. For head, cover one hole of a 25mm bead with a tagboard circle. Paint head light red-brown.

2. Referring to 6–6, paint eyes black and cheeks dark pink. At center back of head, measure and mark ⅝″ from edge of top bead hole. Paint hair black, curving hairline from sides of head up to mark.

3. For body, cut a 1¹¹⁄₁₆″ length of ¾″ dowelling.

4. Draw a line down length of body to indicate center front.

5. Measure and mark position of left and right arms ⅛″ from top of body and ¹¹⁄₁₆″ from center line. At each mark, whittle a ¼″ × ¼″ area flat.

6. Sand bottom edge of head to expose raw wood.

7. Wood-glue head to top of body so head faces slightly towards left.

8. For moccasins, cut two ¹¹⁄₁₆″ lengths from the rounded ends of an ice-cream stick. Sand corners to round them.

9. Referring to 6–3, trim off one back corner of each moccasin so when moccasins are side by side the toes point slightly out.

10. Wood-glue moccasins to bottom of body, making sure toes point slightly out and Little Dove stands upright.

11. For arms, cut two ¹³⁄₁₆″ lengths of ¼″ dowelling.

12. To indicate angle of each elbow cut, measure and mark ⁷⁄₁₆″ from right end. Rotate dowelling so mark is away from you, then measure and mark ⅜″ from left end. Cut angle.

13. At flat end of two lower (longer) arms, attach 8mm-bead hands.

14. To complete the arms, reverse the elbow cuts and wood-glue upper and lower arms together so elbow joints are crooked.

15. For each arm, whittle inside area of upper arm flat.

16. With shoulders even with top of body, wood-glue arms to body so left hand is at chest level and right hand is at cheek level.

17. Paint hands light red-brown.

18. Paint body, arms, and moccasins dark taupe.

19. Repeat steps 23 and 24 of Running Deer.

20. For topknot, wind black floss eight times around the 5¼″ × 5¼″ square of cardboard. Cut end and slip from cardboard. Twist strands together. Tie into a knot at center, then tie twice more. Tuck in ends and tacky-glue to secure. Tacky-glue topknot to center top of head.

21. For long necklace, string a strand of forty-six beads onto a 6″ length of beading thread as follows: * four blue, one red, one yellow, one red *, repeat between *'s six times, end with four blue beads.

22. Knot ends ¼″ from beads at each side so necklace will lie close to neck. Secure knot with tacky glue. Tacky-glue thread portion of necklace to center back of neck.

23. For short necklace, string a strand of thirty-four beads onto a 6″ length of beading thread as follows: * six red, one yellow *, repeat between *'s four times, end with six red beads.

24. Repeat step 23.

CANOE

1. Following 6–7, cut canoe from ¼ × 5¼ lattice. Sand edges on front side to round them.

2. Paint top edge dark brown.

3. Using pinking shears, cut a ¼″-wide (measured from pinked point to pinked point) × 8″-long strip from dark red synthetic suede.

6–6. *Little Dove.*

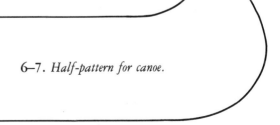

6–7. *Half-pattern for canoe.*

6–8. *Jumping Fox and Many Sparrows.*

4. On right side, tacky-glue strip along upper edge of canoe, easing it around curves and folding ends over edges. Trim ends.

JUMPING FOX

1. For head, cover one hole of a 25mm bead with a tagboard circle.

2. To indicate position of braid holes, draw a line around the equator, parallel with the bead holes, and a line around the meridian. Where lines cross, measure and mark ¼" below the equator towards the open hole side of head.

3. Using a 3/32" bit, drill ⅛"-deep braid holes.

4. Paint head light red-brown.

5. Referring to 6–8, paint eyes black and cheeks dark pink. At center back of head, measure and mark ⅝" from edge of top bead hole. Paint hair black, curving hairline from sides of head up to mark.

6. For body, cut a 1¼" length of ¾" dowelling.

7. Draw a line down length of body to indicate center front.

8. Measure and mark position of left and right arms ⅛" from top of body and ¹¹⁄₁₆" from center line. At each mark, whittle a ¼" × ¼" area flat.

9. To indicate position where left side of body will be glued to canoe, measure and mark ⅜" from center line and ¾" from bottom edge. At mark, whittle a ¼" × ¾" area flat.

10. Sand bottom edge of head to expose raw wood.

11. Wood-glue head to top of body so head faces towards left.

12. For arms, cut two 1¹⁄₁₆" lengths of ¼" dowelling.

13. To indicate angle of each elbow cut, measure and mark ⁹⁄₁₆" from right end. Rotate dowelling so mark is away from you, then measure and mark ⁷⁄₁₆" from left end. Cut angle.

14. At flat end of two lower (shorter) arms, attach 8mm-bead hands.

15. To complete the arms, reverse the elbow cuts and wood-glue upper and lower arms together so elbow joints are crooked.

16. For each arm, whittle inside area of upper arm flat.

17. With shoulder even with top of body, wood-glue right arm to body so right hand is at waist level. Place canoe against whittled area of body. With shoulder even with top of body, wood-glue left arm to body so left elbow touches top of canoe. Set canoe aside.

18. Paint hands light red-brown.

19. Paint body and arms dark taupe.

20. For each braid, cut six 3" lengths of black floss. Tacky-glue ends together at one end to secure.

21. Using two lengths for each section of braid, braid for 1¼". Wrap a 6" length of one strand of floss four times around bottom end of braid to secure. Tie ends in a knot and secure knot with tacky glue.

22. Trim braids so they measure 1⅝" long.

23. Tacky-glue top ends of braids into braid holes.

24. Referring to 6–1, tacky-glue left side of Jumping Fox to wrong side of canoe.

25. Tacky-glue twig to inside of left hand.

MANY SPARROWS

1. Repeat steps 1 to 16 of Jumping Fox.

2. With shoulder even with top of body, wood-glue right arm to body so right hand is at mouth level. Place canoe against whittled area of body. With shoulder even with top of body, wood-glue arm to body so left upper arm is parallel with and ⅛" above top edge of canoe. Set canoe aside.

3. Repeat steps 18 to 23 of Jumping Fox.

4. Referring to 6–1, tacky-glue left side of Many Sparrows to wrong side of canoe.

5. Tacky-glue twig to inside of left arm.

6–9. *Yellow Feather.*

48

YELLOW FEATHER

1. For head, cover one hole of a 25mm bead with a tagboard circle.

2. To indicate position of braid hole at back of head, draw a line around the equator, parallel with the bead holes, and a line around the meridian. Where lines cross, mark for braid hole (back of head).

3. Using a ³⁄₃₂″ bit, drill a ⅛″-deep braid hole.

4. Paint head light red-brown.

5. Referring to 6–9, paint eyes black and cheeks dark pink. At center back of head, measure and mark ⅝″ from edge of top bead hole. Paint hair black, curving hairline from sides of head up to mark.

6. For body, cut a 1″ length of ¾″ dowelling.

7. Draw a line down length of body to indicate center front.

8. Measure and mark position of left and right arms ⅛″ from top of body and ⅝″ from center line. At each mark, whittle a ¼″ × ¼″ area flat.

9. Sand bottom edge of head to expose raw wood.

10. Wood-glue head to body so head faces forward.

11. For legs, cut two 1⅝″ lengths of ⅜″ dowelling.

12. To indicate angle of each knee cut, measure and mark ¹¹⁄₁₆″ from right end. Rotate dowelling so mark is away from you, then measure and mark ¹³⁄₁₆″ from left end. Cut angle.

13. To indicate angle of each hip cut, place an upper (shorter) leg on work surface so the knee end is at top. Rotate leg so the face of the knee angle cut is facing down. At opposite end, measure and mark ⅛″ from flat end. Cut angle.

14. To indicate angle of each ankle cut, place a lower (longer) leg on work surface so the knee end is at top. Rotate leg so the face of the knee angle cut is face down. At opposite end, measure and mark ⅛″ from flat end. Cut angle.

15. To complete the legs, reverse the knee cuts and wood-glue upper and lower legs together so knee joints are crooked.

16. Whittle inside of upper legs flat.

17. With sides of legs flush with sides of body, and centered from front to back, wood-glue hips to bottom of body so knees turn slightly out.

18. For moccasins, cut two ¹¹⁄₁₆″ lengths from the rounded ends of an ice-cream stick. Sand corners to round them.

19. Wood-glue moccasins to bottom of legs so heels are flush with back of ankles, toes point in same direction as knees, and Yellow Feather stands upright.

20. For arms, cut two 1³⁄₁₆″ lengths of ¼″ dowelling.

21. To indicate angle of each elbow cut, measure and mark ⁹⁄₁₆″ from right end. Rotate dowelling so mark is away from you, then measure and mark ⁹⁄₁₆″ from left end. Cut angle.

22. At flat end of two arm halves, attach 8mm-bead hands.

23. To complete the arms, reverse the elbow cuts and wood-glue upper and lower arms together so elbow joints are crooked.

24. With shoulders even with top of body, wood-glue arms to body so right hand points down and left hand points forward and up.

25. Repeat steps 18 to 20 of Chief Standing Tall. Substitute a red, yellow, and blue seed bead for three red.

26. For leg fringe, cut two ¼″ × ¾″ strips of beige synthetic suede. Trim one long edge of each with pinking shears. Tacky-glue long straight edge of each fringe to outside of each lower leg.

27. Repeat steps 23 and 24 of Running Deer.

28. For braid, cut six 3″ lengths of black floss. Tacky-glue ends together at one end to secure.

29. Using two lengths for each section of braid, braid for 1¼″. Wrap a 6″ length of one strand of floss four times around bottom end of braid to secure. Tie ends in a knot and secure knot with tacky glue.

30. Trim braid so it measures 1¾″ long.

31. Tacky-glue top end of braid into braid hole.

32. For headband, cut a ⅛″ × 3⅜″ strip of orange felt. Tacky-glue headband around head, butting short edges at center back.

33. Tacky-glue yellow feather to center back of head so it stands straight up.

CAMPFIRE

1. For base, cut a ¾″ × ¾″ square of tagboard.

2. For logs, cut nine ¾″ and three ⅝″ lengths of ¼″ dowelling.

3. For bottom pile, wood-glue six ¾″ logs to base in a spoked circle so ends at center are ¼″ apart.

4. For top pile, wood-glue remaining logs, alternating sizes, with outside ends flush with work surface and opposite ends pointed towards center of pile.

5. Paint logs light red-brown.

6. To suggest charring, paint ends of logs at center of campfire dark brown.

7. Referring to 6–10, cut four flames from orange felt.

8. Tacky-glue straight ends of flames evenly spaced around center of campfire.

9. Paint flame tips medium yellow.

10. For burning embers, cut ten ½" × ½" squares of aluminum foil. Crumple into ⅛"-diameter balls. Paint bright red.

11. Tacky-glue embers randomly around center of campfire, tucking them between the logs.

SITTING WOLF

1. For head, cover one hole of a 25mm bead with a tagboard circle. Paint head light red-brown.

2. Referring to 6–11, paint eyes black and cheeks dark pink. At center back of head, measure and mark ⅝" from edge of top bead hole. Paint hair black, curving hairline from sides of head up to mark.

3. For body, cut a 1" length of ¾" dowelling.

4. Draw a line down length of body to indicate center front.

5. Measure and mark position of left and right arms ⅛" from top of body and ¾" from center line. At each mark, whittle a ¼" × ¼" area flat.

6. Measure and mark position of left and right legs ³⁄₁₆" from bottom edge of body and ⁷⁄₁₆" from center line. At each mark, whittle a ¼" × ¼" area flat.

7. Sand bottom edge of head to expose raw wood.

8. Wood-glue head to body so head faces forward.

9. For legs, cut two 1⁷⁄₁₆" lengths of ⅜" dowelling.

10. To indicate angle of each knee cut, measure and mark ⅝" from right end. Rotate dowelling so mark is away from you, then measure and mark ¾" from left end. Cut angle.

11. To indicate angle of each hip cut, place an upper (shorter) leg on work surface so the knee end is at top. Rotate leg so the face of the knee angle cut is facing up. At opposite end, measure and mark ⅛" from flat end. Cut angle.

12. To complete the legs, reverse the knee cuts and wood-glue upper and lower legs together so knee joints are crooked.

13. Sit Sitting Wolf on work surface. Wood-glue legs to body so knees point out and sides of legs are flush with work surface.

14. For moccasins, cut two ¹¹⁄₁₆" lengths from the rounded ends of an ice-cream stick. Sand corners to round them.

15. Sit Sitting Wolf on wood surface. Wood-glue moccasins to bottom of legs so heels are flush with back of ankles and outside edges are flush with work surface.

16. For left arm, cut a 1³⁄₁₆" length of ¼" dowelling.

17. To indicate angle of left elbow cut, measure and mark ⁹⁄₁₆" from right end. Rotate dowelling so mark is away from you, then measure and mark ⁹⁄₁₆" from left end. Cut angle.

18. For right arm, cut a 1" length of ¼" dowelling.

19. At flat end of one right arm half and one end of left arm, attach an 8mm-bead hand.

20. To complete the left arm, reverse the elbow cuts and wood-glue upper and lower arms together so elbow joint is crooked.

21. For each arm, whittle inside area of upper arm flat.

22. With shoulders even with top of body, wood-glue arms to body so right hand touches right leg and left hand is at chest level.

23. Paint hands light red-brown.

24. Paint body, arms, legs, and moccasins dark taupe.

25. Repeat step 24 of Running Deer.

26. Repeat step 28 of Yellow Feather.

27. For topknot, wind black embroidery floss five times around four fingers. Cut end and slip from fingers. Twist strands together and tie into a loose knot. Tacky-glue topknot to center top of head, tucking in ends.

28. For long necklace, string a strand of thirty-eight beads onto a 6" length of beading thread as follows: four red, * one blue, one yellow, one blue, six red *,

6–10. *Pattern for flames.* 6–11. *Sitting Wolf.*

50

repeat between *'s three times, end with one blue, one yellow, one blue and four red beads.

29. Knot thread ends ¼″ from beads at each side so necklace will lie close to neck. Secure knot with tacky glue. Tacky-glue thread portion of necklace to center back of neck.

30. For short necklace, string a strand of twenty-seven beads onto a 6″ length of beading thread as follows: * twelve blue, one yellow *, repeat between *'s twice, end with twelve blue beads.

31. Repeat step 29.

BRAVE EAGLE

1. Repeat steps 1 to 5 of Jumping Fox, referring to 6–12.

2. For body, cut a 1″ length of ¾″ dowelling.

3. Draw a line down length of body to indicate center front.

4. Measure and mark position of left and right arms ⅛″ from top of body and 1¹⁄₁₆″ from center line. At each mark, whittle a ¼″ × ¼″ area flat.

5. Sand bottom edge of head to expose raw wood.

6. Wood-glue head to body so head faces forward.

7. For legs, cut two 1⅛″ lengths of ⅜″ dowelling.

8. Sand one side of each leg flat.

9. With whittled sides together, wood-glue legs side by side to bottom of body and centered from front to back.

10. For moccasins, cut two 1¹⁄₁₆″ lengths from the rounded ends of an ice-cream stick. Sand corners to round them.

11. Wood-glue moccasins to bottom of legs so heels are flush with back of ankles, toes point slightly out, and Brave Eagle stands upright.

12. For arms, cut two 1³⁄₁₆″ lengths of ¼″ dowelling.

13. To indicate angle of each elbow cut, measure and mark ⁹⁄₁₆″ from right end. Rotate dowelling so mark is away from you, then measure and mark ⁹⁄₁₆″ from left end. Cut angle.

6–12. *Brave Eagle.*

14. At flat end of two arm halves, attach 8mm-bead hands.

15. To complete the arms, reverse the elbow cuts and wood-glue upper and lower arms together so elbow joints are crooked.

16. For each arm, whittle inside area of upper arm flat.

17. With shoulders even with top of body, wood-glue arms to body so right hand is over left hand and both are at waist level.

18. Repeat steps 18 to 20 of Chief Standing Tall. Substitute a red, yellow, and blue seed bead for three red.

19. Repeat step 28 of Yellow Feather.

20. Repeat steps 23 and 24 of Running Deer.

21. Repeat steps 20 to 23 of Jumping Fox.

22. Repeat steps 35 and 36 of Yellow Feather. Substitute blue feather for yellow feather.

SMALL TOM-TOM

1. For small tom-tom, use a 20mm bead.

2. Paint tom-tom dark brown.

3. For tom-tom skins, use a pencil compass to describe two 1″-diameter circles onto beige synthetic suede. Cut out circles.

4. On each skin, measure and mark eight evenly spaced points around perimeter ¹⁄₁₆″ from edge.

5. Cut an 18″ length of black floss and separate strands. Using two strands in needle, knot one end.

6. Center skins on top and bottom bead holes. Center marks on top skin over marks on bottom skin. Taking care not to scratch paint, lace top and bottom skins together as follows: * insert needle from front to back at a mark on top skin, then insert needle from front to back at a mark on bottom skin *, repeat between *'s to the beginning. Fasten off end securely.

MEDIUM TOM-TOM

1. For medium tom-tom, use a 25mm bead.

2. Paint tom-tom dark brown.

3. For tom-tom skins, use a pencil compass to describe two 1⅛″-diameter circles onto beige synthetic suede. Cut out circles.

4. Repeat steps 4 to 6 of small tom-tom.

LARGE TOM-TOM

1. For large tom-tom, use the 32mm × 22mm bead.

2. Paint tom-tom dark brown.

3. For tom-tom skins, use a pencil compass to describe two 1¼″-diameter circles onto beige synthetic suede. Cut out circles.

4. Repeat steps 4 to 6 of small tom-tom.

CLAY POT

1. For pot, cover one hole of a 20mm bead with a tagboard circle (bottom). Paint pot white.

2. Paint inside of pot dark brown.

3. Referring to 6–1, use dark brown to paint eight inverted triangles evenly spaced around pot rim. Use bright red to paint zigzag pattern below inverted triangles. Use dark brown to paint another zigzag pattern below the first.

TEPEE (MAKE 2)

1. Following 6–13, cut tepee from ¼ × 5¼ lattice.

2. Paint opening dark brown.

3. For tepee poles, cut three 1⅜″ lengths from the pointed ends of three square toothpicks.

4. On wrong side of tepee, wood-glue one pole to center top so it extends ¹⁵⁄₁₆″ beyond top.

5. Wood-glue two remaining tepee poles to wrong side of tepee top so they point up and out and extend 1″ beyond top.

6. Paint tepee poles dark brown.

7. Using pinking shears, cut two ¼″-wide (measured from pinked point to pinked point) × 4″-long strips from dark red synthetic suede.

8. Wrapping ends around tepee sides, tacky-glue first strip on a diagonal, with the left end 2¾″ from bottom edge of tepee and the right end 4⅛″ from bottom edge of tepee. Trim ends. Tacky-glue second strip ¼″ above first strip.

9. For easel stand, cut a triangle with 1¼″ × 2½″ right-angle sides from ¼ × 5¼ lattice.

10. Locate and mark center back of tepee. Hold tepee upright with bottom edge flat against work surface. With 1¼″ edge of easel stand flat against work surface, wood-glue the 2½″ edge vertically to center back of tepee.

TREES

1. Following 6–14, cut three tree trunks from ¼ × 5¼ lattice.

2. Following 6–15, cut three treetops from ¼ × 5¼ lattice.

3. For each tree, wood-glue top ½″ of tree trunk to bottom center of treetop.

4. Following 5–31 (large shrub of Project 5), cut base from ¼ × 5¼ lattice.

5. Wood-glue bottom edge of first tree trunk to base, ¼″ from straight edge of base (back), and 1″ from left edge.

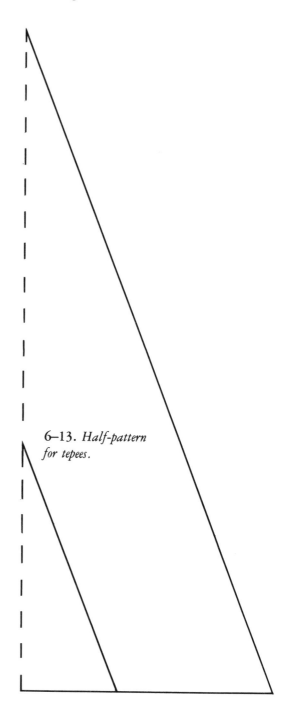

6–13. *Half-pattern for tepees.*

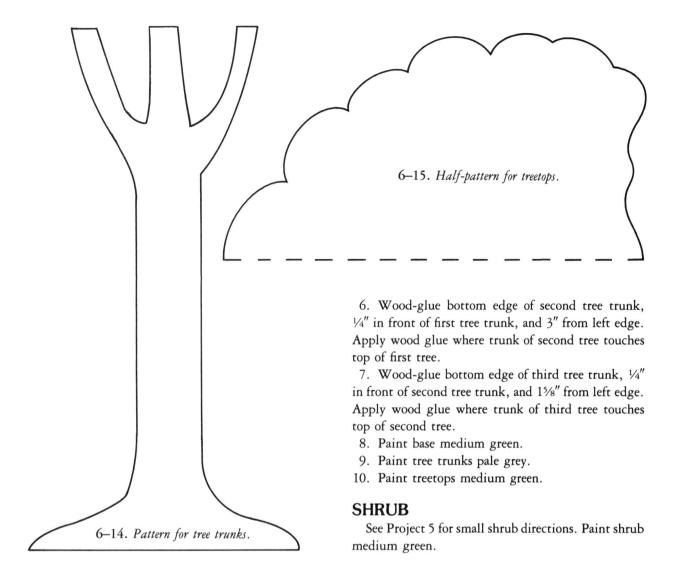

6–15. *Half-pattern for treetops.*

6–14. *Pattern for tree trunks.*

6. Wood-glue bottom edge of second tree trunk, ¼″ in front of first tree trunk, and 3″ from left edge. Apply wood glue where trunk of second tree touches top of first tree.

7. Wood-glue bottom edge of third tree trunk, ¼″ in front of second tree trunk, and 1⅝″ from left edge. Apply wood glue where trunk of third tree touches top of second tree.

8. Paint base medium green.

9. Paint tree trunks pale grey.

10. Paint treetops medium green.

SHRUB

See Project 5 for small shrub directions. Paint shrub medium green.

7 · Into Africa!

MATERIALS

Beads

one white 44mm × 28mm large-hole wood bead
two white 32mm × 22mm large-hole wood beads
nine white 25mm large-hole wood beads
two white 20mm large-hole wood beads
three white 10mm regular-hole wood beads
eighteen white 8mm regular-hole wood beads

Wood

45″ length of ¼″ dowelling
17″ length of ⅜″ dowelling
6″ length of ⁷⁄₁₆″ dowelling
7″ length of ⅝″ dowelling
11″ length of ¾″ dowelling
1⅜″ length of 1″ dowelling
³⁄₁₆″ × ½″ rectangle of ⅛″-thick balsa wood
55″ length of ¼ × 5¼ clear pine lattice
6″ length of ½ × 5½ clear pine lattice

7–1.

twelve ice-cream sticks
four flat wooden ice-cream spoons
fourteen round toothpicks
3½″-long thin twig (see 7–1)
one ½″-diameter × 7″-tall and one ⅝″-diameter × 8⅜″-tall slightly curved tree branches (see 7–1)

Wheels

four 1½″-diameter rubber wheels with fasteners

Paints (Acrylic)

Flesh, black, dark pink, khaki, white, dark brown, pale blue-grey, bright red, dark orange, medium yellow, dark yellow, medium olive green, and light yellow-green

Fabric and Trims

small amount of beige and grey synthetic suede
two 7mm ruby rhinestones
nine gold rochaille beads
8″ length of black sportweight cotton yarn
light brown and black curly chenille hair
4″ × 10″ rectangle of white lightweight cotton fabric
small amount of polyester fibrefill
5″ length of 2mm white rayon satin rattail
small amount of tan fake fur
small amount of white fake fur
1½″ length of yellow worsted-weight yarn

Hardware

four ¾ × 18 wire brads
two 6 × ¾ flathead wood screws.

54

Miscellaneous

small amount of white tagboard
sewing machine (optional)
sewing needle
white sewing thread
paste wood filler

PROFESSOR DAVIS-ROSS

1. For head, cover one hole of a 25mm bead with a tagboard circle. Paint head flesh.

2. Referring to 7–2, paint eyes black and cheeks dark pink.

3. For body, cut a ¹⁵⁄₁₆″ length of ¾″ dowelling.

4. Draw a line down length of body to indicate center front.

5. Measure and mark position of left and right arms ⅛″ from top of body and ¹¹⁄₁₆″ from center line. At each mark, whittle a ¼″ × ¼″ area flat.

6. Measure and mark position of left and right legs ⅛″ from bottom of body and ¼″ from center line. At each mark, whittle a ¼″ × ¼″ area flat.

7. Sand bottom edge of head to expose raw wood.

8. Wood-glue head to top of body so head faces forward.

9. For legs, cut two ⅞″ lengths of ¼″ dowelling.

10. To indicate angle of each hip/knee cut, measure and mark ⁷⁄₁₆″ from right end. Rotate dowelling so mark is away from you, then measure and mark ⅜″ from left end. Cut angle.

11. To indicate angle of each ankle cut, measure and mark ⅛″ from right end of lower (shorter) leg. Cut angle.

12. For each knee notch, place upper (longer) leg on work surface so the face of the hip angle cut is facing up. At opposite end, whittle a ⅛″-deep × ¼″-long notch so knee angle of lower leg will lie close to upper leg and form a right angle (knee bend).

13. Wood-glue hips to body so undersides of upper legs are flush with bottom of body and legs point down slightly.

14. Wood-glue knees to notches of upper legs so legs hang down and jut back.

15. For shoes, cut two ½″ lengths from the rounded ends of an ice-cream stick. Sand corners to round them.

16. Wood-glue shoes to bottom of legs so heels are flush with back of ankles and toes point out slightly.

7–2. *Professor Davis-Ross.*

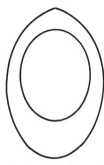

7–3. *Pattern for pith helmet brim.*

17. For arms, cut two $^{13}/_{16}''$ lengths of $^{1}/_4''$ dowelling.

18. To indicate angle of each elbow cut, measure and mark $^3/_8''$ from right end. Rotate dowelling so mark is away from you, then measure and mark $^3/_8''$ from left end. Cut angle.

19. At flat end of two arm halves, attach 8mm-bead hands.

20. To complete the arms, reverse the elbow cuts and wood-glue upper and lower arms together so elbow joints are crooked.

21. For each arm, whittle inside area of upper arm flat.

22. With shoulders even with top of body, wood-glue arms to body so hands are at chest level.

23. Paint hands flesh.

24. For shirt, paint arms, top edge of torso, and torso khaki.

25. For socks, paint bottom $^{1}/_4''$ of legs white.

26. For knees, paint $^3/_8''$ above socks flesh.

27. For shorts, paint top of legs and bottom edge of torso khaki.

28. Paint shoes dark brown.

29. Using dark brown, paint three buttons, spaced $^1/_8''$ apart, down center front of shirt, with the first button $^1/_8''$ from top edge of body.

30. Following 7–3, cut pith helmet brim from beige synthetic suede.

31. To indicate hat crown, pull pith helmet brim down over head so front of brim is $^5/_8''$ from center top of head and back brim is $^{13}/_{16}''$ from center top of head. Trace a line around head underneath pith helmet brim. Remove brim.

32. Using line as a guide, paint top of head khaki.

33. Tacky-glue pith helmet brim to head.

LAND ROVER

1. Following 7–4, cut chassis from $^1/_2'' \times 5^1/_2''$ lattice.

2. For axles, cut one $^9/_{16}'' \times 1^1/_2''$ (front) and one $^9/_{16}'' \times 1^5/_8''$ (rear) rectangle from $^1/_2'' \times 5^1/_2''$ lattice.

3. Placing the $^9/_{16}''$ face of axles against the bottom of chassis, wood-glue front axle $^3/_8''$ from front end and rear axle $^1/_2''$ from rear end of chassis.

4. Turn assembly over and nail chassis to axles, using two wire brads for each axle. Space brads $^1/_2''$ from sides of chassis.

5. At end of each axle, measure and mark for the center. Using a $^1/_{16}''$ bit, drill $^1/_4''$-deep pilot holes for wheel fasteners.

6. For trunk, cut one $^9/_{16}'' \times 1^1/_8''$ (back) and two $^9/_{16}'' \times 1^3/_{16}''$ (sides) rectangles from $^1/_4'' \times 5^1/_4''$ lattice.

7. With back edges flush, wood-glue long edge of trunk back to center back top of chassis. With back edge of sides flush with back of trunk, wood-glue sides to top of chassis.

8. Following 7–5, cut hood from $^1/_2'' \times 5^1/_2''$ lattice.

9. Using a $^3/_{32}''$ bit and angling bit towards the front of the hood, drill a $^1/_4''$-deep column hole as indicated by dot on pattern.

10. With front edges flush, wood-glue hood to top of chassis. Sand the top side edges of hood to round them.

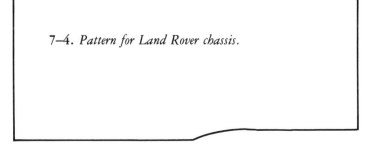

7–4. *Pattern for Land Rover chassis.*

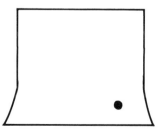

7–5. *Pattern for Land Rover hood.*

55

11. For fenders, cut two 5/16″ × 2⅛″ lengths from ¼ × 5¼ lattice.

12. To indicate position of each angle cut, place fender on work surface so ¼ face is facing up. Measure and mark 1″ from right end and draw a line across width of fender. Turn fender over so mark is on the bottom, then measure and mark 1″ from left end. Cut angle.

13. To complete each fender, wood-glue angled end of one fender half to flat end of other fender half.

14. With flat end of each fender flush with front of hood and angled end of each fender flush with bottom edge of chassis, wood-glue fenders to sides of Land Rover.

15. Paint Land Rover khaki.

16. For bench seat, cut one 1″ × 1 9/16″ rectangle (seat bottom) and two 11/16″ × 11/16″ squares (backrests) from ¼ × 5¼ lattice. On one long edge and two sides of each piece, sand corners to round them. Whittle straight bottom edge of each backrest so they will tilt back at a 105° angle.

17. For bench platform, cut a 5/16″ × 1 7/16″ rectangle from ¼ × 5¼ lattice.

18. Wood-glue seat bottom to platform, with back of seat ¼″ from back edge of platform and centered side to side.

19. With bottom edge of backrests flush with back of seat, wood-glue backrests to seat so they tilt back.

20. Paint platform khaki.

21. Paint bench seat black.

22. Tacky-glue bench-seat platform to chassis floor so back edge of seat bottom is ⅛″ from sides of trunk and centered side to side.

23. For front bumper, cut a 2⅜″ length from an ice-cream stick. Sand cut edges to round them.

24. Paint bumper pale blue-grey.

25. With bottom edge of bumper 3/16″ from bottom edge of chassis and centered from side to side, tacky-glue bumper to front of Land Rover.

26. For headlights, cut a 10mm bead in half. Sand half-bead holes to eliminate them. Sand rounded sides to flatten so headlights will lie close to the front of the hood.

27. Paint front of headlights white. Paint back of headlights khaki.

28. Tacky-glue headlights to front of hood spacing them 3/32″ from sides of hood, centered between top of hood and top of bumper.

29. For rear bumper, cut a 2⅜″ length from an ice-cream stick. Sand cut edges to round them.

30. Paint bumper pale blue-grey.

31. For taillights, tacky-glue a 7mm ruby rhinestone to each side of bumper, spaced 7/16″ from side edges, and centered from top to bottom.

32. Tacky-glue bumper to rear of Land Rover, centered from side to side, spacing bottom edge of bumper ¼″ from bottom edge of chassis.

33. For steering wheel, cut a ⅛″ length of ⅝″ dowelling.

34. Use a 3/32″ bit to drill a steering-column hole through center of steering wheel.

35. For steering column, cut a ¾″ length from the thickest part of a toothpick.

36. Wood-glue column into steering-column hole in wheel.

37. Paint steering wheel and column black.

38. Tacky-glue column into column hole in top of hood.

39. Attach wheels by hammering fasteners into pilot holes.

DOCTOR FORD

1. For head, cover one hole of a 25mm bead with a tagboard circle. Paint head flesh.

2. Referring to 7–6, paint eyes black and cheeks dark pink.

3. For body, cut a 15/16″ length of ¾″ dowelling.

4. Draw a line down length of body to indicate center front.

5. Measure and mark position of left and right arms ⅛″ from top of body and 11/16″ from center line. At each mark, whittle a ¼″ × ¼″ area flat.

6. Sand bottom edge of head to expose raw wood.

7. Wood-glue head to top of body so head faces forward.

7–6. *Doctor Ford.*

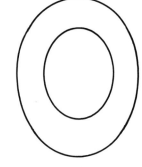

7–7. *Pattern for hat brims.*

8. For legs, cut a 2⅜″ length of ¼″ dowelling.

9. To indicate angle of ankle cut, measure and mark 1⅛″ from right end. Rotate dowelling so mark is away from you, then measure and mark 1⅛″ from left end. Cut angle.

10. To indicate angle of each hip cut, place leg on work surface so ankle end is at top. Rotate leg so the face of the ankle angle cut is facing down. At opposite end, measure and mark ⅛″ from flat end. Cut angle.

11. With side of left leg flush with side of body and centered from front to back, wood-glue left hip to bottom of body so ankle juts forward.

12. With side of right leg flush with side of body and centered from front to back, wood-glue right hip to bottom of body so ankle juts back.

13. For shoes, cut two ¹¹/₁₆″ lengths from the rounded ends of an ice-cream stick. Sand corners to round them.

14. Wood-glue shoes to bottom of legs so heels extend ⅛″ behind ankles, toes point forward, and Doctor Ford stands upright.

15. For arms, cut two 1″ lengths of ¼″ dowelling.

16. To indicate angle of each elbow cut, measure and mark ⁷/₁₆″ from right end. Rotate dowelling so mark is away from you, then measure and mark ⁷/₁₆″ from left end. Cut angle.

17. At flat end of two arm halves, attach 8mm-bead hands.

18. To complete the arms, reverse the elbow cuts and wood-glue upper and lower arms together so elbow joints are crooked.

19. For each arm, whittle inside area of upper arm flat.

20. With shoulders even with top of body, wood-glue arms to body so left hand is at waist level and right hand hangs down.

21. Paint hands and lower arms flesh.

22. For shirt, paint upper arms, top edge of torso, and torso khaki.

23. For socks, paint bottom ⅜″ of legs white.

24. For knees, paint ³/₁₆″ above socks flesh.

25. for shorts, paint top of legs and bottom edge of torso khaki.

26. Paint shoes dark brown.

27. Following 7–7, cut hat brim from beige synthetic suede.

28. To indicate hat crown, pull hat brim down over head so front and back of brim are ½″ from center top of head. Trace a line around head underneath hat brim. Remove brim.

29. Using line as a guide, paint top of head khaki.

30. Tacky-glue hat brim to head.

31. For buttons, tacky-glue three gold rochaille beads, spaced ⅛″ apart, down center front of shirt with the first ⅛″ from top edge of body.

32. For camera body, cut a ⅜″ × ¹¹/₁₆″ rectangle from ¼ × 5¼ lattice.

33. To indicate position of shutter release hole, place one long cut edge (bottom) on work surface. On upper long cut edge (top), measure and mark ⅛″ in from left side and ¹/₁₆″ from long side closest to you (front).

34. Using a ³/₃₂″ bit, drill a ⅛″-deep shutter release hole.

35. To indicate position of camera strap holes, measure and mark sides ⅛″ from top and centered front to back.

36. Using a ³/₃₂″ bit, drill two ⅛″-deep camera strap holes.

37. For shutter release, cut a ¼″ length from the thickest part of a toothpick.

38. Wood-glue shutter release into shutter release hole.

39. For telephoto lens, cut a ⅜″ length of ⅜″ dowelling.

40. With shutter release at left side, wood-glue lens to center front of camera.

41. Paint entire camera black.

42. Paint a small dot bright red on front of camera below shutter release.

43. For camera strap, cut a 2″ length of black yarn. Tacky-glue each end of strap into camera strap holes.

HAROLD

1. For head, cover one hole of a 25mm bead with a tagboard circle. Paint head flesh.

2. Referring to 7–8, paint eyes black and cheeks dark pink.

3. For body, cut a ¹⁵/₁₆″ length of ¾″ dowelling.

4. Draw a line down length of body to indicate center front.

5. Measure and mark position of left and right arms ⅛″ from top of body and ⅝″ from center line. At each mark, whittle a ¼″ × ¼″ area flat.

6. Sand bottom edge of head to expose raw wood.

7. Wood-glue head to body so head faces forward.

7–8. *Harold.*

8. For left leg, cut a 1³⁄16″ length of ¼″ dowelling.

9. To indicate angle of left hip/knee cut, measure and mark 9⁄16″ from right end. Rotate dowelling so mark is away from you, then measure and mark ½″ from left end. Cut angle.

10. To complete the left leg, wood-glue angled end of lower (longer) leg to flat end of upper (shorter) leg, making sure the knee is crooked and the hip angle of the upper leg is parallel with the angled end of the lower leg.

11. For right leg, cut a 1⁵⁄16″ length of ¼″ dowelling.

12. To indicate angle of right hip/knee cut, measure and mark ⅝″ from right end. Rotate dowelling so mark is away from you, then measure and mark ⅝″ from left end. Cut angle.

13. To indicate angle of right ankle cut, place one leg half (lower) on work surface so the knee end is at top. Rotate leg so the face of the knee angle cut is facing down. At opposite end, measure and mark ⅛″ from flat end. Cut angle.

14. To complete the right leg, wood-glue angled end of lower leg to flat end of upper leg, making sure the knee joint is crooked, ankle juts back, and the hip angle of the upper leg is parallel with the angled end of the lower leg.

15. With sides of legs flush with sides of body, and centered from front to back, wood-glue hips to bottom of body so left knee points forward and slightly to the left, and right ankle juts back and towards center.

16. For feet, cut two ⅝″ lengths from the rounded ends of an ice-cream stick. Sand corners to round them.

17. Wood-glue feet to bottom of legs so heels are flush with back of ankles, left toe points forward, right toe points out slightly, side edge of right foot butts inside edge of left heel, and Harold stands upright.

18. For arms, cut two 1″ lengths of ¼″ dowelling.

19. To indicate angle of each elbow cut, measure and mark 7⁄16″ from right end. Rotate dowelling so mark is away from you, then measure and mark 7⁄16″ from left end. Cut angle.

20. At flat end of two arm halves, attach 8mm-bead hands.

21. To complete the arms, reverse the elbow cuts and wood-glue upper and lower arms together so elbow joints are crooked.

22. With shoulders even with top of body, wood-glue arms to body so left hand points forward and up, and right hand points forward and is at chest level.

23. Paint hands, lower arms, bottom ¼″ of upper arms flesh.

24. Paint feet, lower legs, and bottom ¼″ of upper legs flesh.

25. For shirt, paint top of upper arms, top edge of torso, and torso white.

26. For shorts, paint top of legs and bottom of torso white.

27. For hair, cut sufficient ⅛″ lengths of light brown hair to cover head. Tacky-glue hair to head.

28. Use the 3½″ twig for the walking stick.

29. Stand Harold on work surface, with bottom edge of walking stick touching work surface. Tacky-glue stick to inside of wrist.

HANK

1. For head, cover one hole of a 25mm bead with a tagboard circle. Paint head flesh.

2. Referring to 7–9, paint eyes black and cheeks dark pink.

3. For body, cut a 1″ length of ¾″ dowelling.

4. Draw a line down length of body to indicate center front.

5. Measure and mark position of left and right arms ⅛″ from top of body and 11⁄16″ from center line. At each mark, whittle a ¼″ × ¼″ area flat.

6. Sand bottom edge of head to expose raw wood.

7. Wood-glue head to body so head faces forward.

8. For left leg, cut a 1⁷⁄16″ length of ¼″ dowelling.

9. To indicate angle of left hip cut, measure and mark ⅛″ from right end. Cut angle.

10. To indicate angle of left ankle cut, place leg on work surface so the hip end is at top. Rotate the leg so the face of the hip angle cut is facing down. At opposite end, measure and mark ⅛″ from flat end. Cut angle.

11. For right leg, cut a 1¼″ length of ¼″ dowelling.
12. To indicate angle of right hip/knee cut, measure and mark 9/16″ from right end. Rotate dowelling so mark is away from you, then measure and mark ⅝″ from left end. Cut angle.
13. To complete the right leg, wood-glue angled end of lower (shorter) leg to flat end of upper (longer) leg, making sure the knee is crooked and the hip angle of the upper leg is parallel with the angled end of the lower leg.
14. With sides of legs flush with sides of body, and centered from front to back, wood-glue hips to bottom of body so left ankle juts back and slightly to the left, and right knee points forward.
15. For feet, cut two 11/16″ lengths from the rounded ends of an ice-cream stick. Sand corners to round them.
16. Wood-glue feet to bottom of legs so heels extend ⅛″ behind ankles, toes point forward, and Hank stands upright.
17. For arms, cut two 13/16″ lengths of ¼″ dowelling.
18. To indicate angle of each elbow cut, measure and mark ½″ from right end. Rotate dowelling so mark is away from you, then measure and mark ⅝″ from left end. Cut angle.
19. At flat end of two lower (shorter) arms, attach 8mm-bead hands.
20. To complete the arms, reverse the elbow cuts and wood-glue upper and lower arms together so elbow joints are crooked.
21. For each arm, whittle inside area of upper arm flat.
22. Wood-glue arms to body so hands are raised up and lower arms touch the sides of head.
23. Paint hands, lower arms, and bottom ¼″ of upper arms flesh.
24. Paint feet, lower legs, and bottom ⅜″ of upper legs flesh.

7–9. *Hank.*

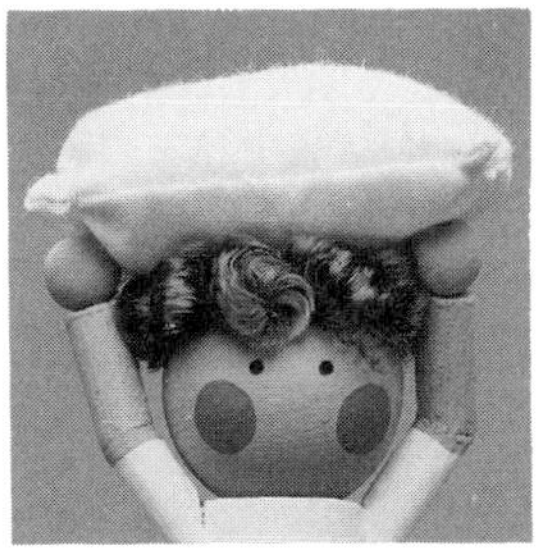

7–10. *Harvey.*

25. For shirt, paint top of upper arms, top edge of torso, and torso white.
26. For shorts, paint top of legs and bottom edge of torso white.
27. For bundle, cut 4″ × 4″ square of white cotton fabric.
28. Place a walnut-size piece of polyester fibrefill in center. Tie one pair of opposite corners together into a square knot, then tie the remaining pair of opposite corners together in an overhand knot.
29. Tacky-glue bundle to center top of head.
30. For hair, cut sufficient ⅛″ lengths of black hair to cover head below bundle. Tacky-glue hair to head.

HARVEY

1. For head, cover one hole of a 25mm bead with a tagboard circle. Paint head flesh.
2. Referring to 7–10, paint eyes black and cheeks dark pink.
3. For body, cut a 15/16″ length of ¾″ dowelling.
4. Draw a line down length of body to indicate center front.
5. Measure and mark position of left and right arms ⅛″ from top of body and ⅝″ from center line. At each mark, whittle a ¼″ × ¼″ area flat.
6. Sand bottom edge of head to expose raw wood.
7. Wood-glue head to body so head faces forward.
8. For left leg, cut a 1⅛″ length of ¼″ dowelling.
9. To indicate angle of left hip/knee cut, measure and mark 9/16″ from right end. Rotate dowelling so mark is away from you, then measure and mark 7/16″ from left end. Cut angle.
10. To complete the left leg, wood-glue angled end of lower (longer) leg to flat end of upper (shorter) leg, making sure the knee is crooked and the hip angle of the upper leg is parallel with the angled end of the lower leg.
11. For right leg, cut a 1½″ length of ¼″ dowelling.
12. To indicate angle of right knee cut, measure and mark 13/16″ from right end. Rotate dowelling so mark is away from you, then measure and mark 9/16″ from left end. Cut angle.
13. To indicate angle of right hip cut, place upper (shorter) leg on work surface so the knee end is at top. Rotate leg so the face of the knee angle cut is facing down. At opposite end, measure and mark ⅛″ from flat end. Cut angle.

14. To indicate angle of right ankle cut, place lower (longer) leg on work surface so hip end is at top. Rotate leg so the face of the hip angle cut is facing down. At opposite end, measure and mark ⅛" from flat end. Cut angle.

15. To complete the right leg, reverse the knee cuts and wood-glue upper and lower legs together so knee joint is crooked.

16. With side of left leg flush with side of body, and slightly to rear of center from front to back, wood-glue left hip to bottom of body so knee points forward.

17. With side of right leg flush with side of body, and centered from front to back, wood-glue right hip to bottom of body so knee points forward.

18. For feet, cut two ⅝" lengths from the rounded ends of an ice-cream stick. Sand corners to round them.

19. Wood-glue feet to bottom of legs so left heel extends ⅛" behind ankle and toe points forward, right heel is flush with back of ankle, toe points slightly to the right, and Harvey stands upright.

20. For arms, cut two 1³⁄₁₆" lengths of ¼" dowelling.

21. To indicate angle of each elbow cut, measure and mark ⁹⁄₁₆" from right end. Rotate dowelling so mark is away from you, then measure and mark ⁹⁄₁₆" from left end. Cut angle.

22. At flat end of two arm halves, attach 8mm-bead hands.

23. To complete the arms, reverse the elbow cuts and wood-glue upper and lower arms together so elbow joints are crooked.

24. For each arm, whittle inside area of upper arm flat.

25. Wood-glue arms to body so hands are raised up.

26. Paint hands, lower arms, and bottom ¼" of upper arms flesh.

27. Paint feet, lower legs, and bottom ⁷⁄₁₆" of upper legs flesh.

28. For shirt, paint top of upper arms, top edge of torso, and torso white.

29. For shorts, paint top of legs and bottom edge of torso white.

30. For flour sack, cut two 2⅛" × 2¹³⁄₁₆" rectangles from white cotton fabric.

31. With right sides facing and using ¼" seam allowance, machine-stitch (or hand-stitch) along three

7–11. *Hugh.*

7–12. *Professor Morse.*

sides, leaving one short end open. Turn right side out.

32. Stuff with polyester fibrefill. Whipstitch opening closed.

33. Tightly wrap each corner of bundle with white sewing thread. Knot thread and trim ends close to knot.

34. Tacky-glue flour sack to center top of head.

35. For hair, cut sufficient ⅛" lengths of light brown hair to cover head below flour sack. Tacky-glue hair to head.

HUGH

1. For head, cover one hole of a 25mm bead with a tagboard circle. Paint head flesh.

2. Referring to 7–11, paint eyes black and cheeks dark pink.

3. For body, cut a 1" length of ¾" dowelling.

4. Draw a line down length of body to indicate center front.

5. Measure and mark position of left and right arms ⅛" from top of body and ⅝" from center line. At each mark, whittle a ¼" × ¼" area flat.

6. Sand bottom edge of head to expose raw wood.

7. Wood-glue head to body so head faces forward.

8. For left leg, cut a 1½" length of ¼" dowelling.

9. To indicate angle of left hip/knee cut, measure and mark ¾" from right end. Rotate dowelling so mark is away from you, then measure and mark ¹¹⁄₁₆" from left end. Cut angle.

10. To indicate angle of left ankle cut, place lower (shorter) leg on work surface so the knee end is at top. Rotate leg so the face of the knee angle cut is facing down. At opposite end, measure and mark ⅛" from flat end. Cut angle.

11. To complete the left leg, wood-glue knee angle end of lower (shorter) leg to flat end of upper (longer)

leg, making sure the knee is crooked and the hip angle of the upper leg is parallel with the angled end of the lower leg.

12. For right leg, cut a 1⁵⁄₁₆" length of ¼" dowelling.

13. To indicate angle of right hip/knee cut, measure and mark ¹¹⁄₁₆" from right end. Rotate dowelling so mark is away from you, then measure and mark ⁹⁄₁₆" from left end. Cut angle.

14. To complete the right leg, wood-glue angled end of lower (shorter) leg to flat end of upper (longer) leg, making sure the knee is crooked and the hip angle of the upper leg is parallel with the angled end of the lower leg.

15. With sides of legs flush with sides of body, and centered from front to back, wood-glue hips to bottom of body so left ankle juts back and right knee points forward.

16. For feet, cut two ¹¹⁄₁₆" lengths from the rounded ends of an ice-cream stick. Sand corners to round.

17. Wood-glue feet to bottom of legs so heels extend ⅛" behind ankles, left toes point slightly towards the left, right toes point slightly towards the right, and Hugh stands upright.

18. For arms, cut two 1³⁄₁₆" lengths of ¼" dowelling.

19. To indicate angle of each elbow cut, measure and mark ⁹⁄₁₆" from right end. Rotate dowelling so mark is away from you, then measure and mark ⁹⁄₁₆" from left end. Cut angle.

20. At angled end of two arm halves, attach 8mm-bead hands.

21. To complete the arms, wood-glue angled ends of upper arms to flat ends of lower arms, making sure the elbow joints are crooked.

22. For each arm, whittle inside area of upper arm flat.

23. Wood-glue arms to body so hands are raised up and lower arms touch the sides of head.

24. Paint hands, lower arms, and bottom ¼" of upper arms flesh.

25. Paint feet, lower legs, and bottom ⁷⁄₁₆" of upper legs flesh.

26. For shirt, paint top of upper arms, top edge of torso, and torso white.

27. For shorts, paint top of legs and bottom edge of torso white.

28. For body of water jug, cover one hole of a 20mm bead with a tagboard circle (bottom).

29. For neck of water jug, cut a ½" length of ⁷⁄₁₆" dowelling.

30. Sand top edge of water jug body to expose raw wood.

31. Wood-glue neck to body.

32. For handle, cut a ⅛" length of ⁷⁄₁₆" dowelling. Whittle off ⅛" from one side to flatten.

33. Wood-glue whittled edge of handle to side of neck and center from top to bottom.

34. For spout, cut a ³⁄₁₆"-long × ⅛"-wide rectangle from ⅛"-thick balsa wood. Whittle one short edge to round it.

35. With rounded side of spout facing up, narrow tip facing out, and top edge even with top of neck, wood-glue spout to side of neck opposite handle.

36. Paint water jug dark orange.

37. For neck opening, use black to paint a ⁵⁄₁₆"-diameter circle on center top of jug.

38. Tacky-glue water jug to center top of head.

39. For hair, cut sufficient ⅛" lengths of black hair to cover head below water jug. Tacky-glue hair to head.

PROFESSOR MORSE

1. For head, cover one hole of a 25mm bead with a tagboard circle. Paint head flesh.

2. Referring to 7–12, paint eyes black and cheeks dark pink.

3. For body, cut a 1" length of ¾" dowelling.

4. Draw a line down length of body to indicate center front.

5. Measure and mark position of left and right arms ⅛" from top of body and ¹¹⁄₁₆" from center line. At each mark, whittle a ¼" × ¼" area flat.

6. Sand bottom edge of head to expose raw wood.

7. Wood-glue head to top of body so head faces forward.

8. For legs, cut two 1³⁄₁₆" lengths of ⅜" dowelling.

9. Wood-glue legs to bottom of body so sides of legs are flush with sides of body and are slightly to the rear of center from front to back.

10. For shoes, cut two ⅝" lengths from the rounded ends of an ice-cream stick. Sand corners to round them.

11. Wood-glue shoes to bottom of legs so heels are flush with back of ankles, toes point out slightly, and Professor Morse stands upright.

12. For arms, cut two 1" lengths of ¼" dowelling.

13. To indicate angle of each elbow cut, measure and

mark ⁷⁄₁₆″ from right end. Rotate dowelling so mark is away from you, then measure and mark ⁷⁄₁₆″ from left end. Cut angle.

14. At flat end of two arm halves, attach 8mm-bead hands.

15. To complete the arms, reverse the elbow cuts and wood-glue upper and lower arms together so elbow joints are crooked.

16. For each arm, whittle inside area of shoulder flat.

17. With shoulders even with top of body, wood-glue tops of arms to body so left hand is at waist level and right hand hangs down.

18. Paint hands flesh.

19. For shirt and pants, paint legs, top and bottom edges of torso, and arms khaki.

20. Repeat steps 26 to 38 of Doctor Ford.

21. For wide-angle lens, cut a ³⁄₁₆″ length from ³⁄₈″ dowelling.

22. Repeat steps 40 to 43 of Doctor Ford. Substitute a 4″ camera strap for a 2″ camera strap.

SIMBA

1. For body, cover both holes of the 44mm × 28mm bead with tagboard circles (front and rear of body).

2. To indicate position of head, tail hole, and legs, draw a line around the equator parallel with the bead holes and a line around the meridian.

3. For head position, measure and mark ¼″ from each side of the meridian and ³⁄₈″ from front of body. Whittle area flat.

4. For tail-hole position on rear of body, measure and mark ³⁄₁₆″ from top edge of bead hole.

5. Using an ice pick, pierce tail hole through tagboard circle.

6. To indicate position of left and right front legs, place body so head position faces down, measure and mark ³⁄₈″ from front of body and ¼″ from the meridian. To indicate position of left and right back legs, measure and mark ⁷⁄₁₆″ from rear of body and ³⁄₁₆″ from the meridian. At each mark, whittle a ⁵⁄₁₆″ × ⁵⁄₁₆″ area flat.

7. For head, cover one hole of a 25mm bead with a tagboard circle.

8. Sand bottom edge of head to expose raw wood.

9. Wood-glue head to body.

10. For muzzle, cut a slice off a 10mm bead, leaving the bead intact. Discard slice.

7–13. *Simba.*

11. Fill bead holes with paste wood filler. Allow to dry and sand smooth.

12. With bead holes horizontal, position muzzle on front of Simba's head so it is centered horizontally and vertically. Trace outline of muzzle. Sand muzzle area of head flat.

13. Wood-glue muzzle to head.

14. For ears, cut two ⅛″ lengths of ³⁄₈″ dowelling. Whittle off a ⅛″ slice from one side of each ear to flatten. Sand sides of head to expose raw wood.

15. Referring to 7–13, wood-glue ears to each side of head.

16. For front legs, cut a 1¾″ length of ¼″ dowelling.

17. To indicate angle of hip cut, measure and mark ¹³⁄₁₆″ from right end. Rotate dowelling so mark is away from you, then measure and mark ¹³⁄₁₆″ from left end. Cut angle.

18. Wood-glue front legs to body so left leg juts back slightly and right leg is straight.

19. For back legs, cut a 2¹⁄₁₆″ length of ³⁄₈″ dowelling.

20. To indicate angle of hip cut, measure and mark 1″ from right end. Rotate dowelling so mark is away from you, then measure and mark 1″ from left end. Cut angle.

21. Wood-glue back legs to body so legs are spread apart and Simba stands upright.

22. For paws, cut four ⅛″ lengths of ⁷⁄₁₆″ dowelling.

23. With one edge of paw flush with back of ankle, wood-glue each paw to bottom of legs.

24. For tail, cut a 3″ length of white rattail. Tacky-glue end of tail into tail hole.

25. Paint entire body khaki.

26. Referring to 7–13, paint eyes, nose, mouth, and whisker dots black. Paint cheeks and tongue dark pink. Paint inside of ears dark brown.

27. For claws, use black to paint three vertical lines

on top front of each paw and extending down edge to bottom of paw.

28. For chest fur, cut a ⅛″ × ½″ strip from tan fake fur. Tacky-glue to center front of neck.

29. For mane, cut a ⅜″ × 3″ strip from tan fake fur. Butting short edges to shoulders, tacky-glue over head, just behind ears. Cut a 1¼″-wide half-circle from fake fur to fit back of head. Tacky-glue to back of head.

30. For tail fur, cut a ¼″ × ⅜″ rectangle from tan fake fur. Tacky-glue around tip of tail.

DUMA

1. For body, cover both holes of a 32mm × 22mm bead with tagboard circles (front and rear of body).

2. To indicate position of head, tail hole, and legs, draw a line around the equator parallel with the bead holes and a line around the meridian.

3. For head position, measure and mark ¼″ from each side of the meridian and ⅜″ from front of body. Whittle area flat.

4. For tail-hole position on rear of body, measure and mark ³⁄₁₆″ from top edge of bead hole.

5. Using an ice pick, pierce tail hole through tagboard circle.

6. To indicate position of left and right front legs, place body so head position faces down, measure and mark ¼″ from front of body and ¼″ from the meridian. To indicate position of left and right back legs, measure and mark ¼″ from rear of body and ¼″ from the meridian. At each mark, whittle a ³⁄₁₆″ × ³⁄₁₆″ area flat.

7. For head, cover one hole of a 20mm bead with a tagboard circle.

8. Sand bottom edge of head to expose raw wood.

7-14. *Duma*.

7-15. *Duma*.

9. Wood-glue head to body.

10. For muzzle, cut a 10mm bead in half. Discard one half.

11. With half-holes of bead horizontal, position muzzle on front of Duma's head so it is centered from top to bottom and slightly off-centered towards Duma's left. Trace outline of muzzle. Sand muzzle area flat.

12. Wood-glue muzzle to head.

13. Fill half-bead holes with paste wood filler. Allow to dry and sand smooth.

14. For ears, cut two ⅛″ lengths of ¼″ dowelling. Whittle off a ¹⁄₁₆″ slice from one side of each ear to flatten. Sand sides of head to expose raw wood.

15. Referring to 7–14, wood-glue ears to each side of head.

16. For front legs, cut a 1″ length of ¼″ dowelling.

17. To indicate angle of hip cut, measure and mark ⁷⁄₁₆″ from right end. Rotate dowelling so mark is away from you, then measure and mark ⁷⁄₁₆″ from left end. Cut angle.

18. Wood-glue front legs to body so points of hip angles are on outside of body and legs are straight.

19. For back legs, cut a 1⅛″ length of ¼″ dowelling.

20. To indicate angle of hip cut, measure and mark ½″ from right end. Rotate dowelling so mark is away from you, then measure and mark ½″ from left end. Cut angle.

21. To indicate angle of each ankle cut, place leg on work surface so the hip end is at top. Rotate leg so the face of the hip angle cut is facing up. At opposite end, measure and mark ⅛″ from flat end. Cut angle.

22. Wood-glue back legs to body so legs jut back and are spread apart, and Duma stands upright.

23. For paws, cut four ³⁄₃₂″ lengths of ⅜″ dowelling.

24. With one edge of paw flush with back of ankle, wood-glue each paw to bottom of legs.

25. For tail, cut a 1⅞″ length of white rattail. Tacky-glue end of tail into tail hole.

26. Paint entire body medium yellow.

27. Referring to 7–14, paint eyes black, cheeks dark pink, and bottom two-thirds of muzzle white. Paint nose, mouth, and inner ears black. Paint tongue dark pink.

28. Referring to 7–15, paint a line down center of chest, underbelly, and insides of legs white. Paint bottom of paws, bottom half of paws' sides, and spots black.

29. For claws, use black to paint three vertical lines

on top front of each paw and extending down edge to bottom of paw.

30. For chest fur, cut a ¼"-diameter circle from white fake fur. Tacky-glue to chest.

31. For tail fur, cut a ¼" × ⅜" rectangle from white fake fur. Tacky-glue around tip of tail.

TWIGA

1. For body, use the 1⅜" length of 1" dowelling.

2. Whittle a ¾"-wide area along length of body (bottom) until flat.

3. To indicate position of tail hole, turn body so flattened side faces down. On rear of body, measure and mark 3⁄16" from center top edge.

4. Using a 3⁄32" bit, drill a ⅛"-deep tail hole.

5. To indicate position of neck, turn body so flattened side faces down. On top of body, measure and mark 3⁄16" from each side of center and ⅜" from front. Whittle area flat.

6. For neck, cut a 2¼" length of 7⁄16" dowelling.

7. For neck/head angle, measure and mark ⅛" from one cut end. Cut angle.

8. For head, whittle a ⅝"-wide × ⅝"-long × ¼"-deep area at a hole end of a 32mm × 22mm bead. Test-fit flat end of neck with whittled end of head to make sure they form a right angle.

9. With whittled side of head towards you and facing down, draw a line down center top of head. Measure and mark for two horn holes ⅝" from end nearest you and ⅛" from each side of center line.

10. Using a 3⁄32" bit, drill ⅛"-deep horn holes.

11. For nose hole, measure and mark 1⁄16" from opposite end along center line.

12. Using a 3⁄32" bit, drill a ⅛"-deep nose hole, angling bit towards bottom rear of head.

13. Wood-glue flat end of neck to body.

14. Wood-glue head to neck, making sure head faces forward.

15. Cover bead holes with tagboard circles.

16. For legs, cut two 3⅞" lengths of ⅜" dowelling.

17. To indicate angle of hip cuts, measure and mark 1⅞" from right end. Rotate dowelling so mark is away from you, then measure and mark 1⅞" from left end. Cut angle.

18. To indicate angle of each ankle cut, place leg on work surface so the hip end is at top. Rotate leg so the face of the hip angle cut is facing down. At opposite end, measure and mark ⅛" from flat end. Cut angle.

19. With front legs flush with front of body, wood-glue top of legs to bottom of body so hips touch at the top, and ankles jut forward and are spaced ⅝" apart.

20. With back legs ⅛" from rear end of body, wood-glue top of legs to bottom of body so hips are 1⁄16" apart and ankles jut back.

21. For hooves, cut four ⅝" lengths from the rounded ends of ice-cream sticks. Sand cut edges to round them (front).

22. With heel of hooves flush with back of ankles, wood-glue hooves to bottom of legs.

23. For each horn, wood-glue the pointed end of a toothpick into an 8mm bead. Trim tip extending beyond hole. Sand until smooth. Trim so overall length is ⅞".

24. Wood-glue horns into horn holes.

25. For nose, cut a 3⁄16" length from the thickest part of a toothpick.

26. Wood-glue nose into nose hole.

27. Following 7–16, cut ears from tagboard.

28. Dot bottom edge with tacky glue, fold over, and pinch to secure.

29. Referring to 7–17, tacky-glue ears to each side of head ⅛" below horns and ¼" from rear of head.

30. Paint entire body dark yellow.

31. Referring to 7–17, paint eyes and mouth black, cheeks dark pink, and nose dark brown. Paint spots on legs, body, neck, and back of head dark brown.

32. Use dark brown to paint a vertical line in center front of each hoof.

33. For mane, cut a ⅛" × 3½" strip from tan fake fur. Taper one end into a narrow point (top).

34. With point of mane at center top of head, tacky-glue mane to head and down back of neck.

35. For tail, use the 1¼" length of yellow yarn. Tacky-glue tail into tail hole.

7–16. *Pattern for Twiga's ears.*

7–17. *Twiga.*

64

7–18. *Doctor Noonan.*

36. For tail fur, cut a ⅛″ × ⅜″ strip from tan fake fur. Tacky-glue around tip of tail.

DOCTOR NOONAN

1. For head, cover one hole of a 25mm bead with a tagboard circle. Paint head flesh.

2. Referring to 7–18, paint eyes black, cheeks dark pink, and hair light red-brown.

3. For body, cut a ¹⁵⁄₁₆″ length of ¾″ dowelling.

4. Draw a line down length of body to indicate center front.

5. Measure and mark position of left and right arms ⅛″ from top of body and ¹¹⁄₁₆″ from center line. At each mark, whittle a ¼″ × ¼″ area flat.

6. To indicate position of peg hole (used for sitting Doctor Noonan on Tembo), locate and mark center bottom of body.

7. Using a ³⁄₃₂″ bit, drill a ¼″-deep peg hole.

8. Sand bottom edge of head to expose raw wood.

9. Wood-glue head to top of body so head faces towards right.

10. For legs, cut two 1³⁄₁₆″ lengths of ¼″ dowelling.

11. To indicate angle of each hip/knee cut, measure and mark ⁹⁄₁₆″ from right. Rotate dowelling so mark is away from you, then measure and mark ⁹⁄₁₆″ from left end. Cut angle.

12. To complete each leg, wood-glue angled end of lower leg to flat end of upper leg, making sure the knee is crooked and the hip angle of the upper leg is parallel with the angled end of the lower leg.

13. With sides of legs flush with sides of body and centered from front to back, wood-glue hips to bottom of body so knees point out slightly.

14. For shoes, cut two ¹¹⁄₁₆″ lengths from the rounded ends of an ice-cream stick. Sand corners to round them.

15. Wood-glue shoes to bottom of legs so heels extend ⅛″ behind ankles and toes point out.

16. For arms, cut two 1⅛″ lengths of ¼″ dowelling.

17. To indicate angle of each elbow cut, measure and mark ⁷⁄₁₆″ from right end. Rotate dowelling so mark is away from you, then measure and mark ½″ from left end. Cut angle.

18. At flat end of two lower (shorter) arms, attach 8mm-bead hands.

19. To complete the arms, reverse the elbow cuts and wood-glue upper and lower arms together so elbow joints are crooked.

20. For each arm, whittle inside area of upper arm flat.

21. With shoulders even with top of body, wood-glue arms to body so left hand is raised up and right hand is slightly above waist level.

22. Paint hands flesh.

23. For shirt, paint arms, top edge of torso, and torso khaki.

24. Repeat steps 26 to 31 of Doctor Ford.

25. For binocular lenses, cut two ¹¹⁄₁₆″ lengths of ¼″ dowelling.

26. For focusing mechanism, cut a ³⁄₁₆″ × ¼″ rectangle of ⅛″-thick balsa wood.

27. Contour focusing mechanism so front of binocular lenses will angle out slightly. To contour, place ³⁄₁₆″ side of focusing mechanism on work surface. Whittle off a ¹⁄₃₂″ wedge from upper surface. Turn over; repeat for other side at same end.

28. Wood-glue focusing mechanism between lenses so narrow end of contour is ⅛″ below top edge of lenses and front of lenses angles out slightly.

29. For binocular strap, cut a 2″ length of black yarn.

30. Fold strap in half and tacky-glue ends to center back of focusing mechanism so loop is at top.

TEMBO

1. Following 7–19, cut Tembo from ¼ × 5¼ lattice. Transfer tusk position, indicated by the dot, to each side of trunk.

2. Using a ³⁄₃₂″ bit, drill a ⅛″-deep tusk hole on each side, angling the drill bit towards the back of the head.

3. For peg hole (used for sitting Doctor Noonan on Tembo) measure and mark ⅞″ from base of neck along top edge of back.

4. Using a ³⁄₃₂″ bit, drill a ⅛″-deep peg hole.

5. For peg, cut a ¼″ length from the thickest part of a toothpick.

6. Wood-glue peg into peg hole.

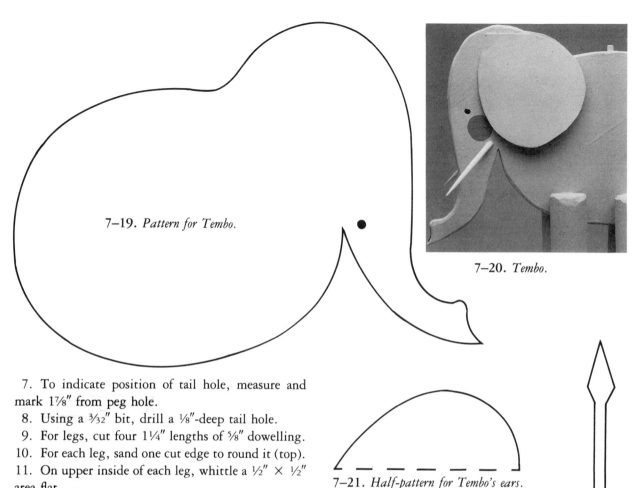

7–19. *Pattern for Tembo.*

7–20. *Tembo.*

7–21. *Half-pattern for Tembo's ears.*

7–22. *Pattern for Tembo's tail.*

7. To indicate position of tail hole, measure and mark 1⅞″ from peg hole.

8. Using a ³⁄₃₂″ bit, drill a ⅛″-deep tail hole.

9. For legs, cut four 1¼″ lengths of ⅝″ dowelling.

10. For each leg, sand one cut edge to round it (top).

11. On upper inside of each leg, whittle a ½″ × ½″ area flat.

12. Wood-glue flattened side of front legs to each side of body 2″ from tip of trunk. Wood-glue flattened side of back legs to each side of body ⅝″ from front legs.

13. For feet, cut four ¾″ lengths from the handle ends of four flat wooden ice-cream spoons. Sand cut edges (heels) to round them.

14. Wood-glue feet to bottom of legs so heels are flush with back of ankles, toes point forward, and Tembo stands upright.

15. For tusks, cut two 1⅜″ lengths from the pointed ends of two toothpicks.

16. Wood-glue cut ends into tusk holes.

17. Paint body, legs, and feet pale blue-grey.

18. Paint tusks and three toenails on each foot white.

19. Referring to 7–20, paint eyes black and cheeks dark pink.

20. At tip of trunk, use black to paint a ⅛″ × ³⁄₁₆″ opening.

21. Following 7–21, cut two ears from tagboard.

22. Paint ears pale blue-grey.

23. Referring to 7–20, tacky-glue ears to each side of head.

24. Following 7–22, cut tail from grey synthetic suede.

25. Tacky-glue end of tail into tail hole.

LOW BUSH (MAKE 2)

1. Following 7–23, cut low bush from ¼ × 5¼ lattice.

2. For easel stand, cut a triangle with ⅞″ × 1¼″ right-angle sides from ¼ × 5¼ lattice.

3. Locate and mark center back of bush. Hold bush upright with bottom edge flat against work surface. With ⅞″ edge of easel stand flat against work surface, wood-glue the 1¼″ edge vertically to center back of bush.

4. Paint bush medium olive green.

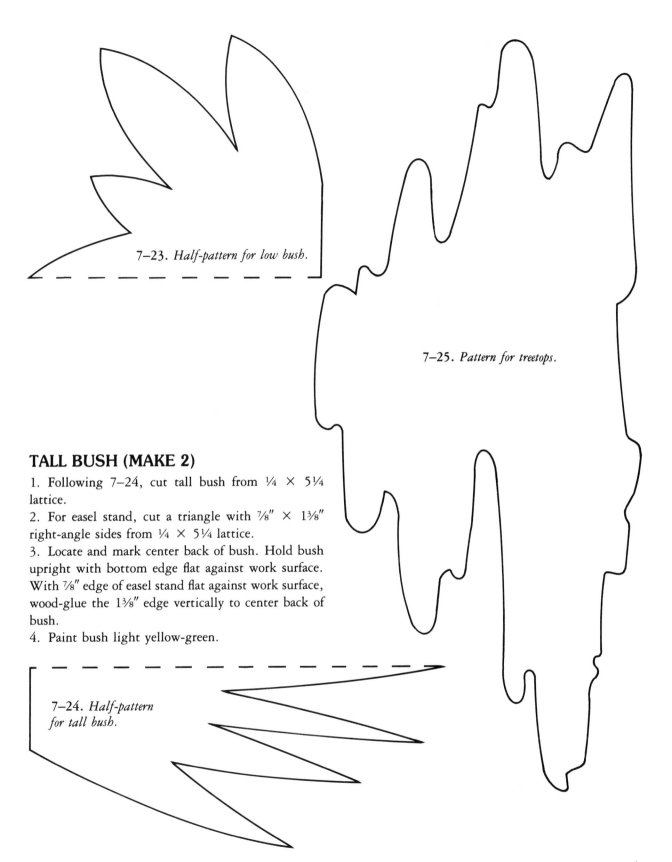

7–23. Half-pattern for low bush.

7–25. Pattern for treetops.

TALL BUSH (MAKE 2)

1. Following 7–24, cut tall bush from ¼ × 5¼ lattice.

2. For easel stand, cut a triangle with ⅞″ × 1⅜″ right-angle sides from ¼ × 5¼ lattice.

3. Locate and mark center back of bush. Hold bush upright with bottom edge flat against work surface. With ⅞″ edge of easel stand flat against work surface, wood-glue the 1⅜″ edge vertically to center back of bush.

4. Paint bush light yellow-green.

7–24. Half-pattern for tall bush.

ACACIA TREES

1. Following 7–25, cut two treetops from ¼ × 5¼ lattice.

2. For tree trunks, use the ⅝″-diameter × 8⅜″-tall and the ½″-diameter × 7″-tall branches.

3. Lie taller trunk on work surface so it curves towards the right. At top of trunk, whittle a ¼″-deep × 1¼″-long area to flatten so trunk will lie close to treetop.

4. Lie shorter trunk on work surface so it curves towards the left. At top of trunk, whittle a ¼″-deep × ⅞″-long area to flatten so trunk will lie close to treetop.

5. Following 5–31 (large shrub of Project 5), cut tree base from ¼ × 5¼ lattice.

6. To indicate position of taller tree, measure and mark 2½″ from right edge and ⅝″ from straight edge of base (back).

7. To indicate position of shorter tree, measure and mark 4″ from left edge and 1¼″ from back edge.

8. Using a 1/16″ bit, drill pilot holes through base.

9. Using a 1/16″ bit, drill ½″-deep pilot holes into center bottom of each tree trunk.

10. Matching pilot holes in base to pilot holes in trunks, wood-glue and screw trunks to base.

11. Wood-glue treetops to trunks, making sure bottom edges of treetops are parallel with the base.

12. Paint base and treetops medium olive green.

8 · Yo-ho-ho and a Bottle of Rum!

MATERIALS

Beads

one white 32mm × 22mm large-hole wood bead
five white 25mm large-hole wood beads
one white 20mm large-hole wood bead
two white 10mm regular-hole wood beads
eleven white 8mm regular-hole wood beads

Wood

37″ length of 3/16″ dowelling
46″ length of ¼″ dowelling
15″ length of ⅜″ dowelling
2⅛″ length of 7/16″ dowelling
4¼″ length of ⅝″ dowelling
8″ length of ¾″ dowelling
1¾″ length of 1¼″ dowelling
36″ length of ¼ × 5¼ clear pine lattice
42″ length of ½ × 5½ clear pine lattice
six ice-cream sticks
seventy-two round toothpicks

Hardware

one ⅞ × 17 wire brad

8–1.

Paints (Acrylic)

Flesh, black, dark pink, pale grey, bright red, white, dark ultramarine, ochre, light red-brown, medium yellow-green, khaki, dark-brown, off-white, medium orange, dark red-brown, medium yellow, dark blue-grey, medium aqua, and light blue

Fabric and Trims

black curly crepe hair
small amount of red calico fabric
2½" length of narrow gold tubular cording
small amount of brown synthetic suede
1½" length of white worsted-weight cotton yarn
6" length of ¼"-wide olive green satin ribbon
four yards of beige sportweight cotton yarn
two 5" × 14" rectangles of unbleached muslin
one package of fusible webbing
small amount of red, yellow, and black heavyweight cotton fabric

Miscellaneous

small amount of white tagboard
small amount of chrome, brass, and black decorative adhesive vinyl
two 4" × 4" squares of brass decorative adhesive vinyl
cardboard tube from paper towelling
sharp-tip, large-eye needle

Additional Equipment

³⁄₃₂" nail set
hole punch

QUIGGLEY

1. For head, cover one hole of a 25mm bead with a tagboard circle. Paint head flesh.

2. Referring to 8–2, paint eyes black and cheeks dark pink.

3. For body, cut a ¹⁵⁄₁₆" length of ¾" dowelling.

4. Draw a line down length of body to indicate center front.

5. Measure and mark position of left and right arms ⅛" from top of body and ⅝" from center line. At each mark, whittle a ¼" × ¼" area flat.

8–2. *Quiggley.*

6. Sand bottom edge of head to expose raw wood.

7. Wood-glue head to body so head faces forward.

8. For pantaloon legs, use the 2⅛" length of ⁷⁄₁₆" dowelling.

9. To indicate angle of hip cut, measure and mark 1" from right end. Rotate dowelling so mark is away from you, then measure and mark 1" from left end. Cut angle.

10. To indicate angle of each knee cut, place pantaloon leg on work surface so the hip end is at top. Rotate leg so the face of the hip angle cut is facing down. At opposite end, measure and mark ³⁄₁₆" from flat end. Cut angle.

11. Whittle inside of pantaloon legs flat.

12. For lower legs, cut a 1⅞" length of ¼" dowelling.

13. To indicate angle of knee cut, measure and mark ⅞" from right end. Rotate dowelling so mark is away from you, then measure and mark ⅞" from left end. Cut angle.

14. To indicate angle of each ankle cut, place lower leg on work surface so the knee end is at top. Rotate leg so the face of the knee angle cut is facing down. At opposite end, measure and mark ⅛" from flat end. Cut angle.

15. Wood-glue left pantaloon leg hip to bottom of body so side of leg is flush with side of body, hip is centered from front to back, and knee juts forward.

16. Wood-glue right pantaloon leg hip to bottom of body so side of leg is flush with side of body, hip is centered from front to back, and knee juts back.

17. Wood-glue left lower leg knee to bottom of left pantaloon leg so front edge of lower leg is ⅛" from edge of pantaloon knee and ankle juts straight back.

18. Wood-glue right lower leg knee to bottom of right pantaloon leg so front edge of lower leg is ⅛" from edge of pantaloon knee and ankle juts back towards Quiggley's left.

19. For shoes, cut two ¹¹⁄₁₆" lengths from the rounded ends of an ice-cream stick. Sand corners to round them.

20. Wood-glue shoes to bottom of legs so heels extend ⅛" behind ankles, left toe points in slightly, right toe points out slightly, and Quiggley stands upright.

21. For right arm, cut a 1¹⁄₁₆" length of ¼" dowelling.

22. To indicate angle of right elbow cut, measure

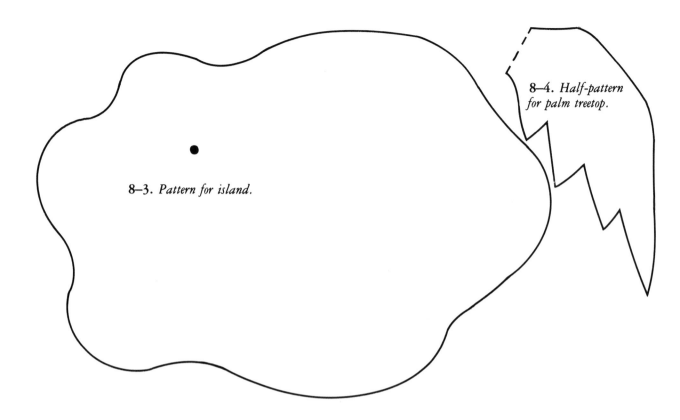

8–4. *Half-pattern for palm treetop.*

8–3. *Pattern for island.*

and mark ½″ from right end. Rotate dowelling so mark is away from you, then measure and mark ½″ from left end. Cut angle.

23. For left arm, cut a 1¹⁄₁₆″ length of ¼″ dowelling.

24. At one flat end of left arm, attach an 8mm-bead hand. Place right lower (longer) arm on work surface so point of elbow angle is at top and at your left. Attach half of an 8mm bead for hand, making sure rounded side of bead is facing up.

25. For pointing finger of left hand, cut a ⁵⁄₁₆″ length from the thickest part of a toothpick. Wood-glue into bead hole of left hand.

26. To complete the right arm, reverse the elbow cuts and wood-glue upper and lower arms together so elbow joint is crooked.

27. For each arm, whittle inside area of upper arm flat.

28. With shoulders even with top of body, wood-glue arms to body so left hand is at shoulder level and right hand is at eye level.

29. Paint hands and lower legs flesh.

30. Paint lower right arm and lower ⅛″ of right upper arm flesh.

31. Paint lower ⅝″ of left arm flesh.

32. Paint shoes and bottom ⅛″ of lower legs black.

33. For socks, paint ⅜″ above top of shoes pale grey.

34. For pantaloons, paint top ⅛″ of lower legs, upper legs, bottom edge of torso, and bottom ⅜″ of torso bright red.

35. For shirt, paint upper arms and upper ⅝″ of torso white. Use dark ultramarine to paint top edge of torso and ⅛″-wide stripes around torso and arms.

36. For shoe buckles, cut two ³⁄₁₆″ × ⁵⁄₁₆″ rectangles from chrome adhesive vinyl. Trim corners to round them. Adhere to insteps.

37. For hair, cut sufficient ½″ lengths of black hair to cover head. Tacky-glue hair to head.

38. For headband, cut a ³⁄₁₆″ × 3½″ strip from red calico. Referring to 8–2, wrap headband around head at an angle and overlapping short edges at center back of head. Tack-glue ends to secure.

39. For spyglass, cut a 1⅛″ length of ³⁄₁₆″ dowelling.

40. Paint spyglass black.

41. Paint lens at each end pale grey.

42. Cut a ½″ length of gold cording.

43. Wrap gold cording twice around front end of spyglass, tacky-gluing ends to secure.

44. Tacky-glue spyglass to flat side of right hand.

70

ISLAND

1. Following 8–3, cut island from ½ × 5½ lattice.

2. Following 8–4, cut palm treetop from ¼ × 5¼ lattice.

3. For tree trunk, use the 4¼" length of ⅝" dowelling. Cut trunk into nine unequal segments, cutting some pieces at a slight angle so when trunk is constructed it will bend.

4. Wood-glue and nail longest trunk segment to top of island where indicated by dot on pattern. Use nail set to sink nail head into trunk segment.

5. Stack and wood-glue seven trunk segments on top of first, forming a gentle S-curve.

6. Whittle a ¼"-wide × ⅛"-deep notch at top of each side of last trunk segment.

7. Wood-glue treetop to last trunk segment.

8. Wood-glue last trunk segment to top of trunk so front of treetop is parallel with front of island.

9. Paint island ochre.

10. Paint tree trunk light red-brown, using a fairly dry brush so some raw wood is still visible.

11. Paint treetop medium yellow-green.

TREASURE CHEST

1. For bottom, cut two 1¼" × 1¾" rectangles from ½ × 5½ lattice. Wood-glue faces together.

2. To indicate position of two handle holes on each side, measure and mark ¼" from top edge and ⅜" from front and back edge.

3. Using a 3⁄32" bit, drill two ⅛"-deep handle holes on each side.

4. For lid, use the 1¾" length of 1¼" dowelling. On end of dowel, measure and mark ½" from edge. Cut dowel lengthwise at ½" mark. Discard larger piece.

5. Paint bottom and lid khaki.

6. Referring to 8–5, use a dry brush and light red-brown to paint spaces between slats. On top of chest bottom and underside of lid, use black to paint rectangles spaced ⅛" from edge on all sides.

7. For hinge, cut a 1¾" length from the thickest part of a toothpick. Paint center 1½" black and ⅛" at each end light red-brown.

8. Tacky-glue hinge ¼" from back edge of trunk. Tacky-glue lid to back edge of trunk and hinge.

9. For bottom front straps, cut two ¼" × ¾" strips from brown synthetic suede. Tacky-glue straps to

8–5. *Treasure chest.*   8–6. *Jean de la Mer.*

trunk, spacing them 3⁄16" from sides of trunk and flush with bottom.

10. For top and back straps, cut two ¼" × 3⅛" strips from brown synthetic suede. Trim one end of each strap to round it. With straight end of straps flush with bottom back of trunk, tacky-glue straps to trunk, spacing them 3⁄16" from side edges.

11. For rope handles, cut the 1½" length of white yarn in half.

12. Tacky-glue ends of rope handles into handle holes at each side of chest.

13. For gold doubloons, adhere two 4" × 4" squares of brass adhesive vinyl together.

14. Using a hole punch, punch out thirty-five doubloons.

15. Tacky-glue layers of doubloons to top of chest bottom.

JEAN DE LA MER

1. For head, cover one hole of a 25mm bead with a tagboard circle. Paint head flesh.

2. Referring to 8–6, paint eyes and hair black. Paint cheeks dark pink.

3. For body, cut a 1" length of ¾" dowelling.

4. Draw a line down length of body to indicate center front.

5. Measure and mark position of left and right arms ⅛" from top of body and ⅝" from center line. At each mark, whittle a ¼" × ¼" area flat.

6. Sand bottom edge of head to expose raw wood.

7. Wood-glue head to top of body so head faces forward.

8. For left leg, cut a 1¾" length of ⅜" dowelling.

9. To indicate angle of left knee cut, measure and mark ¾" from right end. Rotate dowelling so mark is away from you, then measure and mark ⅞" from left end. Cut angle.

10. To indicate angle of left hip cut, place upper (longer) leg on work surface so the knee end is at top.

8–7. *Pattern for Jean's sword blade.*

Rotate leg so the face of the knee angle cut is facing down. At opposite end, measure and mark ¼″ from flat end. Cut angle.

11. To indicate angle of left ankle cut, place lower (shorter) leg on work surface so the knee end is at top. Rotate leg so the face of the knee angle cut is facing down. At opposite end, measure and mark ⅛″ from flat end. Cut angle.

12. To complete the left leg, reverse the knee cuts and wood-glue lower and upper legs together so knee joint is crooked.

13. For right leg, cut a 1⁷⁄₁₆″ length of ⅜″ dowelling.

14. Wood-glue legs to bottom of body so sides of legs are flush with sides of body, both are positioned ¹⁄₁₆″ closer to the back of body than the front, and left knee juts forward.

15. For feet, cut two 1¹⁄₁₆″ lengths from the rounded ends of an ice-cream stick. Sand corners to round them.

16. Wood-glue feet to bottom of legs so heels are flush with back of ankles, left toe points straight, right toe points out slightly, and Jean de la Mer stands upright.

17. For arms, cut two 1³⁄₁₆″ lengths of ¼″ dowelling.

18. To indicate angle of left elbow cut, measure and mark ⅜″ from right end. Rotate dowelling so mark is away from you, then measure and mark ⁵⁄₁₆″ from left end. Cut angle.

19. To indicate angle of right elbow/shoulder cut, measure and mark ⅜″ from right end. Rotate dowelling so mark is away from you, then measure and mark ⁵⁄₁₆″ from left end. Cut angle.

20. At flat end of lower (longer) arms, attach 8mm-bead hands.

21. To complete the left arm, reverse the elbow cuts and wood-glue upper and lower arms together so elbow joint is crooked.

22. To complete the right arm, place upper arm on work surface so shoulder angle end is at top. Rotate arm so the face of the shoulder angle cut is facing up. At opposite end, wood-glue angled end of lower arm to flat end of upper arm, making sure the elbow is

crooked and the hand points towards your right.

23. With shoulders even with top of body, wood-glue left arm to body so hand is at lower chest level. Wood-glue right arm to body so hand is at waist level.

24. Paint hands and bottom ⁵⁄₁₆″ of lower arms flesh.

25. Paint feet and lower legs flesh.

26. For pantaloons, paint upper legs, bottom edge of torso, and bottom ¼″ of torso dark brown.

27. For shirt, paint top edge of torso, ¾″ of torso, and top of arms off-white.

28. Referring to 8–6, paint vest medium orange.

29. Using black, paint three evenly spaced buttons down center front of shirt and slash pockets on vest.

30. Paint toes and knee dimples dark brown.

31. For belt, cut a ⅛″ × 2¾″ strip from black adhesive vinyl.

32. Adhere around waist, overlapping short edges at center back.

33. For headband, use the 6″ length of olive green satin ribbon. Referring to 8–6, wrap headband around head and tie ends in a knot at left back neck. Trim ends at an angle.

34. For gold earring, cut a ½″ length of gold cording and form into a circle.

35. Tacky-glue earring to right side of head, tucking ends under headband.

36. Following 8–7, cut sword blade from an ice-cream stick.

37. For sword hilt, cut a 10mm bead in half at the equator. Discard one half.

38. For sword handle, cut a ⁷⁄₁₆″ length from the thickest part of a toothpick.

39. Wood-glue handle into bead hole on the flat side of hilt. Wood-glue end of blade into bead hole on other side of hilt.

40. Spray-paint sword silver metallic.

41. Tacky-glue sword handle into bead hole of left hand.

42. Wrap remaining gold cording around sword handle, tacky-gluing ends to secure.

JOLLY ROGER

1. Following 8–8, cut two hulls from ½ × 5½ lattice. Wood-glue hulls together.

2. For forward deck, cut a 1⁹⁄₁₆″ × 5⁹⁄₁₆″ rectangle from ¼ × 5¼ lattice.

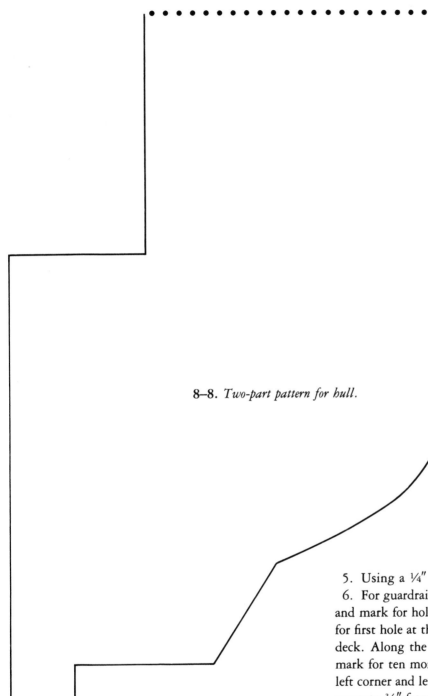

8–8. *Two-part pattern for hull.*

3. Wood-glue forward deck to hull with front edge extending ⅝″ beyond bow, and centered over hull side to side.

4. For forward mast hole, measure and mark 3¼″ from front edge of deck, centered from side to side.

5. Using a ¼″ bit, drill a ½″-deep mast hole.

6. For guardrail postholes on forward deck, measure and mark for holes. Measuring ³⁄₁₆″ from edge, mark for first hole at the right corner of the bow end of the deck. Along the right edge, working towards stern, mark for ten more holes spaced ½″ apart. Repeat for left corner and left edge towards stern. At front edge, measure ⅜″ from both corner posts.

7. Using a ³⁄₃₂″ bit, drill ⅛″-deep guardrail postholes.

8. For middle deck, cut a 1⅜″ × 3¼″ rectangle from ¼ × 5¼ lattice.

9. Wood-glue middle deck to hull, centering it from side to side.

10. For center mast hole, mark center of middle deck.

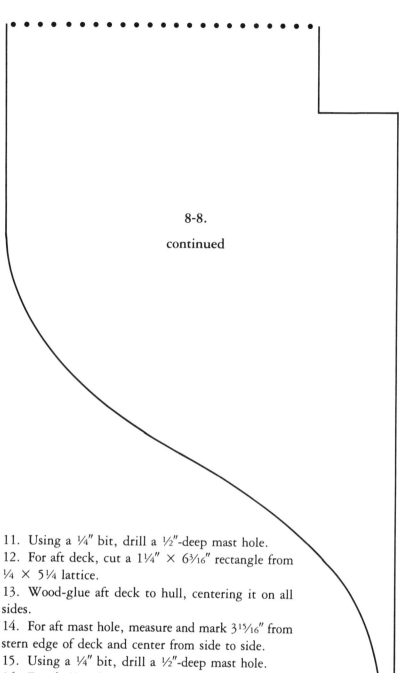

8-8.

continued

8–9. *Thompson and Lightfoote.*

11. Using a ¼″ bit, drill a ½″-deep mast hole.

12. For aft deck, cut a 1¼″ × 6³⁄₁₆″ rectangle from ¼ × 5¼ lattice.

13. Wood-glue aft deck to hull, centering it on all sides.

14. For aft mast hole, measure and mark 3¹⁵⁄₁₆″ from stern edge of deck and center from side to side.

15. Using a ¼″ bit, drill a ½″-deep mast hole.

16. For skull and crossbones flagpole hole, measure and mark center of stern between bottom of aft deck and top of stern.

17. Using a ³⁄₁₆″ bit, drill a ¼″-deep flagpole hole.

18. To stain the hull, mix a small amount of dark red-brown with an equal amount of water. Brush on, then wipe off excess with paper towelling.

19. For portholes, slit the cardboard tube along its length. Cut six ⁵⁄₁₆″-wide strips from the width of the tubing.

20. For each porthole, wind a strip into a 1″-diameter circle; tacky-glue ends to secure. Butt one end of next strip to end of wound circle and tacky-glue to secure. Wind strip around circle and tacky-glue end to secure.

21. Tacky-glue center porthole to hull ³⁄₈″ below middle deck and center on the mast hole.

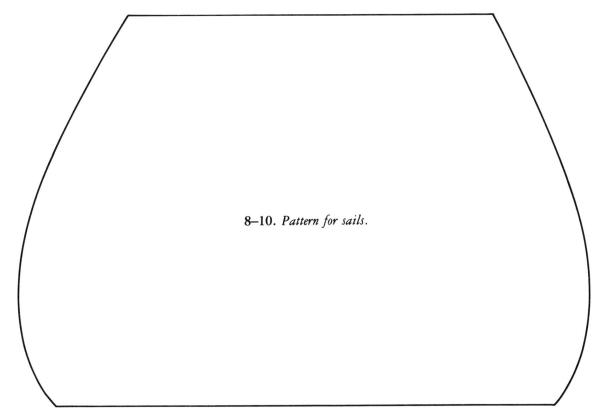

8–10. *Pattern for sails.*

22. Tacky-glue forward and aft portholes ⅜″ from center porthole.

23. Paint inside of portholes pale grey.

24. Paint porthole rims black.

25. For Thompson's and Lightfoote's heads, cut the 20mm bead in half. Cover half-bead holes at top with half-circles of tagboard. Paint heads flesh.

26. Referring to 8–9, paint Thompson's eyes black, cheeks dark pink, and bandana bright red.

27. Referring to 8–9, paint Lightfoote's eyes black, cheeks dark pink, and hair dark brown.

28. For Lightfoote's headband, cut a ⅛″ × 3″ strip from red calico. Referring to 8–9, wrap headband around head and tie ends in a knot at left side of head. Trim ends at an angle.

29. Tacky-glue Thompson into center porthole and Lightfoote into aft porthole.

30. For forward mast, cut a 7¼″ length of ¼″ dowelling.

31. Wood-glue forward mast into forward mast hole.

32. For guardrail posts, cut twenty-four 1″ lengths from the thickest part of toothpicks.

33. Wood-glue guardrail posts into guardrail postholes.

34. For crow's nest platform, use a pencil compass to describe a 2⅝″-diameter circle onto ½ × 5½ lattice. Cut out circle.

35. For guardrail postholes, measure and mark for holes. Measuring ¼″ from edge, mark for sixteen holes spaced ⁷⁄₁₆″ around the perimeter.

36. Using a ³⁄₃₂ bit, drill ⅛″-deep guardrail postholes.

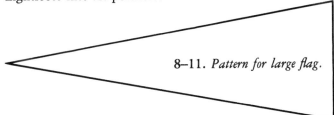

8–11. *Pattern for large flag.*

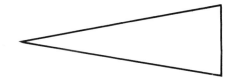

8–12. *Pattern for small flags.*

37. For crow's nest base, use a pencil compass to describe a 1⅜″-diameter circle onto ½ × 5½ lattice. Cut out circle.

38. Wood-glue base to center bottom of platform.

39. Using a ¼″ bit, drill a hole through center of platform assembly.

40. For guardrail posts, cut sixteen ¹⁵⁄₁₆″ lengths from the thickest part of toothpicks.

41. Wood-glue guardrail posts into guardrail post-holes.

42. For center mast, cut an 11¼″ length of ¼″ dowelling.

43. Using a ³⁄₃₂″ bit, drill a ⅛″-deep peg hole for sea gull.

44. Wood-glue center mast into crow's nest so it extends 3⅛″ above platform.

45. Wood-glue center mast into center mast hole.

46. For aft mast, cut a 7¼″ length of ¼″ dowelling.

47. Wood-glue aft mast into aft mast hole.

48. Paint center deck black.

49. Use dark red-brown to paint forward and aft decks, crow's nest, guardrail posts, and masts.

50. Cut a 24″ length of beige yarn for rope along forward deck guardrail posts. Beginning with bow of ship towards your left, begin at first post at right and wrap yarn once around each post from front to back to front. Trim ends and secure with tacky glue.

51. Cut an 18″ length of beige yarn for rope around crow's nest guardrail posts. Beginning at any post, wrap yarn once around each post from front to back to front. Trim ends and secure with tacky glue.

52. For sailcloth, fuse the two 5″ × 14″ rectangles of muslin together, using fusible webbing and following manufacturer's directions.

53. Following 8–10, cut two sails from sailcloth.

54. For sail beams, cut two 4⅝″ lengths (top) and two 7¼″ lengths (bottom) of ³⁄₁₆″ dowelling.

55. In center of each beam, whittle a ¼″-wide × ⅛″-deep notch so beams will lie close to masts.

56. Paint beams dark red-brown.

57. To attach beams to each sail, place a sail on work surface with long edge at bottom. Run a bead of tacky glue along top and bottom edges. Adhere top and bottom beams to sail with beams centered on width of sail and notched sides facing away from sail.

58. To lace each beam to a sail, cut an 18″ length of beige yarn, thread into needle and knot one end.

Overcast stitch along the width of sail. Trim end and tacky-glue to secure.

59. With top beam 1″ from top of forward mast, tacky-glue top and bottom beam notches to back of mast. Repeat for aft mast.

60. Following 8–11, cut large flag from red fabric.

61. Tacky-glue short edge of flag to top back of center mast so tip of flag is at left.

62. Following 8–12, cut two small flags from yellow fabric.

63. Tacky-glue short edge of flags to top back of forward mast and aft mast so tips of flags are at left.

64. For skull and crossbones flagpole, cut a 3″ length of ³⁄₁₆″ dowelling. Paint black.

65. For skull and crossbones flag, use the 2⅜″ × 4¾″ rectangle of black fabric.

66. To fuse flag together and form a casing along top fold, cut a 2⅜″ × 2″ rectangle of fusible webbing. With 2⅜″ edge of webbing even with 2⅜″ edge of fabric, fuse, following manufacturer's directions. Fold fabric over to fused side so edges are even and fuse again.

67. Following 8–13, cut skull and crossbones from tagboard. Tacky-glue to center front of flag.

68. Insert flagpole through casing at top of flag.

69. Tacky-glue flagpole in flagpole hole.

70. For sea gull's head, use an 8mm bead.

71. To indicate position of beak hole, measure and mark at the equator.

72. Using a ¹⁄₁₆″ bit, drill a ¹⁄₁₆″-deep beak hole.

73. For body, use a 10mm bead.

74. Sand one hole of head (bottom) and one bead hole of body (top) to expose raw wood.

75. Insert a toothpick through bottom hole of body and exit at top of body.

76. Wood-gluing head to body, insert toothpick at

8–13. *Pattern for skull and crossbones.*

8–14. *Pattern for sea gull's tail and wings.*

top of body through hole at bottom of head and exit at top of head.

77. Trim toothpick that extends from top hole so it is flush with top of head. Trim toothpick at bottom of body so only ⅛″ extends beyond hole.

78. For beak, cut a ³⁄₁₆″ length from the pointed end of a toothpick.

79. Wood-glue cut end into beak hole.

80. Following 8–14, cut one tail and two wings from tagboard.

81. With pointed tip facing up and opposite end flush with bottom edge of body, tacky-glue tail to center back of body.

82. With pointed tips facing back and tilted slightly up, tacky-glue wings to each side of body.

83. Paint entire sea gull white. Paint eyes black and beak medium yellow.

84. Wood-glue sea gull peg into peg hole at top of center mast.

ROPE LADDER

1. For ladder sides, cut two 10″ lengths of beige yarn.

2. For rungs, cut twenty 1″ lengths from the thickest part of toothpicks.

3. Place ladder sides on work surface with their ends aligned and spaced 1¹⁄₁₆″ apart.

4. Beginning at the bottom and working up, tacky-glue rungs to sides at ½″ intervals.

5. Trim yarn ends close to top and bottom rungs.

WOODEN LADDER

1. For ladder sides, cut two 2⅝″ lengths of ³⁄₁₆″ dowelling.

2. Whittle along length of each ladder side to flatten so rungs will lie close to sides.

3. For rungs, cut six ¾″ lengths from the thickest part of toothpicks.

4. Wood-glue rungs to sides at ⅜″ intervals beginning and ending ¼″ from top and bottom.

BARREL

1. For barrel, cover both holes of the 32mm × 22mm bead with tagboard circles.

2. Paint barrel khaki.

3. Referring to 8–15, use a dry brush and light red-brown to paint spaces between staves. Paint top, bottom, and rings dark grey.

8–15. *Barrel.*

8–16. *Old Pegleg.*

OLD PEGLEG

1. For head, cover one hole of a 25mm bead with a tagboard circle. Paint head flesh.

2. Referring to 8–16, paint eyes black and cheeks dark pink.

3. For body, cut a 1″ length of ¾″ dowelling.

4. Draw a line down length of body to indicate center front.

5. Measure and mark position of left and right arms ⅛″ from top of body and ⅝″ from center line. At each mark, whittle a ¼″ × ¼″ area flat.

6. Sand bottom edge of head to expose raw wood.

7. Wood-glue head to top of body so head faces forward.

8. For left upper leg, cut a ⅞″ length of ⅜″ dowelling.

9. For peg leg, cut a 1¹⁄₁₆″ length of ³⁄₁₆″ dowelling. Whittle bottom end to taper it.

10. Wood-glue top of peg leg to center bottom of upper leg.

11. For right leg, cut a 1⁷⁄₁₆″ length of ⅜″ dowelling.

12. Wood-glue legs to bottom of body so sides of legs are flush with sides of body and are centered from front to back.

13. For shoe portion of right boot, cut a 1¹⁄₁₆″ length from the rounded end of an ice-cream stick. Sand corners to round them.

14. Wood-glue shoe to bottom of right leg so heel extends ⅛″ behind ankle, toe points straight, and Old Pegleg stands upright.

15. For left arm, cut a 1³⁄₁₆″ length of ¼″ dowelling.

16. To indicate angle of left elbow/shoulder cut, measure and mark ½″ from right end. Rotate dowelling so mark is away from you, then measure and mark ⁹⁄₁₆″ from left end. Cut angle.

17. For right arm, cut a 1³⁄₁₆″ length of ¼″ dowelling.

8–17. *Pattern for Old Pegleg's eyepatch.*

18. To indicate angle of right elbow cut, measure and mark ½″ from right end. Rotate dowelling so mark is away from you, then measure and mark 9/16″ from left end. Cut angle.

19. At flat end of left lower (shorter) and right lower (shorter) arms, attach an 8mm-bead hand.

20. To complete the left arm, wood-glue angled end of lower arm to flat end of upper arm, making sure the elbow is crooked and the shoulder angle of the upper arm is parallel with the angled end of the lower arm.

21. To complete the right arm, reverse the elbow cuts and wood-glue upper and lower arms together so elbow joint is crooked.

22. For right arm, whittle inside area of upper arm flat.

23. With shoulders even with top of body, wood-glue left arm to body so hand is raised up and slightly forward. Wood-glue right arm to body so hand is at chest level.

24. Paint hands flesh.

25. For boot, paint shoe and bottom ¾″ of right leg black.

26. Paint peg leg and bottom ⅛″ of upper left leg light red-brown.

27. For pants, paint upper legs, bottom edge of torso, and bottom 3/16″ of torso dark blue-grey.

28. For shirt, paint top edge of torso, top 13/16″ of torso, and arms white.

29. Use bright red to paint ⅛″-wide stripes around torso and arms.

30. For belt, cut a ⅛″ × 2¾″ strip from black adhesive vinyl. Adhere around waist, overlapping short edges at center back.

31. Following 8–17, cut eyepatch from black adhesive vinyl.

32. Referring to 8–16, adhere eyepatch over right eye.

33. For bandana, cut a 4½″ × 4½″ square from red calico. Fold in half diagonally. For tie, cut a ¼″ × ¾″ strip from red calico. Fold in half lengthwise and

finger-press along fold. Referring to 8–16, wrap bandana around head, gathering ends together at left back neck. Wrap and tacky-glue bandana tie around base of gathers. Cut bandana ends ⅜″ from tie.

CAPTAIN BLACKHEART

1. For head, cover one hole of a 25mm bead with a tagboard circle. Paint head flesh.

2. Referring to 8–18, paint right eye black and cheeks dark pink.

3. For body, cut a 1″ length of ¾″ dowelling.

4. Draw a line down length of body to indicate center front.

5. Measure and mark position of left and right arms ⅛″ from top of body and ⅝″ from center line. At each mark, whittle a ¼″ × ¼″ area flat.

6. Sand bottom edge of head to expose raw wood.

7. Wood-glue head to top of body so head faces forward.

8. For pantaloon legs, cut a 1⅜″ length of ⅜″ dowelling.

9. To indicate angle of hip cut, measure and mark ⅝″ from right end. Rotate dowelling so mark is away from you, then measure and mark ⅝″ from left end. Cut angle.

10. For lower legs, cut a 1⅝″ length of ¼″ dowelling.

11. To indicate angle of knee cut, measure and mark ¾″ from right end. Rotate dowelling so mark is away from you, then measure and mark ¾″ from left end. Cut angle.

12. To indicate angle of right ankle cut, place lower leg on work surface so the knee end is at top. Rotate leg so the face of the knee angle cut is facing down. At opposite end, measure and mark ⅛″ from flat end. Cut angle.

13. Wood-glue left pantaloon leg hip to bottom of

8–18. *Captain Blackheart.*   8–20. *Smythe.*

78

8–19. *Pattern for Captain Blackheart's eyepatch.*

body so side of leg is flush with side of body, hip is positioned $\frac{1}{16}''$ closer to the back of body than the front, and knee juts forward.

14. Wood-glue right pantaloon leg hip to bottom of body so side of leg is flush with side of body, hip is positioned $\frac{1}{16}''$ closer to the front of body than the back, and knee juts back.

15. Wood-glue lower left leg knee to center bottom of left pantaloon knee so lower leg is vertical.

16. Wood-glue lower right leg knee to center bottom of right pantaloon knee so ankle juts back towards Captain Blackheart's left.

17. For shoes, cut two $\frac{11}{16}''$ lengths from the rounded ends of an ice-cream stick. Sand corners to round them.

18. Wood-glue shoes to bottom of legs so left heel extends $\frac{1}{8}''$ behind ankle and toe points out, right heel is flush with back of ankle and toe points slightly out, and Captain Blackheart stands upright.

19. For right arm, cut a $1\frac{3}{8}''$ length of $\frac{1}{4}''$ dowelling.

20. To indicate angle of right elbow cut, measure and mark $\frac{9}{16}''$ from right end. Rotate dowelling so mark is away from you, then measure and mark $\frac{3}{4}''$ from left end. Cut angle.

21. To indicate angle of right shoulder cut, place upper (longer) arm on work surface so the elbow end is at top. Rotate arm so the face of the elbow angle cut is facing up. At opposite end, measure and mark $\frac{1}{8}''$ from flat end. Cut angle.

22. For left arm, cut a $1\frac{1}{16}''$ length of $\frac{1}{4}''$ dowelling.

23. At flat end of lower (shorter) right arm and at one end of left arm attach an 8mm-bead hand.

24. To complete the right arm, place upper arm on work surface so shoulder angle end is at top. Rotate arm so point of shoulder angle is at your left. At opposite end, wood-glue angled end of lower arm to bottom end of upper arm, making sure elbow is crooked and hand points towards your right.

25. For left arm, whittle inside area of upper arm flat.

26. With shoulders even with top of body, wood-glue arms to body so left hand is at upper chest level and right hand is raised up and slightly forward.

27. Paint hands and lower legs flesh.

28. Using a dry brush, paint leg hair dark red-brown.

29. Paint shoes and bottom $\frac{1}{8}''$ of lower legs black.

30. For pantaloons, paint top $\frac{1}{8}''$ of lower legs, upper legs, bottom edge of torso, and bottom $\frac{3}{8}''$ of torso bright red.

31. For shirt, paint arms, upper $\frac{5}{8}''$ of torso, and top edge of torso medium yellow.

32. Referring to 8–18, paint vest black.

33. For shoe buckles, cut two $\frac{3}{16}'' \times \frac{5}{16}''$ rectangles from brass adhesive vinyl. Trim corners to round them. Adhere to insteps.

34. For belt buckle, cut a $\frac{1}{4}'' \times \frac{5}{16}''$ rectangle from brass adhesive vinyl. Adhere to center front of waist.

35. Following 8–19, cut eyepatch from black adhesive vinyl.

36. Referring to 8–18, adhere eyepatch over left eye.

SMYTHE

1. For head, cover one hole of a 25mm bead with a tagboard circle. Paint head flesh.

2. Referring to 8–20, paint eyes black, cheeks dark pink, and hair dark red-brown.

3. For body, cut a $\frac{15}{16}''$ length of $\frac{3}{4}''$ dowelling.

4. Draw a line down length of body to indicate center front.

5. Measure and mark position of left and right arms $\frac{1}{8}''$ from top of body and $\frac{5}{8}''$ from center line. At each mark, whittle a $\frac{1}{4}'' \times \frac{1}{4}''$ area flat.

6. Measure and mark position of right and left legs $\frac{3}{16}''$ from bottom edge of body and $\frac{5}{16}''$ from center line. At each mark, whittle a $\frac{1}{4}'' \times \frac{1}{4}''$ area flat.

7. Sand bottom edge of head to expose raw wood.

8. Wood-glue head to body so head faces forward.

9. For pantaloon legs, cut a $1\frac{5}{16}''$ length of $\frac{3}{8}''$ dowelling.

10. To indicate angle of knee cut, measure and mark $\frac{9}{16}''$ from right end. Rotate dowelling so mark is away from you, then measure and mark $\frac{9}{16}''$ from left end. Cut angle.

11. For lower legs, cut a $1\frac{9}{16}''$ length of $\frac{1}{4}''$ dowelling.

12. To indicate angle of each knee cut, measure and

mark $1\frac{1}{16}''$ from right end. Rotate dowelling so mark is away from you, then measure and mark $1\frac{1}{16}''$ from left end. Cut angle.

13. To complete the legs, reverse the knee cuts and wood-glue pantaloon legs and lower legs together so knee joints are crooked. Whittle back of each upper leg flat.

14. Wood-glue pantaloon legs to body so knees point out, lower legs hang down, and backs of legs are flush with bottom of torso.

15. For feet, cut two $\frac{5}{8}''$ lengths from the rounded ends of an ice-cream stick. Sand corners to round them.

16. Wood-glue feet to bottom of legs so heels extend $\frac{1}{16}''$ behind ankles and toes point out.

17. For arms, cut two $1''$ lengths of $\frac{1}{4}''$ dowelling.

18. To indicate angle of left elbow/shoulder cut, measure and mark $\frac{5}{16}''$ from right end. Rotate dowelling so mark is away from you, then measure and mark $\frac{9}{16}''$ from left end. Cut angle.

19. To indicate angle of right elbow cut, measure and mark $\frac{5}{16}''$ from right end. Rotate dowelling so mark is away from you, then measure and mark $\frac{9}{16}''$ from left end. Cut angle.

20. To indicate angle of right shoulder cut, place upper (longer) arm on work surface so the elbow end is at top. Rotate arm so the face of the elbow angle cut is facing up. At opposite end, measure and mark $\frac{1}{8}''$ from flat end. Cut angle.

21. At one flat end of right lower (shorter) arm, attach an 8mm-bead hand. Place left lower (shorter) arm on work surface so point of elbow angle is at top and at your right. Attach half of an 8mm bead for hand, making sure rounded side of bead is facing up.

22. To complete the left arm, wood-glue elbow cut end of lower arm to elbow cut end of upper arm, making sure elbow is crooked and the shoulder angle of upper arm is parallel with the angled end of lower arm.

23. To complete the right arm, reverse the elbow cuts and wood-glue upper and lower arms together so elbow joint is crooked and the shoulder angle of the upper arm is parallel with the angled end of lower arm.

24. With shoulders even with top of body, wood-glue arms to body so left hand is raised up and right hand rests on right knee.

25. Paint hands, arms, top edge of torso, and top $\frac{1}{2}''$ of torso flesh.

26. Paint feet and bottom $\frac{3}{4}''$ of lower legs flesh.

27. For pantaloons, paint upper $\frac{1}{8}''$ of lower legs, upper legs, bottom edge of torso, and bottom $\frac{1}{2}''$ of torso medium aqua.

28. Using a dry brush, paint chest, arm, and leg hair dark red-brown.

29. Paint chest detail and toes dark red-brown.

30. For belt, cut a $\frac{3}{32}'' \times 2\frac{3}{4}''$ strip from black adhesive vinyl. Adhere around waist, overlapping short edges at center back.

WAVES (MAKE 4)

See Project 2 for wave directions.

9 · Down on the Farm

MATERIALS

Beads

one white 32mm × 22mm large-hole wood bead
one white 20mm × 30mm large-hole wood bead
three white 25mm large-hole wood beads
three white 20mm large-hole wood beads
three white 16mm × 15mm large-hole wood beads
two white 16mm 6mm-hole wood beads
five white 10mm regular-hole wood beads
seven red 10mm regular-hole wood beads
one white 5mm regular-hole wood bead
one 3mm gold-plated bead
two 3mm × 6mm gold-plated beads

Wood

24″ length of $\frac{1}{4}''$ dowelling
9″ length of $\frac{3}{16}''$ dowelling
14″ length of $\frac{5}{16}''$ dowelling
4″ length of $\frac{5}{8}''$ dowelling

9–1.

12" length of ¾" dowelling
1⁹⁄₁₆" length of ⅞" dowelling
6" length of 1" dowelling
30" length of ¼ × 5¼ clear pine lattice
7¼" × 9" rectangle of ¾" plywood
two 1¹¹⁄₁₆" wooden eggs
two ⅞"-diameter ready-to-finish wood balls
two 1⅝"-long × ⅜"-diameter axle pegs
eleven round toothpicks
6"-tall forked tree branch (see 7–1)

Paints (Acrylic)

Flesh, black, medium pink, dark blue-grey, dark ultramarine, white, beige, light pink, dark purple, bright red, dark brown, ecru, light red-brown, pale pink, light grey, light yellow-green and medium yellow.

Fabric and Trims

small amount of beige Aida cloth
white, yellow, and orange curly chenille hair
2¼" length of 1"-wide ecru pregathered lace
6" length of ¹⁄₁₆"-wide lavender satin ribbon
2⅜" length of ⅛"-wide black satin ribbon
small amount of black, taupe, white, and pink synthetic suede
8" × 8" square of polyester batting
small amount of red, yellow, and green felt

Hardware

three 1¼ × 17 wire brads
eight ⅞ × 17 wire brads

Miscellaneous

small amount of white tagboard
7" × 7" square of white tagboard
five paper-covered twist ties
three ¾"-long white down feathers
3" × 5" piece of white decorative adhesive covering
natural-color raffia
tennis ball can
36" length of waxed ribbon dental floss
masking tape
1⅛"-tall cork with a top diameter of 1⅜" and a bottom diameter of 1⅛"

FARMER BROWN

1. For head, cover one hole of the 32mm × 22mm bead with a tagboard circle. Paint head flesh.
2. Referring to 9–2, paint eyes black and cheeks medium pink.
3. For body, cut a 2½" length of ¾" dowelling.
4. Draw a line down length of body to indicate center front.
5. Sand bottom edge of head to expose raw wood.
6. Wood-glue head to top of body so head faces forward.
7. For shirt, paint top edge of body and top 1" of body dark blue-grey.
8. For overall pants, paint rest of body dark ultramarine.
9. Referring to 9–2 for overall bib, use dark ultramarine to paint a ¾"-wide × ½"-high rectangle at center front.
10. For overall straps, use dark ultramarine to paint ³⁄₁₆"-wide front and back straps. Have straps crisscross at center back. Continue straps onto top edge of body.
11. Use white to paint a button each side of upper bib.
12. Following 9–3, cut hat brim from beige Aida cloth.
13. To indicate hat crown, pull hat brim down over head so front brim is ³⁄₁₆" from edge of bead and back brim is ⅝" from edge of bead. Trace a line around head underneath hat brim. Remove brim.
14. Using line as a guide, paint top of head beige.
15. Tacky-glue hat brim to head.
16. Cut a ¼" length of white hair and tacky-glue to center forehead, just beneath hat brim.

9-2. *Farmer Brown.*

9-3. *Pattern for Farmer Brown's hat.*

9-4, 9-5. *Mrs. Brown.*

9-6. *Junior Brown.*

MRS. BROWN

1. For head, cover one hole of a 25mm bead with a tagboard circle. Paint head flesh.

2. Referring to 9-4, paint eyes black and cheeks medium pink.

3. For body, cut a 2½" length of ¾" dowelling.

4. Draw a line down length of body to indicate center front.

5. Sand bottom edge of head to expose raw wood.

6. Wood-glue head to top of body so head faces forward.

7. For blouse, paint top edge of body and top ¹⁵⁄₁₆" of body light pink.

8. For skirt, paint rest of body dark purple.

9. For apron bib, cut a ¾" length of ecru lace. Trim off gathered edge. With cut edge at skirt waist, tacky-glue bib to center front.

10. For apron skirt, tacky-glue gathered edge of remaining lace around waist, covering raw bottom edge of bib on center front and overlapping short edges at center back.

11. Referring to 9-5, cut a 14" length of yellow hair. Working from left to right, tacky-glue one end to center back of neck. Framing face first, tacky-glue hair around head. Butting each row, continue around head to ½" from center top of head. Fold hair, change

direction, and continue back around head to ½" from center top of opposite side of head. Fold hair, change direction, fill back of head with a loop and continue around front of head, ending with a topknot at top.

12. Using lavender satin ribbon, tie a bow around neck. Tacky-glue knot to secure. Trim ribbon ends at an angle.

JUNIOR BROWN

1. For head, cover one hole of a 20mm bead with a tagboard circle. Paint head flesh.

2. Referring to 9-6, paint eyes black and cheeks medium pink.

3. For body, cut a 1⅝" length of ¾" dowelling.

4. Draw a line down length of body to indicate center front.

5. Sand bottom edge of head to expose raw wood.

6. Wood-glue head to top of body so head faces forward.

7. For shirt, paint top edge of body and top ¾" of body white. Use bright red to paint ¹⁄₁₆"-wide horizontal stripes around body. Paint one stripe around top edge of body.

8. For pants, paint rest of body dark ultramarine.

9. For belt, tacky-glue black satin ribbon around waist, overlapping short edges at center back.

10. Referring to 9-6, cut two 1¼" lengths of orange hair. Set one aside. Tacky-glue ¼" of one end vertically above left eye. Fold hair and tacky-glue rest of length to frame left side of face. Repeat for right side. Cut two 2" lengths of hair. Set one aside. Fold hair in half. Tacky-glue to right side of back of head placing the fold behind folds of forehead hair and butting the hair on the right side of head. Fold the other length in half and tacky-glue it to the left of and butted against the first length. Cut a 1" length of hair and fold in half. With fold at top, tacky-glue to left side of back of head to fill remaining space.

BOSCO

1. For body, cut a $^{15}/_{16}''$ length of $^5/_8''$ dowelling.

2. To indicate position of first two leg holes, measure and mark $^3/_{16}''$ from each end of body. To indicate position of the last two leg holes, measure $^3/_{16}''$ from each end of body and $^5/_{16}''$ from the first two leg holes.

3. Using a $^3/_{32}''$ bit, drill $^1/_4''$-deep leg holes, angling the bit slightly towards the center top of body.

4. To indicate position of tail hole, turn body so leg holes face down. At center back, measure and mark $^1/_8''$ from end.

5. Using a $^3/_{32}''$ bit, drill a $^1/_8''$-deep tail hole.

6. To indicate position of neck hole, turn body so leg holes face down. At center front, measure and mark $^1/_8''$ from end.

7. Using a $^3/_{32}''$ bit, drill a $^3/_{16}''$-deep neck hole.

8. For legs, cut four $^{11}/_{16}''$ lengths from thickest part of four toothpicks.

9. Wood-glue legs into leg holes.

10. Make one paw at a time. Using a $^1/_8''$ bit, drill a $^1/_{16}''$-deep hole (close to edge) of $^5/_{16}''$ dowelling. Cut a $^1/_8''$ length from drilled end of dowelling. Make four paws.

11. With the widest part of each paw facing forward, wood-glue bottom of legs into holes in paws.

12. For head, cover both holes of a 16mm bead with tagboard circles.

13. To indicate position of neck hole, draw a line around the equator parallel with the covered bead holes.

14. Use a $^3/_{32}''$ bit to drill a $^3/_{16}''$-deep neck hole on the line.

15. Cut a $^3/_8''$ length from the thickest part of a toothpick. Wood-glue one end into head hole and other end into neck hole.

16. For nose hole at top of muzzle, use a $^3/_{32}''$ bit to drill a $^1/_{16}''$-deep perpendicular hole, close to edge of $^5/_{16}''$ dowelling. Cut a $^3/_{16}''$ length from drilled end of dowelling.

17. For nose, trim $^1/_8''$ from the pointed end of a toothpick. Wood-glue cut end into nose hole. Trim so only $^1/_8''$ extends from muzzle.

18. With nose pointed up, position muzzle on front of head, centered from top to bottom, but slightly off-centered towards Bosco's left. Trace outline of muzzle position. Sand muzzle area of head flat.

19. Wood-glue muzzle to head.

20. For tail, cut a $^1/_2''$ length from the pointed end of a toothpick.

21. Wood-glue cut end of tail into tail hole.

22. Paint body, legs, and head dark brown. Paint muzzle, nose, paws, and tail black.

23. Referring to 9–7, paint eyes black. Use white to paint mouth and to highlight nose and eyes. Paint tongue light pink.

24. Following 9–8, cut two ears from black synthetic suede. On wrong side of ears, apply a dot of tacky glue to each short straight edge. Glue ears to each side of head.

25. For dog tag, tacky-glue a 3mm gold bead to center front of neck.

HORATIO HORSE

1. For body, use the $1^9/_{16}''$ length of $^7/_8''$ dowelling.

2. To indicate position of first two leg holes, measure and mark $^5/_{16}''$ from each end of body. To indicate position of last two leg holes, measure $^5/_{16}''$ from each end of body and $^5/_8''$ from first two leg holes.

3. Using a $^1/_4''$ bit, drill $^1/_4''$-deep right and left back leg holes and right front leg hole, angling the bit slightly towards the center top of body.

4. To indicate position of tail hole, turn body so leg holes face down. At center back, measure and mark $^3/_{16}''$ from end.

5. Using a $^3/_{32}''$ bit, drill a $^1/_8''$-deep tail hole.

6. To indicate position of neck, turn body so leg holes face down. At center front, measure and mark $^1/_4''$ from each side of center and $^5/_8''$ from end. Whittle area flat.

7. For neck, cut a $^7/_8''$ length of $^5/_8''$ dowelling.

8. For neck/body angle, measure and mark $^1/_8''$ from one cut end. Cut angle.

9. For head, whittle a $^5/_8''$-wide $\times$ $^5/_8''$-long $\times$ $^1/_4''$-deep area at a hole end of the 20mm $\times$ 30mm bead. Test-fit flat end of neck with whittled end of head to make sure they form a right angle. Wood-glue head to neck.

9–7. *Bosco.*

9–8. *Pattern for Bosco's ears.*

9–9. *Horatio Horse.*

9–10. *Patterns for Horatio's mane, ears, and tail.*

10. Wood-glue angled end of neck to body so head juts forward.

11. Cover bead holes with tagboard circles.

12. For straight legs, cut two 1 9/16″ (back legs) and one 1 3/4″ (right front leg) lengths of 1/4″ dowelling.

13. Wood-glue legs into leg holes.

14. For left front leg, cut an 1 1/16″ (upper leg), a 3/4″ (lower leg), and a 1/8″ (hoof) length from 1/4″ dowelling.

15. At one end of upper leg, whittle a 1/8″-deep × 5/16″-long notch so upper leg will lie close to body.

16. At each end of lower leg, and on same side, whittle a 1/8″-deep × 1/4″-long notch for knee and ankle bends. With notched side of upper leg facing up, wood-glue opposite end to a lower leg notch. Wood-glue hoof to other lower leg notch. Wood-glue upper leg notch to body at mark.

17. Paint entire body ecru.

18. For hooves, paint bottom 1/8″ of each leg dark brown.

19. Referring to 9–9, paint eyes black, and nostrils light red-brown.

20. Following 9–10, cut mane, ears, and tail from taupe synthetic suede.

21. Tacky-glue straight edge of mane to center top of head and down back of neck.

22. On right side of ears, dot straight edge with

tacky glue. Fold over and pinch to secure. Tacky-glue ears to each side of head.

23. Tacky-glue end of tail into tail hole.

FLOSSIE AND BOSSIE COWS (MAKE 2)

1. For body, cut a 2″ length of 1″ dowelling.

2. Draw a line down length of body to indicate center of underside.

3. To indicate position of left and right front leg holes, measure 1/2″ from front end of body and 1/4″ from center line. To indicate position of left and right back leg holes, measure 5/16″ from back end of body and 1/4″ from center line.

4. Using a 1/4″ bit, drill 1/4″-deep leg holes, angling the bit slightly towards the center top of body.

5. For tail-hole position on rear of body, turn body so leg holes face down. On rear of body, measure and mark 3/16″ from center top edge.

6. Using a 3/32″ bit, drill a 1/8″-deep tail hole.

7. To indicate position of udder, turn body so leg holes face up. Measure and mark 7/8″ from front of body, 3/8″ from center line, 7/16″ from rear of body, and 3/8″ from center line. Whittle area flat.

8. For legs, cut four 1 1/4″ lengths of 5/16″ dowelling.

9. Wood-glue legs into leg holes.

10. For udder, cut a 20mm bead in half.

11. To indicate position of udder's teat holes, draw a center line from half-bead hole to half-bead hole. For first two teat holes, measure and mark 5/16″ from edge of one half-bead hole and 1/8″ from center line. For last two teat holes, measure and mark 5/16″ from edge of other half-bead hole and 1/8″ from center line.

12. Using a 3/32″ bit, drill 1/8″-deep teat holes.

13. Test-fit udder to underside of body, placing half-bead holes of udder parallel with front and back edge

9–11. *Flossie and Bossie Cow.*

of body. Whittle side edges of udder so they are the same width as the body.

14. For teats, cut four ⅜″ lengths from the thickest part of a toothpick.

15. Wood-glue teats into teat holes.

16. Wood-glue udder to underside of body.

17. For head, cover one hole of a 25mm bead with a tagboard circle (back of head).

18. Draw a line from bead hole to bead hole to indicate center of head.

19. For left and right horn holes, measure and mark ⁵⁄₁₆″ from edge of tagboard circle and ⁷⁄₃₂″ from center line.

20. Using a ³⁄₃₂″ bit, drill ⅛″-deep horn holes, angling bit towards center line.

21. For muzzle, cut the shank from an axle peg. Discard the shank. Sand the bottom of the cap to remove any remaining shank.

22. Sand the hole edge of the head to expose raw wood. Wood-glue muzzle to the hole.

23. For horns, cut two ⁷⁄₁₆″ lengths from the pointed ends of a toothpick.

24. Wood-glue cut ends of horns in horn holes.

25. Paint head, muzzle, and horns white.

26. Referring to 9–11, paint eyes black and muzzle detail medium pink.

27. Following 9–12, cut ears from white synthetic suede.

28. Paint center of ears light pink.

29. On right side of ears, dot straight edge with tacky glue. Fold over and pinch to secure. Tacky-glue ears to each side of head.

30. Cut a ½″ length of white hair and tacky-glue it horizontally between the horns.

31. Position Flossie's head at the center top front of body so she faces forward. Using very short strokes and firm, even pressure, scrape the head against the body to remove paint from the back of head. Sand area where the paint has been removed until flat. Repeat

9–12. Pattern for
Flossie's and Bossie's ears.

9–13. Pattern for Flossie's and Bossie's tail.

9–14. Fuzzy and Fluffy Sheep.

9–15. Pattern for Fuzzy's and Fluffy's ears.

for Bossie, making sure she faces slightly down and towards her left.

32. Wood-glue head to body.

33. Following 9–13, cut tail from a twist tie.

34. Tacky-glue end of tail into tail hole.

35. Paint body, legs, and tail white.

36. Paint udder medium pink.

37. For hooves, paint bottom ⅛″ of legs black.

38. Paint spots on back and tip of tail black.

39. For cow bell, tacky-glue a 3mm × 6mm gold bead vertically to center front of neck.

FUZZY AND FLUFFY SHEEP (MAKE 2)

1. For body, cut a 1⅜″ length of ¾″ dowelling.

2. To indicate position of first two leg holes, measure and mark ³⁄₁₆″ from each end of body. To indicate position of last two leg holes, measure ³⁄₁₆″ from each end of body and ⅜″ from first two leg holes.

3. Using a ³⁄₁₆″ bit, drill ¼″-deep leg holes, angling the bit slightly towards the center top of body.

4. For tail-hole position on rear of body, turn body so leg holes face down. On rear of body, measure and mark ³⁄₁₆″ from center top edge.

5. Using a ³⁄₃₂″ bit, drill a ⅛″-deep tail hole.

6. To indicate position of neck hole, turn body so leg holes face down. At center front, measure and mark ⅛″ from end.

7. Using a ³⁄₃₂″ bit, drill a ³⁄₁₆″-deep neck hole.

8. For legs, cut four ¾″ lengths of ³⁄₁₆″ dowelling.

9. Wood-glue legs into leg holes.

10. For head, use a ³⁄₃₂″ bit to drill a ³⁄₁₆″-deep hole into a ⅞″ ready-to-finish wood ball.

11. Cut a ⅜″ length from the thickest part of a toothpick. Wood-glue one end into head hole and other end into neck hole.

12. For muzzle, cut a 10mm bead in half.

13. With half-holes of bead horizontal, position muzzle on front of Fuzzy's head, centered from top to bottom, but slightly off-centered towards Fuzzy's left. Trace outline of muzzle. Sand muzzle area flat. For Fluffy, position muzzle on front of head, centered from top to bottom and left to right, so Fluffy faces forward. Trace outline of muzzle and sand area flat.

14. Tacky-glue muzzle to head.

15. Referring to 9–14, paint eyes and muzzle black.

16. Paint legs black.

17. To cover head with fleece, cut a 1¼″ × 2½″ rectangle from batting. Tacky-glue to head, cutting a Y-shaped seam at center back of head to accommodate roundness and cutting away batting at center front to reveal eyes and muzzle.

18. To cover body with fleece, cut a 1⅜″ × 2½″ rectangle from batting. With seam centered along top of body, tacky-glue to body, cutting out holes to accommodate legs and cutting away batting around neck.

19. To cover front and back of body, cut two ¾″-diameter circles from batting. Tacky-glue in place.

20. Following 9–15, cut ears from black synthetic suede.

21. On wrong side of ears, apply a dot of tacky glue to each short straight edge. Glue ears to each side of head.

22. For tail, cut a ¼″ × ½″ triangle from batting.

23. Tacky-glue point of tail into tail hole using an ice pick to pierce batting and to guide end of tail into hole.

PINKIE AND PEGGY PIGS (MAKE 2)

1. For head/body, use a 1¹¹⁄₁₆″ wooden egg.

2. To indicate position of two back leg holes, measure and mark ½″ from flat end of body (rear) and space marks ⅜″ apart. To indicate position of two front leg holes, measure and mark ¹³⁄₁₆″ from pointed end of body (front) and space marks ⅜″ apart and parallel with back-leg marks.

9–16. *Pinkie and Peggy Pig.*

9–17. Pattern for Pinkie's and Peggy's ears.

86

3. Using a ¼″ bit, drill ¼″-deep leg holes, angling the bit slightly towards the center top of body.

4. To indicate position of tail hole, turn body so leg holes face down. Measure and mark ¹⁄₁₆″ from center top edge of rear of body.

5. Using a ³⁄₃₂″ bit, drill a ⅛″-deep tail hole.

6. For legs, cut four ½″ lengths of ¼″ dowelling.

7. Wood-glue legs into leg holes.

8. Paint entire body light pink.

9. For hooves, use black to paint a ¹⁄₁₆″-long vertical line at bottom center front of each leg.

10. Referring to 9–16, paint eyes black and snout pale pink. Paint nostrils light pink and outline with light grey. Paint mouth black.

11. Following 9–17, cut ears from pink synthetic suede.

12. On right side of ears, dot straight edge with tacky glue. Fold over and pinch to secure. Tacky-glue ears to each side of head.

13. For tail, cut a 1¾″ length of twist tie. Trim paper from sides so tail measures ⅛″ wide.

14. Paint tail light pink.

15. Wind tail around a pencil to curl.

16. Tacky-glue end of tail into tail hole.

HARRIET, HENRIETTA, AND HORTENSE HENS (MAKE 3)

1. For body, cover one hole of a 16mm × 15mm bead with a tagboard circle (top).

2. For head, cover one hole of a 10mm bead with a tagboard circle (top).

3. Tacky-glue bottom of head to top of body so one-third of head extends from body.

4. Paint head and body white.

5. Referring to 9–18, paint eyes black.

6. For comb, cut a ⁵⁄₁₆″-long crescent shape from red felt.

7. Tacky-glue comb to center top of head.

8. For beak, cut a ⅛″ × ⅛″ × ⅛″-triangle from yellow felt.

9. Referring to 9–18, tacky-glue beak to face. Separate layers to "open" beak.

10. For wattle, cut a tiny triangle from red felt and tacky-glue under beak.

11. For tail feathers, tacky-glue the right side of a down feather to center back of body so feather stands up and curves back.

9–18. *Harriet, Henrietta, and Hortense Hen.*

9–19. *Half-pattern for barn.*

BARN

1. For base, cut a 1⅝″ × 8¾″ rectangle from ¼ × 5¼ lattice.

2. Following 9–19, cut barn from ¾″ plywood.

3. Center base on bottom of barn. Wood-glue and nail with three evenly spaced 1¼ × 17 wire brads.

4. For roof, cut two 1⅝″ × 2¹¹⁄₁₆ (gable) and two 1⅝″ × 3½″ (eaves) rectangles from ¼ × 5¼ lattice.

5. Butt the two gable pieces together at the peak. Sand underside edges of both gable pieces at an angle so they butt tightly together.

6. Place gable pieces at peak, centered side to side over barn. Wood-glue and nail each to barn with two evenly spaced ⅞ × 17 wire brads.

7. On each side, butt an eave piece to the gable. Sand underside edge of eave piece at an angle so it butts tightly against gable.

8. Place eave pieces on each side of gable, centered side to side over barn. Wood-glue and nail each to barn with two evenly spaced ⅞ × 17 wire brads.

9. Paint barn bright red, base light yellow-green, and roof black.

10. For barn door, cut two ¼″ × 4¼″ (top and bottom) and two ¼″ × 4″ (sides) strips from white adhesive vinyl.

11. Adhere bottom strip flush with bottom edge of barn and centered side to side.

12. Adhere side strips, butting their bottom ends with top edge of bottom strip, and parallel with sides of barn.

13. Adhere top strip, butting top edge of side strips.

14. For crisscross, cut two ¼″ × 5⅝″ strips from white adhesive vinyl.

15. Adhere in a crisscross, trimming ends into points with an art knife so they fit neatly into the corners.

16. For loft opening, cut two ¼″ × 2″ (top and bottom) and two ¼″ × 1⅛″ (sides) strips from white adhesive vinyl.

17. Adhere bottom strip 1⅛″ from top of door and centered side to side.

18. Adhere sides strips same as for barn door.

19. Adhere top strip.

20. For hay, cut thirty-four ¾″-long pieces of raffia.

21. Referring to 9–1, tacky-glue to lower center of loft opening.

9–20. *Pattern for Roosting Roberta's outline.*

9–21. *Pattern for Big Bertha's outline.*

22. Following 9–20, cut Roosting Roberta's outline from tagboard.

23. For body, cut a 10mm bead in half. Discard one half.

24. For head, cut the 5mm bead in half. (Save one half for Big Bertha's head.) With head and body half-bead holes horizontal, tacky-glue head and body to tagboard outline.

25. Paint head and body white.

26. Paint eye black, comb and wattle bright red, and beak medium yellow.

27. Tacky-glue Roosting Roberta on top of hay in loft opening.

28. Following 9–21, cut Big Bertha's outline from white tagboard.

29. For body, cut a 16mm bead in half.

30. With head half-bead holes horizontal and body half-bead holes vertical, tacky-glue head and body to tagboard outline.

31. Paint head and body white.

32. Paint eye black, comb and wattle bright red, and beak medium yellow.

33. Referring to 9–1, tacky-glue Big Bertha to left side of barn.

SILO

1. For silo base, paint tennis ball can light grey.

2. For roof, use a pencil compass to describe a 5½"-diameter circle on 7" × 7" tagboard square. Cut out circle.

3. Cut a slit from the edge of the circle to the center. Overlap slit edges 1" to form a shallow cone and tacky-glue to secure.

4. Paint roof black.

5. Tacky-glue roof to top of base.

FENCE

1. For base, cut one 1" × 8¾" length of ¼ × 5¼ lattice.

2. Draw a line down center of base.

3. To indicate position of postholes, measure and mark along center line. Mark center, 2¹⁄₁₆" from either side of center mark and ½" from each end.

4. Using a ¼" bit, drill ³⁄₁₆"-deep postholes.

5. For posts, cut five 2" lengths of ¼" dowelling.

6. Wood-glue posts into postholes.

7. Paint posts white.

8. Paint base light yellow-green.

9. To string bottom row of posts, use a square knot to tie one end of dental floss around first post ½" from base. Dot knot with tacky glue. Working from front to back to front, wrap floss once around each of next three posts, dotting wraps with tacky glue. Use a square knot to tie end to last post. Dot knot with tacky glue and cut end close to knot.

10. String top row of posts ¹¹⁄₁₆" above first row.

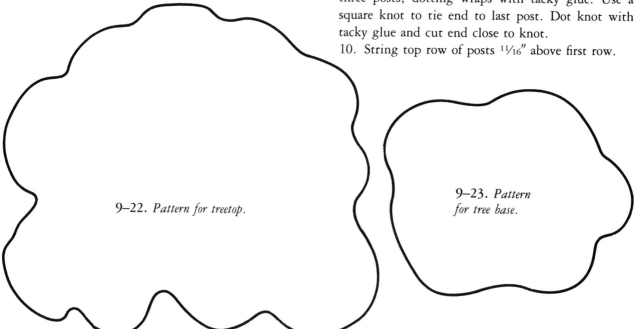

9–22. *Pattern for treetop.*

9–23. *Pattern for tree base.*

9–24. *Bushel basket of apples.*

APPLE TREE

1. Following 9–22, cut treetop from ¼ × 5¼ lattice.

2. Test-fit forked branch to treetop by placing branch on wrong side of treetop with its main stem approximately perpendicular to the bottom edge of treetop. Prune limbs so only 1″ extends onto wrong side of treetop. Use masking tape to hold branch in position. Stand tree/branch assembly on end and adjust position if necessary. Prune bottom of trunk so tree is 7″ tall.

3. Remove tape. Trace outline of forked branches onto back of treetop. Rout out two ⅛″-deep depressions so branches will lie close to treetop.

4. Wood-glue forked branches to back of treetop.

5. Following 9–23, cut base from ¼ × 5¼ lattice.

6. Using a bit that matches diameter of tree trunk (we used a ⅜″ bit), drill a ³⁄₁₆″-deep hole in center of base.

7. Wood-glue tree trunk into hole.

8. Paint treetop and base light yellow-green.

9. For apples on tree, cut two 10mm red beads in half. Discard one half. Referring to 9–1, tacky-glue three apple halves to treetop.

10. Tacky-glue a whole 10mm red bead to base.

11. Cut a ¹⁄₁₆″ × ⅜″ stem from black synthetic suede and tacky-glue into hole in apple.

BUSHEL BASKET OF APPLES

1. Paint the cork beige.

2. Using light red-brown, paint a 1″-diameter circle on center top of basket.

3. Referring to 9–24, paint basket weave pattern, using a dry brush and light red-brown.

4. For handles, cut two 1¼″ lengths of paper twist ties. Strip paper from each end, leaving ⅛″ of wire core exposed. Bend twist ties into handles. Tacky-glue and embed wire ends into top of basket.

5. Paint handles ecru.

6. For half-apples, cut three 10mm red beads in half.

7. Tacky-glue apple halves in a circle around top of basket.

8. For whole apple, tacky-glue one 10mm red bead, hole side up, to center top of basket.

9. Cut a ⅜″-long leaf shape from green felt and a ¹⁄₁₆″ × ⅜″ stem from black synthetic suede.

10. Tacky-glue leaf and stem into bead hole of center apple.

HAYSTACKS (MAKE 4)

1. Cut a 6″ length of raffia. Set aside.

2. Wind raffia around your hand 25 times. Cut end. Slip raffia loops off your hand.

3. Tie securely around middle with the 6″ length of raffia.

4. Cut top and bottom loops. Trim ends evenly.

5. Referring to 9–1, to stand haystacks, fan the ends out at top and bottom.

10 · A Day at the Beach

MATERIALS

Beads

five white 25mm large-hole wood beads
two white 20mm large-hole wood beads
one white 10mm regular-hole wood bead
twelve white 8mm regular-hole wood beads
one 3mm × 6mm gold-plated bead

Wood

18″ length of ³⁄₁₆″ dowelling
57″ length of ¼″ dowelling
6″ length of ⅝″ dowelling
5″ length of ¾″ dowelling
3″ length of ¼ × 5¼ clear pine lattice
ten ice-cream sticks
nine round toothpicks

10–1.

Wheel

one 1½″-diameter wooden spoked wheel

Paints (Acrylic)

Flesh, black, dark pink, light blue, white, dark brown, medium purple, light red-brown, medium orange, bright red, dark ultramarine and medium pink metallic

Fabric and Trims

orange and light brown curly chenille hair

4⅝″ × 5½″ rectangle of yellow lightweight cotton fabric

6″ of ⅛″-wide pink grosgrain ribbon

small amount of white synthetic suede

3¾″ of black sportweight cotton yarn

6″ of white worsted-weight cotton yarn

Miscellaneous

white tagboard

small amount of aluminum foil

black fine-tip permanent marker

5½″ length of 20-gauge galvanized steel wire

three ½″-tall corks with a top diameter of ⅜″ and a bottom diameter of ⁵⁄₁₆″

two ¹¹⁄₁₆″-tall corks with a top diameter of ½″ and a bottom diameter of ⅜″

one ¹⁵⁄₁₆″-tall cork with a top diameter of ⅝″ and a bottom diameter of ¾″

fine-grain sand

red-bead-head straight pin

small amount of red, yellow, and blue adhesive vinyl.

90

TRACY

1. For head, cover one hole of a 25mm bead with a tagboard circle. Paint head flesh.

2. Referring to 10–2, paint cheeks dark pink and eyelashes black.

3. For body, cut a ⅞″ length of ¾″ dowelling.

4. Draw a line down length of body to indicate center front.

5. Measure and mark position of left and right arms ⅛″ from top of body and ¹³⁄₁₆″ from center line. At each mark, whittle a ¼″ × ¼″ area flat.

6. Measure and mark position of left and right bikini bra ¼″ from top of body and ³⁄₁₆″ from center line. At each mark, whittle a ¼″ × ¼″ area flat.

7. Sand bottom edge of head to expose raw wood.

8. Wood-glue head to top of body so bottom edge of head is flush with front edge of body and faces slightly towards the left.

9. For legs, cut two 1¾″ lengths of ¼″ dowelling.

10. To indicate angle of each knee cut, measure and mark ¹⁵⁄₁₆″ from right end. Rotate dowelling so mark is away from you, then measure and mark ¾″ from left end. Cut angle.

11. To indicate angle of each hip cut, place upper (shorter) leg on work surface so the knee end is at top. Rotate leg so the face of the knee angle cut is facing down. At opposite end, measure and mark ⅛″ from flat end. Cut angle.

12. To indicate angle of left ankle cut, place lower (longer) leg on work surface so the knee end is at top. Rotate leg so the face of the knee angle cut is facing down. At opposite end, measure and mark ⅛″ from flat end. Cut angle.

13. To complete the legs, reverse the knee cuts and wood-glue upper and lower legs together so knee joints are crooked.

14. Lie Tracy face up on work surface. With sides of legs flush with sides of body, wood-glue hips to bot-

10–2. *Tracy.*

10–3. *Tracy.*

tom of body so knees point up and backs of ankles are flush with work surface.

15. For feet, cut two $^{11}/_{16}''$ lengths from the rounded ends of an ice-cream stick. Sand corners to round them.

16. Lie Tracy face up on work surface. Wood-glue feet to bottom of legs so toes point up and heels are flush with work surface.

17. For arms, cut two $^{15}/_{16}''$ lengths of $^{1}/_{4}''$ dowelling.

18. To indicate angle of each elbow cut, measure and mark $^{3}/_{8}''$ from right end. Rotate dowelling so mark is away from you, then measure and mark $^{3}/_{8}''$ from left end. Cut angle.

19. At flat end of two arm halves, attach 8mm-bead hands.

20. To complete the arms, reverse the elbow cuts and wood-glue upper and lower arms together so elbow joints are crooked.

21. For each arm, whittle inside area of shoulder flat.

22. With shoulders even with top of body, wood-glue arms to body so hands are at hip level.

23. For bikini bra, cut the 10mm bead in half.

24. With half-bead holes vertical, wood-glue bra halves to chest.

25. Paint body flesh.

26. For bikini bottom, paint bottom edge of torso and bottom $^{3}/_{16}''$ of torso light blue.

27. Referring to 10–2, paint bikini bra light blue. For ties, continue a $^{1}/_{16}''$-wide horizontal line across back. On back, paint a bow in center of line.

28. Referring to 10–2, for bangs, cut three $^{1}/_{2}''$ lengths of orange hair. Place side by side and tacky-glue them vertically across center of forehead, $^{1}/_{8}''$ above eyes. Referring to 10–3, cut three 4$''$ lengths of hair. Placing them side by side, tacky-glue first length over top of head, butting bangs and framing face. Tacky-glue second and third lengths in place. Cut two 2$^{1}/_{2}''$ lengths of hair. Tacky-glue one length in place. Fold last length of hair in half. Tacky-glue fold to center back of head to fill in empty space.

MARYANN

1. For head, cover one hole of a 25mm bead with a tagboard circle. Paint head flesh.

2. Referring to 10–4, paint eyes black and cheeks dark pink.

3. For body, cut a 1$''$ length of $^{3}/_{4}''$ dowelling.

10–4. *Maryann.*

10–5. *Simon.*

4. Whittle a $^{1}/_{2}''$-wide area down length of body to flatten so Maryann will lie flat.

5. Draw a line down length of body, centered on whittled area, to indicate center front.

6. Measure and mark position of left and right arms $^{1}/_{8}''$ from top of body and $^{9}/_{16}''$ from center line. At each mark, whittle a $^{1}/_{4}'' \times ^{1}/_{4}''$ area flat.

7. Sand bottom edge of head to expose raw wood.

8. Wood-glue head to top of body, making sure head faces left.

9. For left leg, cut a 1$^{1}/_{2}''$ length of $^{1}/_{4}''$ dowelling.

10. To indicate angle of left knee cut, measure and mark $^{11}/_{16}''$ from right end. Rotate dowelling so mark is away from you, then measure and mark $^{3}/_{4}''$ from left end. Cut angle.

11. To indicate angle of left ankle cut, place lower (shorter) leg work on surface so the knee end is at top. Rotate leg so the face of the knee angle cut is facing down. At opposite end, measure and mark $^{1}/_{8}''$ from flat end. Cut angle.

12. To complete the left leg, reverse the knee cuts and wood-glue upper and lower legs together so knee joint is crooked.

13. For right leg, cut a 1$^{3}/_{8}''$ length of $^{1}/_{4}''$ dowelling.

14. To indicate angle of right ankle cut, measure and mark $^{1}/_{8}''$ from right end. Cut angle.

15. With front of left leg $^{1}/_{16}''$ from front of body and $^{1}/_{16}''$ to the left of center, wood-glue left hip to bottom of body so ankle is raised.

16. With front of right leg $^{1}/_{16}''$ from front of body and $^{1}/_{16}''$ to the right of center, wood-glue right hip to bottom of body so the point of the ankle angle is on the outside of the leg.

17. For feet, cut two $^{5}/_{8}''$ lengths from the rounded ends of an ice-cream stick. Sand corners to round them.

18. Lie Maryann face down on work surface. Wood-glue left foot to bottom of left leg so heel is flush with

back of ankle and toes point down and slightly towards her left. Wood-glue right foot to bottom of right leg so heel is flush with back of ankle, toes point towards her right, and inside edge of foot is flush with work surface.

19. For arms, cut two $^{15}/_{16}''$ lengths of $^{1}/_{4}''$ dowelling.

20. To indicate angle of each elbow cut, measure and mark $^{7}/_{16}''$ from right end. Rotate dowelling so mark is away from you, then measure and mark $^{7}/_{16}''$ from left end. Cut angle.

21. At flat end of two arm halves, attach 8mm-bead hands.

22. To complete the arms, reverse the elbow-cuts and wood-glue upper and lower arms together so elbow joints are crooked.

23. Wood-glue arms to body so they are raised up.

24. Paint body flesh.

25. For bikini bottom, paint bottom edge of torso and bottom $^{3}/_{16}''$ of torso medium pink metallic.

26. Referring to 10–4, paint bikini top medium pink metallic. For ties, continue a $^{1}/_{16}''$-wide horizontal line across back. On back, paint a bow in center of line.

27. For hair, cut sufficient $^{1}/_{8}''$ lengths of light brown hair to cover head. Tacky-glue hair to head.

BEACH BLANKET

1. For beach blanket, use the $4^{5}/_{8}'' \times 5^{1}/_{2}''$ rectangle of yellow fabric.

2. For fringe, ravel each short edge for $^{1}/_{4}''$.

RADIO

1. For body, cut a $^{11}/_{16}'' \times 1^{7}/_{16}''$ rectangle from $^{1}/_{4} \times 5^{1}/_{4}$ lattice. On one long edge, sand corners to round them (top).

2. To indicate position of antenna hole at top, measure and mark $^{3}/_{16}''$ from right edge.

3. Using a $^{1}/_{16}''$ bit, drill a $^{1}/_{8}''$-deep antenna hole.

4. For speaker, cut a $^{1}/_{8}''$ length of $^{5}/_{8}''$ dowelling.

5. Wood-glue speaker to radio $^{1}/_{8}''$ from left edge and centered top to bottom.

6. For control knobs, cut two $^{3}/_{32}''$ lengths of $^{3}/_{16}''$ dowelling.

7. Wood-glue control knobs at lower right, spacing them $^{1}/_{8}''$ from right edge and bottom, and $^{1}/_{16}''$ apart.

8. Paint radio black.

9. Paint front of control knobs white.

10. Cut a $^{5}/_{8}''$-diameter circle from aluminum foil.

11. Tacky-glue to front of speaker.

12. Using black fine-tip permanent marker, draw closely spaced diagonal grid lines.

13. For antenna, cut a $2^{1}/_{4}''$ length of wire.

14. Tacky-glue antenna into antenna hole.

SIMON

1. For head, cover one hole of a 20mm bead with a tagboard circle. Paint head flesh.

2. Referring to 10–5, paint eyes black, cheeks dark pink, and hair dark brown.

3. For body, cut a $1''$ length of $^{5}/_{8}''$ dowelling.

4. Draw a line down length of body to indicate center front.

5. Measure and mark position of left and right arms $^{1}/_{8}''$ from top of body and $^{1}/_{2}''$ from center line. At each mark, whittle a $^{1}/_{4}'' \times ^{1}/_{4}''$ area flat.

6. Sand bottom edge of head to expose raw wood.

7. Wood-glue head to top of body so head faces forward.

8. For legs, cut two $^{7}/_{8}''$ lengths of $^{1}/_{4}''$ dowelling.

9. To indicate angle of each knee/hip cut, measure and mark $^{1}/_{2}''$ from right end. Rotate dowelling so mark is away from you, then measure and mark $^{5}/_{16}''$ from left end. Cut angle.

10. To indicate each knee placement, place upper (shorter) leg on work surface so the hip angle is at top. Rotate leg so the face of the hip angle cut is facing down. At opposite end, measure and mark $^{1}/_{4}''$ from flat end. Beginning at same end, whittle a $^{1}/_{4}'' \times ^{1}/_{4}''$ area to flatten so lower legs will lie close to upper legs.

11. To complete each leg, wood-glue angled end of lower (longer) leg to whittled area of upper (shorter) leg, making sure knee is crooked.

12. Wood-glue legs to bottom of body so sides of legs are flush with sides of body, centered from front to back, and Simon kneels.

13. For feet, cut two $^{1}/_{2}''$ lengths from the rounded ends of an ice-cream stick. Sand corners to round them.

14. Kneel Simon on work surface. Wood-glue feet to bottom of lower legs so toes point out, outside edges of feet are flush with work surface, and heels butt.

15. For arms, cut two $^{7}/_{8}''$ lengths of $^{1}/_{4}''$ dowelling.

16. To indicate angle of each elbow cut, measure and mark $^{7}/_{16}''$ from right end. Rotate dowelling so mark is away from you, then measure and mark $^{5}/_{16}''$ from left end. Cut angle.

17. At flat end of two lower (shorter) arms, attach 8mm-bead hands.

18. To complete the arms, reverse the elbow cuts and wood-glue upper and lower arms together so elbow joints are crooked.

19. Whittle inside area of each upper arm flat.

20. With shoulders even with top of body, wood-glue arms to body so left hand is at chest level and right hand is at cheek level.

21. Paint body flesh.

22. For bathing suit, paint bottom edge of torso and bottom ⁵⁄₁₆″ of torso medium purple.

SAND CASTLES

1. For small sand castles, coat the tops and sides of two ½″-tall corks with tacky glue. Press glued sides into fine-grain sand.

2. For large sand castle, tacky-glue the bottom of a ½″-tall cork to center top of the ¹⁵⁄₁₆″-tall cork.

3. Coat tops and sides with tacky glue. Press glued sides into fine-grain sand.

4. Use the red-bead-head straight pin for flagpole.

5. Following 10–6, cut flag from red adhesive vinyl. To assemble flag, remove protective paper, place flagpole (below bead) across center, and adhere the two sides together.

6. Tacky-glue flagpole into center top of sand castle.

PAIL AND SHOVEL

1. For pail, use a ¹¹⁄₁₆″-tall cork.

2. Cover sides with red adhesive vinyl.

3. Cut a ⅜″-diameter circle from red adhesive vinyl and adhere to bottom of pail.

4. To indicate position of wire handle, measure and mark ⅛″ from top edge on each side of pail.

5. Use an ice pick to make a shallow indentation in center of each mark to accommodate wire handle ends.

6. For handle, cut a 1⅝″ length of wire. Using needle-nose pliers, bend into a handle shape.

7. Use needle-nose pliers to embed handle ends into indentations in pail. Dot with tacky glue to secure.

8. For shaft of shovel handle, cut a ¾″ length from the pointed end of a toothpick.

9. Insert ice pick into center top of pail at an angle, making a ⅛″-deep hole.

10. Tacky-glue pointed end of handle shaft into hole.

11. For top of handle, cut a ⁷⁄₁₆″ length from the

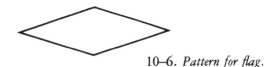

10–6. *Pattern for flag.*

thickest part of a toothpick. Sand one side to flatten slightly.

12. Wood-glue flattened side of handle top to end of shaft, making sure it is centered from side to side.

BEACH BALL

1. Cover both holes of a 25mm bead with tagboard circles.

2. Divide ball into eight sections.

3. Alternating colors, paint sections white and medium pink metallic.

EMILY

1. For head, cover one hole of a 20mm bead with a tagboard circle. Paint head flesh.

2. Referring to 10–7, paint eyes black, cheeks dark pink, and hair light red-brown.

3. For body, cut a 1″ length of ⅝″ dowelling.

4. Draw a line down length of body to indicate center front.

5. Measure and mark position of left and right arms ⅛″ from top of body and ¹¹⁄₁₆″ from center line. At each mark, whittle a ¼″ × ¼″ area flat.

6. Measure and mark position of left and right legs ⅛″ from bottom of body and ⁷⁄₁₆″ from center line. At each mark, whittle a ¼″ × ¼″ area flat.

7. Sand bottom edge of head to expose raw wood.

8. Wood-glue head to top of body, making sure head faces slightly towards the left.

9. For legs, cut two 1″ lengths of ¼″ dowelling.

10. To indicate angle of each knee/hip cut, measure and mark ½″ from right end. Rotate dowelling so mark is away from you, then measure and mark ⁷⁄₁₆″ from left end. Cut angle.

11. To complete each leg, wood-glue angled end of lower (shorter) leg to flat end of upper (longer) leg, making sure the knee is crooked and the hip angle of upper leg is parallel with the angled end of lower leg.

12. Sit Emily on work surface. With knee joints facing out and legs even with bottom edge of body, wood-glue top of legs to body.

10–7. *Emily.*   10–8. *Emily.*

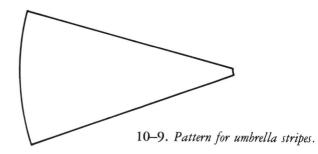

10–9. *Pattern for umbrella stripes.*

13. For feet, cut two ½" lengths from the rounded ends of an ice-cream stick. Sand corners to round them.

14. Wood-glue left foot to bottom of left lower leg so heel is flush with back of ankle and outside edge of foot is flush with work surface. Wood-glue right foot to bottom of right lower leg so heel is flush with back of ankle and toes point up and slightly towards her right.

15. For arms, cut two 1" lengths of ¼" dowelling.

16. To indicate angle of each elbow cut, measure and mark ½" from right end. Rotate dowelling so mark is away from you, then measure and mark ⅜" from left end. Cut angle.

17. At flat end of two lower (shorter) arms, attach 8mm-bead hands.

18. To complete the arms, reverse the elbow cuts and wood-glue upper and lower arms together so elbow joints are crooked.

19. For each arm, whittle inside area of upper arm flat.

20. With shoulders even with top of body, wood-glue arms to body so left hand is at mouth level and right hand is at chest level.

21. Paint body flesh.

22. Referring to 10–7 and 10–8, paint bathing suit (including bottom edge of torso) medium orange.

23. Paint a button at base of each bathing suit strap white. Use black to paint two tiny holes on each button.

24. Make a tiny bow, using pink ribbon. Secure knot with tacky glue. Trim ends at an angle. Tacky-glue to center top of head.

SAND PAIL

Follow steps 1–7 of pail and shovel directions substituting yellow for red adhesive vinyl.

BEACH UMBRELLA

1. For umbrella top, use a pencil compass to describe a 6"-diameter circle onto tagboard. Cut out.

2. Describe a ⁵⁄₁₆"-diameter circle in center of umbrella top.

3. Cut across the radius to the center and cut out center circle.

4. Following 10–9, cut three stripes each from blue, red, and yellow adhesive vinyl.

5. Starting at right side of cut radius, adhere a blue stripe to umbrella top so the left edge of stripe is flush with edge of cut.

6. Working from left to right and butting edges, adhere a red stripe and a yellow stripe to umbrella top. Continue to adhere stripes, alternating colors. (Last section has no stripe.)

7. Use pinking shears to trim outer edge.

8. Overlap right edge over left and tacky-glue to secure.

9. For pole, cut a 5¾" length of ¼" dowelling.

10. For cap, cut a ⅛" length of ⅝" dowelling.

11. Wood-glue one end of pole to center of cap.

12. Insert pole through umbrella hole. Tacky-glue top of umbrella to underside of cap to secure.

STEPHEN

1. For head, cover one hole of a 25mm bead with a tagboard circle. Paint head flesh.

2. Referring to 10–10, paint eyes black and cheeks dark pink.

3. For body, cut a ¹⁵⁄₁₆" length of ¾" dowelling.

4. Draw a line down length of body to indicate center front.

5. Measure and mark position of left and right arms ⅛" from top of body and ⅝" from center line. At each mark, whittle a ¼" × ¼" area flat.

6. Measure and mark position of left leg ⅛" from bottom of body and ⅜" from center line. Measure and

94

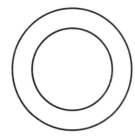

10–10. *Stephen.*

10–11. *Pattern for Stephen's and Harry's hat brims.*

mark position of right leg ⅛" from bottom of body and at center line. At each mark, whittle a ¼" × ¼" area flat.

7. Sand bottom edge of head to expose raw wood.

8. Wood-glue head to top of body, making sure head faces forward.

9. For legs, cut two 1⅜" lengths of ¼" dowelling.

10. To indicate angle of each knee cut, measure and mark ¹¹⁄₁₆" from right end. Rotate dowelling so mark is away from you, then measure and mark ⁹⁄₁₆" from left end. Cut angle.

11. To indicate angle of each hip cut, place upper (shorter) leg on work surface so the knee end is at top. Rotate leg so the face of the knee angle cut is facing up. At opposite end, measure and mark ⅛" from flat end. Cut angle.

12. To complete the legs, reverse the knee cuts and wood-glue upper and lower legs together so knee joints are crooked.

13. Wood-glue hips to body so knees point up.

14. For feet, cut two ⅝" lengths from the rounded ends of an ice-cream stick. Sand corners to round them.

15. Wood-glue feet to bottom of legs so heels extend ⅛" behind ankles and toes point up and out.

16. For left arm, cut a ⅞" length of ¼" dowelling.

17. To indicate angle of left elbow cut, measure and mark ⅜" from right end. Rotate dowelling so mark is away from you, then measure and mark ⅜" from left end. Cut angle.

18. For right arm, cut a 1⅛" length of ¼" dowelling.

19. At flat end of one left arm half and one end of right arm, attach an 8mm-bead hand.

20. To complete the left arm, reverse the elbow cut and wood-glue upper and lower arm together so elbow joint is crooked.

21. For each arm, whittle inside area of shoulder flat.

22. With shoulders even with top of body, wood-glue arms to body so left hand is at cheek level and right hand is straight up.

23. Paint body flesh.

24. For bathing trunks, paint upper ⅛" of legs, bottom edge of torso, and bottom ⅜" of torso white.

25. Referring to 10–10, paint tank top bright red.

26. Following 10–11, cut hat brim from white synthetic suede.

27. To indicate hat crown, pull hat brim down over head so front is ⁹⁄₁₆" from center top of head and back is ¾" from center top of head. Trace a line around head underneath hat brim. Remove brim.

28. Using line as a guide, paint top of head white.

29. Tacky-glue hat brim in place.

30. Paint top of hat brim white.

31. For whistle, tacky-glue both ends of the 3¾" length of black yarn into one hole of the 3mm × 6mm gold-plated bead.

LIFEGUARD CHAIR

1. For seat, cut a 1⅜"-wide × 1⅛"-deep rectangle from ¼ × 5¼ lattice.

2. To indicate position of armrest support holes at each side of seat top, measure and mark ⅜" from front edge and ⅛" from side edge.

3. Using a ³⁄₃₂" bit, drill ⅛"-deep armrest support holes.

4. For armrest supports, cut two ⁷⁄₁₆" lengths from the thickest part of a toothpick.

5. Wood-glue armrest supports into holes.

6. For chair back slats, cut three 1⅛" lengths from the rounded ends of ice-cream sticks.

7. With bottom edges even, wood-glue center chair back slat to center back edge of seat.

8. Wood-glue right and left chair back slats to back edge of seat so they are spaced ⁵⁄₁₆" from center slat at the top and ⅛" at the base.

9. To complete chair back, cut two ³⁄₁₆" lengths from the thickest part of a toothpick. Wood-glue each horizontally between slats.

10. For armrests, cut a 1⅛" length from the rounded end of an ice-cream stick. Draw line down center. Cut in half to make two armrests.

11. With rounded edges of armrests facing the outside, wood-glue supports to bottom of armrests, and flat end of armrests to chair back. Place aside.

12. For legs, cut two 8⅝" lengths of ¼" dowelling.

13. To indicate angle of leg cuts, measure and mark 4¼″ from right end. Rotate dowelling so mark is away from you, then measure and mark 4¼″ from left end. Cut angle.

14. To indicate position of lower and upper cross-pieces, place leg on work surface so angled end is at top. Rotate leg so the face of the angle cut is facing down. Draw a line down length of leg to indicate center. For lower crosspieces, measure and mark ¾″ from flat end (bottom) and ¹⁄₁₆″ from each side of center line. For upper crosspieces, measure and mark 3″ from bottom end and ⅛″ from each side of center line. Whittle a ³⁄₁₆″-wide × ³⁄₁₆″-high × ¹⁄₁₆″-deep notch at each mark. Repeat for three remaining legs.

15. With notches facing in, wood-glue angled end of legs to underside of seat ⅛″ from corners.

16. For front and back upper crosspieces, cut two 1⅜″ lengths of ³⁄₁₆″ dowelling. For side upper crosspieces, cut two 1¼″ lengths of ³⁄₁₆″ dowelling.

17. Wood-glue upper crosspieces to legs, whittling ends if necessary for a proper fit.

18. For front, back, and side lower crosspieces, cut four 2⅛″ lengths of ³⁄₁₆″ dowelling.

19. Wood-glue lower crosspieces to legs, whittling ends if necessary for a proper fit.

20. Paint entire chair white.

LIFE PRESERVER

1. For life preserver, use a knife to cut away spokes from the spoked wheel. Paint white.

2. Divide the preserver into quarters around the outer edge.

3. Referring to 10–12 and with right side of preserver facing you, tacky-glue one end of the 6″ length of white yarn at a mark so loose end of yarn is at your right. This is now 12 o'clock.

4. Cut four ³⁄₁₆″ × 1¾″ strips of red adhesive vinyl. Starting at 3 o'clock, loosely wrap yarn around outer edge of preserver and secure with a red strip. Repeat at 6 and 9 o'clock. At 12 o'clock, trim excess yarn, tacky-glue end, and wrap with a red strip.

HARRY

1. For head, cover one hole of a 25mm bead with a tagboard circle. Paint head flesh.

2. Referring to 10–13, paint eyes black and cheeks dark pink.

10–12. *Life preserver.*

10–13. *Harry.*

3. For body, cut a 1″ length of ¾″ dowelling.

4. Draw a line down length of body to indicate center front.

5. Measure and mark position of left and right arms ⅛″ from top of body and ⅝″ from center line. At each mark, whittle a ¼″ × ¼″ area flat.

6. Sand bottom edge of head to expose raw wood.

7. Wood-glue head to top of body, making sure head faces slightly towards the left.

8. For legs, cut a 2⅝″ length of ¼″ dowelling.

9. To indicate angle of ankle cut, measure and mark 1¼″ from right end. Rotate dowelling so mark is away from you, then measure and mark 1¼″ from left end. Cut angle.

10. To indicate angle of each hip cut, place leg on work surface so the ankle end is at top. Rotate leg so the face of the ankle angle cut is facing down. At opposite end, measure and mark ⅛″ from flat end. Cut angle.

11. With side of left leg ¹⁄₁₆″ from side of body and centered from front to back, wood-glue left hip to bottom of body so ankle juts back.

12. With side of right leg ¹⁄₁₆″ from side of body and centered from front to back, wood-glue right hip to bottom of body so ankle juts forward.

13. For feet, cut two ⅝″ lengths from the rounded ends of an ice-cream stick. Sand corners to round them.

14. Wood-glue feet to bottom of legs so heels extend ⅛″ behind ankles, toes point forward, and Harry stands upright.

15. For arms, cut two ⅞″ lengths of ¼″ dowelling.

16. To indicate angle of each elbow cut, measure and mark ⅜″ from right end. Rotate dowelling so mark is away from you, then measure and mark ⁷⁄₁₆″ from left end. Cut angle.

17. At flat end of lower (shorter) arms, attach 8mm-bead hands.

18. To complete the arms, reverse the elbow cuts and wood-glue upper and lower arms together so elbow joints are crooked.
19. For each arm, whittle inside area of shoulder flat.
20. With shoulders even with top of body, wood-glue tops of arms to body so hands are raised up.
21. Paint body flesh.

22. For bathing trunks, paint upper ⅛″ of legs, bottom edge of torso, and bottom ¼″ of torso dark ultramarine.
23. Using a dry brush, paint chest hair light red-brown.
24. Repeat steps 26 to 30 of Stephen.

11 · Cathy and Kittie

MATERIALS

Beads

one white 20mm large-hole wood bead
one white 16mm large-hole wood bead
one white 10mm regular-hole wood bead
two white 8mm regular-hole wood beads
one white 7mm regular-hole wood bead

Wood

4″ length of ³⁄₁₆″ dowelling
5″ length of ¼″ dowelling
¾″ length of ⁷⁄₁₆″ dowelling
1⅛″ length of ⅝″ dowelling
2″ square of ⅛″-thick balsa wood
one ice-cream stick
two round toothpicks

Paints (Acrylic)

Flesh, black, medium pink, dark brown, light blue, white, bright red, medium orange, medium purple, dark ultramarine, light yellow-green, and medium yellow

Fabric and Trims

small amount of raspberry pink synthetic suede
medium brown curly crepe hair
6″ length of ¹⁄₁₆″-wide pink satin ribbon
6″ length of ¹⁄₁₆″-wide lavender satin ribbon
2″ length of white 4-ply yarn
small amount of white fake fur

Miscellaneous

small amount of white tagboard
small wisp of brown or black human hair
paste wood filler

11–1.

CATHY

1. For head, cover one hole of the 20mm bead with a tagboard circle. Paint head flesh.
2. Referring to 11–2, paint eyes black, cheeks medium pink, and hair dark brown.
3. For body, use the 1⅛″ length of ⅝″ dowelling.
4. Draw a line down length of body to indicate center front.
5. Measure and mark position of left and right arms ⅛″ from top of body and ⁷⁄₁₆″ from center line. At each mark, whittle a ¼″ × ¼″ area flat.
6. Measure and mark position of left leg ⅛″ from bottom of body and ³⁄₁₆″ from center line. Measure and mark position of right leg ⅛″ from bottom of body and ⅜″ from center line. At each mark, whittle a ¼″ × ¼″ area flat.
7. Sand bottom edge of head to expose raw wood.
8. Wood-glue head to top of body so head faces forward.
9. For arms, cut two ¹¹⁄₁₆″ lengths of ¼″ dowelling.

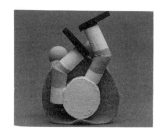

11–2, 11–3. *Cathy.*

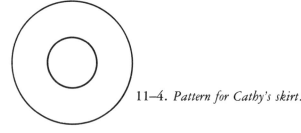

11–4. *Pattern for Cathy's skirt.*

10. To indicate angle of each elbow cut, measure and mark ⁵⁄₁₆″ from right. Rotate dowelling so mark is away from you, then measure and mark ¼″ from left end. Cut angle.

11. At flat end of lower (shorter) arms, attach 8mm-bead hands.

12. To complete the arms, reverse the elbow cuts and wood-glue upper and lower arms together so elbow joints are crooked.

13. For each arm, whittle inside area of upper arm flat.

14. With shoulders even with top of body, wood-glue arms to body so left hand is at waist and right hand is at mouth level.

15. For legs, cut two 1″ lengths of ¼″ dowelling.

16. To indicate angle of each knee cut, measure and mark ½″ from right end. Rotate dowelling so mark is away from you, then measure and mark ⁷⁄₁₆″ from left end. Cut angle.

17. To complete the legs, reverse the knee cuts and wood-glue upper (longer) and lower (shorter) legs together so knee joints are crooked.

18. Whittle a ¼″ × ¼″ area on upper back of right leg flat.

19. Referring to 11–3, sit Cathy on work surface. With knee joint facing out and leg even with bottom edge of body, wood-glue upper back of right leg to body. With knee joint facing out and leg even with bottom edge of body, wood-glue hip of left leg to body.

20. For shoes, cut two ½″ lengths from the rounded ends of the ice-cream stick. Sand corners to round them.

21. Wood-glue right shoe to bottom of right lower leg so heel is flush with back of ankle and outside edge of shoe is flush with work surface. Wood-glue left shoe to bottom of left lower leg so heel is flush with back of ankle and outside corner of heel is flush with work surface.

22. Paint hands flesh.

23. For blouse, paint arms, top edge of torso, and top ¾″ of torso light blue.

24. For bloomers, paint bottom edge of torso, bottom ⅜″ of torso, top ¼″ of right leg, and top ³⁄₁₆″ of left leg white.

25. For socks, paint bottom ⅜″ of each leg and upper shoe white.

26. Paint leg area between top of socks and bottom of bloomer legs flesh.

27. For Mary Jane shoes, paint soles, sides, a ¹⁄₁₆″ band around shoe uppers, and shoe straps black.

28. Following 11–4, cut skirt from raspberry pink synthetic suede. Slip over legs, position at waist, and tacky-glue to secure.

29. Cut a tiny lock of crepe hair and tacky-glue to top of head.

30. Make a tiny bow using ¹⁄₁₆″-wide pink satin ribbon. Secure knot with tacky glue. Trim ends at an angle. Tacky-glue bow to top of head, in front of hair lock.

KITTIE

1. For body, use the ¾″ length of ⁷⁄₁₆″ dowelling.

2. Whittle a ¼″-wide area along one side of body (bottom) flat.

3. To indicate position of tail hole, turn body so flat side faces down. At center back, measure and mark ⅛″ from end.

4. Using a ³⁄₃₂″ bit, drill a ⅛″-deep tail hole.

5. For head, sand bottom edge of the 16mm bead to expose raw wood.

6. Referring to 11–5, test-fit head to body, fitting the top front edge of body into the bead hole (whittle notches on each side of bead hole for a close fit) and angling the head downwards. Wood-glue head to body.

7. Cover bead hole at top of head with a tagboard circle.

8. For muzzle, cut the 7mm bead in half. Discard one half.

11–5. *Kittie.*

11–6. *Pattern for Kittie's ears.*

11–7. *Kittie.*

9. With half-holes of bead horizontal, position muzzle on front of Kittie's head so it is centered horizontally and vertically. Trace outline of muzzle. Sand muzzle area of head flat.

10. Wood-glue muzzle to head.

11. Following 11–6, cut ears from ⅛"-thick balsa wood.

12. Referring to 11–7, tacky-glue ears to each side of head.

13. For legs, cut four ⁹⁄₁₆" lengths of ³⁄₁₆" dowelling.

14. Whittle top ⅛" of each leg to taper.

15. With front and back pairs of legs flush with ends of body, wood-glue top of legs to bottom of body so each pair of legs touches at the top and ankles are spread slightly apart.

16. For paws, cut four ¹⁄₁₆" lengths of ¼" dowelling.

17. With one edge of paw flush with back edge of ankle, wood-glue each paw to bottom of leg.

18. Paint entire body white.

19. Referring to 11–7, paint irises light blue, cheeks and inner ears medium pink. Paint pupils, nose, and mouth black.

20. For claws, use black to paint three vertical lines on front of each paw.

21. For whiskers, cut human hair wisp into 1" strands. For each side of muzzle, gather four strands of hair and tacky-glue into half-hole of muzzle. Trim whiskers to ½".

22. For tail, tacky-glue the 2" length of white yarn into tail hole. Trim tail to 1¼".

23. Cut a ¼"-wide half-circle from white fake fur to fit chest area. Tacky-glue to chest.

24. Tie lavender ribbon around neck and make a bow. Tacky-glue knot to secure. Trim ends at an angle.

BALL

1. Fill holes of a 10mm bead with paste wood filler. Allow to dry and sand smooth.

2. Using a pencil, divide ball in half. Divide one of the halves into thirds and the other half into quarters.

3. Paint each section in the following order: bright red, medium orange, medium purple, light blue, dark ultramarine, light yellow-green, and medium yellow.

12 · Big Top Circus

MATERIALS

Beads

three white 44mm × 28mm large-hole wood beads
two white 32mm × 22mm large-hole wood beads
six white 25mm large-hole wood beads
two white 20mm large-hole wood beads
twelve white 10mm regular-hole wood beads
six white 8mm regular-hole wood beads

Wood

3¾" length of ⅛" dowelling
22" length of ¼" dowelling
26" length of ⅜" dowelling

12–1.

11⁄16″ length of 5⁄8″ dowelling
12″ length of 3⁄4″ dowelling
1⁄4″ length of 1″ dowelling
96″ length of 1⁄4 × 51⁄4 clear pine lattice
36″ length of 1⁄2 × 51⁄2 clear pine lattice
eight ice-cream sticks
eight flat wooden ice-cream spoons
fifteen round toothpicks

Paints (Acrylic)

Flesh, black, dark pink, white, bright red, medium purple, light blue, medium orange, light red-brown, medium pink, pale blue-grey, medium yellow, very dark green, and dark green

Fabric and Trims

black, white, and medium brown curly crepe hair
pink, orange, and white curly chenille hair
1″-diameter circle of black synthetic suede
small amount of grey and navy synthetic suede
80″ length of 1⁄4″-wide gold military braid
4″ length of 2mm-diameter white rayon satin rattail
small amount of white fake fur
12″ length of 1⁄8″-wide pink grosgrain ribbon
two 5mm orchid cup sequins
11⁄2″ × 13″ rectangle of pink tulle
11″ length of 1⁄2″-wide yellow satin ribbon
33″ length of 3⁄8″-wide blue satin ribbon
35″ length of 3⁄8″-wide white satin ribbon
five 5mm light blue acrylic pompons
two 5mm white acrylic pompons
one 3⁄4″ white acrylic pompon
54″ length of gold elastic cord

Hardware

one 3⁄4 × 18 wire brad
six 6 × 3⁄4 flathead wood screws

Miscellaneous

white tagboard
small amount of chrome, yellow, blue, and red decorative adhesive vinyl
three 33⁄4″ circles of both brass and white decorative adhesive vinyl
paste wood filler
cardboard tube from paper towel
sewing needle

pink, yellow, blue, and white sewing thread
four red-bead-head straight pins

JEAN-CLAUDE PICADILLY

1. For head, cover one hole of a 25mm bead with a tagboard circle. Paint head flesh.

2. Referring to 12–2, paint eyes black and cheeks dark pink.

3. For body, cut a 11⁄16″ length of 3⁄4″ dowelling.

4. Draw a line down length of body to indicate center front.

5. Measure and mark position of left and right arms 1⁄8″ from top of body and 5⁄8″ from center line. At each mark, whittle a 5⁄16″ × 5⁄16″ area flat.

6. Sand bottom edge of head to expose raw wood.

7. Wood-glue head to top of body so head faces forward.

8. For legs, cut two 2″ lengths of 3⁄8″ dowelling.

9. Wood-glue legs to bottom of body so sides of legs are flush with sides of body and centered from front to back.

10. For shoes, cut two 11⁄16″ lengths from the rounded ends of an ice-cream stick. Sand corners to round them.

11. Wood-glue shoes to bottom of legs so heels extend 1⁄16″ behind ankles, toes point out, inner corners of heels butt, and Jean-Claude stands upright.

12. For arms, cut a 21⁄8″ length of 3⁄8″ dowelling.

13. To indicate angle of shoulder cut, measure and mark 1″ from right end. Rotate dowelling so mark is away from you, then measure and mark 1″ from left end. Cut angle.

14. At flat end of arms, attach 10mm-bead hands.

15. With shoulders even with top of body, wood-glue arms to body so hands are raised and slightly forward.

16. For tails, cut two 11⁄16″ lengths from the rounded ends of an ice cream stick.

17. Referring to 12–3, wood-glue cut ends of tails to center back bottom edge of torso so top outer corners butt back of legs and tails point slightly up.

18. For gloves and shirt cuffs, paint hands and bottom 1⁄8″ of arms white.

19. For shirt, measure and mark a 7⁄16″ × 9⁄16″ triangle at center front of body. Paint triangle and top edge of torso white.

20. Paint shoes, legs, rest of arms and torso black.

12–2, 12–3. Jean-Claude Picadilly.

21. Referring to 12–2, paint bow tie black. Using black, paint five buttons evenly spaced down center front of shirt and one on upper side of each cuff.

22. Using bright red, paint a $\frac{1}{16}''$ wide $\times$ $\frac{3}{16}''$-high cummerbund at base of shirt.

23. For hair, cut sufficient $\frac{1}{8}''$ lengths of black crepe hair to cover head. Tacky-glue hair to head.

24. For top hat crown, use the $\frac{11}{16}''$ length of $\frac{5}{8}''$ dowelling.

25. To indicate position of hand hole, locate center of one cut end (bottom).

26. Using a $\frac{3}{32}''$ bit, drill a $\frac{1}{4}''$-deep hand hole.

27. Paint crown black.

28. For hat brim, use the 1″-diameter circle of black synthetic suede. Tacky-glue hat brim to center bottom of crown.

29. Use an ice pick to pierce a hole through brim into hand hole.

30. Cut a $\frac{3}{8}''$ length from the thickest part of a tooth-pick.

31. Tacky-glue one end of toothpick into hand hole and opposite end into bead hole of left hand.

RINGS (MAKE 3)

1. Using a pencil compass, inscribe a $4\frac{3}{4}''$ circle onto $\frac{1}{4} \times 5\frac{1}{4}$ lattice. Cut out circle.

2. Cover one side with brass adhesive vinyl and the other side with white adhesive vinyl.

3. Cut a 16″ length of $\frac{1}{4}''$-wide gold braid. Tacky-glue gold braid around outer edge, overlapping short edges.

FEARLESS FELIX

1. For head, cover one hole of a 25mm bead with a tagboard circle. Paint head flesh.

2. Referring to 12–4, paint eyes black and cheeks dark pink.

3. For body, cut a $1\frac{1}{16}''$ length of $\frac{3}{4}''$ dowelling.

4. Draw a line down length of body to indicate center front.

5. Measure and mark position of left and right arms $\frac{1}{8}''$ from top of body and $\frac{1}{2}''$ from center line. At each mark, whittle a $\frac{1}{4}'' \times \frac{1}{4}''$ area flat.

6. Sand bottom edge of head to expose raw wood.

7. Wood-glue head to top of body so head faces forward.

8. For legs, cut two $1\frac{1}{2}''$ lengths of $\frac{1}{4}''$ dowelling.

9. Wood-glue legs to bottom of body so sides of legs are $\frac{1}{16}''$ from sides of body and centered from front to back.

10. For ballet slippers, cut two $\frac{11}{16}''$ lengths from the rounded ends of an ice-cream stick. Sand corners to round them.

11. Wood-glue ballet slippers to bottom of legs so heels extend $\frac{1}{8}''$ behind ankles, toes point out slightly, and Felix stands upright.

12. For arms, cut two 1″ lengths of $\frac{1}{4}''$ dowelling.

13. To indicate angle of each elbow cut, measure and mark $\frac{7}{16}''$ from right end. Rotate dowelling so mark is away from you, then measure and mark $\frac{7}{16}''$ from left end. Cut angle.

14. At flat end of two arm halves, attach 10mm-bead hands.

15. To complete the arms, reverse the elbow cuts and wood-glue upper and lower arms together so elbow joints are crooked.

16. With shoulders even with top of body, wood-glue arms to body so hands are raised and slightly forward.

17. Paint hands, arms, top edge of torso, and top $\frac{3}{4}''$ of torso flesh.

18. Paint top of ballet slippers, legs, bottom edge of torso, and bottom $\frac{5}{16}''$ of torso (tights) medium purple.

19. Referring to 12–4, paint tank top light blue.

12–4. Fearless Felix.

20. For ballet slippers, paint soles, sides, and a ⅛″ band around slipper uppers light blue.

21. For hair, cut sufficient ⅛″ lengths of white crepe hair to cover head. Tacky-glue hair to head.

22. For belt, cut a ⁵⁄₃₂″ × 2¾″ strip from chrome adhesive vinyl. Adhere around waist, overlapping short edges at center back.

23. For armbands, cut two ³⁄₃₂″ × 1″ strips from chrome adhesive vinyl. Adhere around center of upper arms, overlapping short edges at underside of arms.

24. For whip handle, cut a ¹³⁄₁₆″ length from the thickest part of a toothpick. Using an art knife, cut a ⅛″-deep slit at one end to accommodate whip tails.

25. Paint whip handle light blue.

26. For whip tails, cut a ³⁄₃₂″ × 2¼″ strip from the center of ¼″-wide gold braid. Tacky-glue one end of braid into slit in handle. Ravel braid to make single-ply gold threads.

27. Tacky-glue bottom of whip handle into bead hole of left hand.

RANEE

1. For body, cover both holes of a 32mm × 22mm bead with tagboard circles (front and rear of body).

2. To indicate position of head, tail hole, and bottom peg hole, draw a line around the equator, parallel with the bead holes, and a line around the meridian.

3. For head position, measure and mark ¼″ from each side of the meridian and ⅜″ from one end. Whittle area flat.

4. For tail-hole position, measure and mark on the meridian ⅛″ from other end.

5. Using a ³⁄₃₂″ bit, drill a ⅛″-deep tail hole.

6. For peg hole (used for supporting Ranee on the hoop), use a ³⁄₃₂″ bit to drill a ¼″-deep hole where lines cross at center bottom of body.

7. For head, cover one hole of a 20mm bead with a tagboard circle.

8. Sand bottom edge of head to expose raw wood.

9. Wood-glue head to body.

10. For muzzle, cut a 10mm bead in half. (Reserve one half for Raja.)

11. With half-holes of bead horizontal, position muzzle on front of Ranee's head so it is centered horizontally and vertically. Trace outline of muzzle. Sand muzzle area flat.

12. Wood-glue muzzle to head.

12–5. *Ranee.*

12–6. *Ranee.*

13. Fill half-bead holes with paste wood filler. Allow to dry and sand smooth.

14. For ears, cut two ⅛″ lengths of ¼″ dowelling. Whittle off a ¹⁄₁₆″ slice from one side of each ear to flatten. Sand sides of head to expose raw wood.

15. Referring to 12–5, wood-glue ears to each side of head.

16. For front legs, cut a 1⅜″ length of ¼″ dowelling.

17. To indicate angle of ankle cut, measure and mark ⅝″ from right end. Rotate dowelling so mark is away from you, then measure and mark ⅝″ from left end. Cut angle.

18. With side and bottom edges of front legs flush with side and bottom edges of body, tacky-glue front legs to front of body so the face of ankle angle cuts faces down.

19. For back legs, cut a 1⅞″ length of ¼″ dowelling.

20. To indicate angle of hip cut, measure and mark ⅞″ from right end. Rotate dowelling so mark is away from you, then measure and mark ⅞″ from left end. Cut angle.

21. To indicate angle of each ankle cut, place leg on work surface so the hip end is at top. Rotate leg so the face of the hip angle cut is facing down. At opposite end, measure and mark ⅛″ from flat end. Cut angle.

22. With sides of back legs flush with sides of body and centered from top to bottom, tacky-glue back legs to rear of body so the face of the ankle angle cuts faces up.

23. For paws, cut four ³⁄₃₂″ lengths of ⅜″ dowelling.

24. With one edge of paw flush with back of ankle, wood-glue each paw to bottom of legs.

25. For tail, cut a 2″ length of white rattail. Tacky-glue end of tail into tail hole.

26. Paint entire body medium orange.

27. Referring to 12–5, paint eyes black, cheeks dark pink, and muzzle white. Paint nose, mouth, and inner ears black.

28. Referring to 12–6, paint chest and top of paws white. Using a dry brush, paint underside of body white. Paint sides and bottom of paws, and stripes black.

29. For claws, use black to paint three vertical lines on top front of each paw.

30. For chest fur, cut a ¼″-diameter circle from white fake fur. Tacky-glue to chest.

31. For tail fur, cut a ¼″ × ⅜″ rectangle from white fake fur. Tacky-glue around tip of tail.

HOOP

1. For base, use the ¼″ length of 1″ dowelling.

2. For post, cut a 1⁷⁄₁₆″ length of ⅜″ dowelling.

3. To accommodate peg used for supporting Ranee on the hoop, use a ³⁄₃₂″ bit to drill a ¼″-deep peg hole in center top of post.

4. Wood-glue and nail opposite end of post to center top of base.

5. Paint top of base light blue.

6. Paint post and star pattern on top of base medium purple.

7. For peg, cut a ⅝″ length from the thickest part of a toothpick.

8. Wood-glue peg into peg hole.

9. Cut a 3½″ length of ¼″-wide gold braid. Tacky-glue braid around base, overlapping short edges.

10. For hoop, cut a ⅜″ length of paper-towel tubing.

11. Cut a 24″ length of ¼″-wide gold braid. Wrap around hoop, overlapping edges. Tacky-glue end to secure (bottom).

12. Use an ice pick to pierce a hole through center bottom of hoop.

13. Insert peg through hole and tacky-glue hoop to top of post.

14. Place Ranee on hoop.

RAJA

1. For body, cover both holes of a 32mm × 22mm bead with tagboard circles (front and rear of body).

2. To indicate position of head, tail hole, and legs, draw a line around the equator, parallel with the bead holes, and a line around the meridian.

3. For head position, measure and mark ¼″ from each side of the meridian and ⅜″ from one end. Whittle area flat.

4. For tail-hole position, measure and mark on the meridian ⅛″ from other end.

12–7. *Raja.*   12–8. *Raja.*

5. Using a ³⁄₃₂″ bit, drill a ⅛″-deep tail hole.

6. To indicate position of left and right front legs, measure and mark ³⁄₁₆″ from front of body and ³⁄₁₆″ from the meridian. To indicate position of left and right back legs, measure and mark ⅜″ from rear of body and ³⁄₁₆″ from the meridian. At each mark, whittle a ³⁄₁₆″ × ³⁄₁₆″ area flat.

7. For head, cover one hole of a 20mm bead with a tagboard circle.

8. Sand bottom edge of head to expose raw wood.

9. Wood-glue head to body.

10. For muzzle, use the reserved bead-half from Ranee.

11. With half-holes of bead horizontal, position muzzle on front of Raja's head so it is centered horizontally and vertically. Trace outline of muzzle. Sand muzzle area flat.

12. Wood-glue muzzle to head.

13. Fill half-bead holes with paste wood filler. Allow to dry and sand smooth.

14. For ears, cut two ⅛″ lengths of ¼″ dowelling. Whittle off a ¹⁄₁₆″ slice from one side of each ear to flatten. Sand sides of head to expose raw wood.

15. Referring to 12–7, wood-glue ears to each side of head.

16. For front legs, cut a ⅞″ length of ¼″ dowelling.

17. To indicate angle of hip cut, measure and mark ⅜″ from right end. Rotate dowelling so mark is away from you, then measure and mark ⅜″ from left end. Cut angle.

18. Wood-glue front legs to body so points of hip angles are on outside of body, and legs are straight.

19. For back legs, cut a ¹³⁄₁₆″ length of ¼″ dowelling.

20. To indicate angle of hip cut, measure and mark ⅜″ from right end. Rotate dowelling so mark is away

from you, then measure and mark ⅜" from left end. Cut angle.

21. Wood-glue back legs to body so points of hip angles are on outside of body, legs are straight, and Raja stands upright.

22. For paws, cut four ³⁄₃₂" lengths of ⅜" dowelling.

23. With one edge of paw flush with back of ankle, wood-glue each paw to bottom of legs.

24. Repeat steps 25 to 31 of Ranee. Refer to 12–7 and 12–8.

ATHENA

1. For head, cover one hole of a 25mm bead with a tagboard circle. Paint head flesh.

2. Referring to 12–9, paint eyes black, hair light red-brown, and cheeks dark pink.

3. For body, cut a ⅞" length of ¾" dowelling.

4. Draw a line down length of body to indicate center front.

5. Measure and mark position of left and right arms ⅛" from top of body and ½" from center line. At each mark, whittle a ¼" × ¼" area flat.

6. Sand bottom edge of head to expose raw wood.

7. Wood-glue head to top of body so head faces forward.

8. For right leg, cut a 1⁷⁄₁₆" length of ¼" dowelling.

9. To indicate angle of right hip cut, measure and mark ⅛" from one end. Cut angle.

10. For left leg, cut a 1⅜" length of ¼" dowelling.

11. Wood-glue left leg to center bottom of body.

12. With side of right leg flush with side of body and centered from front to back, wood-glue right hip to bottom of body so ankle juts out and back.

13. For ballet slippers, cut two ¹¹⁄₁₆" lengths from the rounded ends of an ice-cream stick. Sand corners to round them.

14. Wood-glue ballet slippers to bottom of legs so heels are flush with back of ankles, toes point in slightly, and Athena stands upright.

12–9. *Athena.*

15. To indicate position of peg hole used for standing Athena on Colossus, locate center and mark bottom of left heel.

16. Using a ³⁄₃₂" bit, drill a ¼"-deep peg hole.

17. For arms, cut two ¹⁵⁄₁₆" lengths of ¼" dowelling.

18. To indicate angle of left shoulder/elbow cut, measure and mark ⁷⁄₁₆" from right end. Rotate dowelling so mark is away from you, then measure and mark ⅜" from left end. Cut angle.

19. To indicate angle of right elbow cut, measure and mark ⁷⁄₁₆" from right end. Rotate dowelling so mark is away from you, then measure and mark ⅜" from left end. Cut angle.

20. At flat end of lower (shorter) arms, attach 10mm bead hands.

21. To complete the right arm, reverse the elbow cuts and wood-glue upper and lower arm together so elbow joint is crooked. To complete the left arm, wood-glue angled end of lower arm to flat end of upper arm making sure the elbow is crooked and the shoulder angle of the upper arm is parallel with the angled end of the lower arm.

22. With shoulders even with top of body, wood-glue arms to body so hands are raised up.

23. Paint hands flesh.

24. Paint legs white (tights).

25. Paint arms, top and bottom edge of torso, and torso medium pink (leotard).

26. Paint ballet slippers medium pink.

27. For each ballet slipper tie, cut two 1¼" lengths of pink grosgrain ribbon.

28. For each leg, tacky-glue one ribbon end to center back of ankle. Wrap ribbon around front of leg, then to back of leg, so end of ribbon is ⅞" from bottom back of ankle. Tacky-glue and wrap second ribbon in the opposite direction.

29. To accent ballet slippers, tacky-glue a 5mm orchid cup sequin to center top of each slipper.

30. For tutu, use the 1½" × 13" rectangle of pink tulle. Fold in half lengthwise. With pink thread doubled in needle, run small gathering stitches along the fold. Draw threads at each end to gather.

31. Place tutu around waist and tie thread ends securely at center back. Dot knot with tacky glue and trim thread ends close to knot.

32. For ponytail, cut a 1½" length of medium brown crepe hair. Tacky-glue ponytail to center top of head.

33. Make a tiny bow using pink grosgrain ribbon.

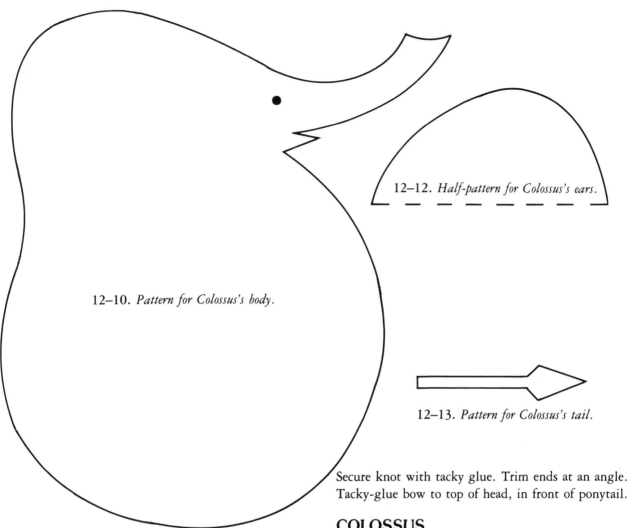

12–12. Half-pattern for Colossus's ears.

12–10. Pattern for Colossus's body.

12–13. Pattern for Colossus's tail.

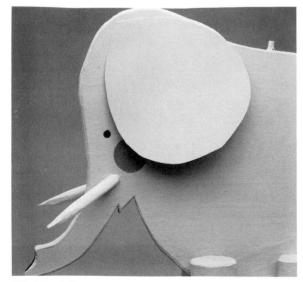

12–11. Colossus.

Secure knot with tacky glue. Trim ends at an angle. Tacky-glue bow to top of head, in front of ponytail.

COLOSSUS

1. Following 12–10, cut Colossus from ¼ × 5¼ lattice. Transfer tusk position, indicated by the dot, to each side of trunk.

2. For peg hole used for standing Athena on Colossus, measure and mark ⅞″ from base of neck along top edge of back.

3. Using a ³⁄₃₂″ bit, drill a ⅛″-deep peg hole.

4. For peg, cut a ¼″ length from the thickest part of a toothpick.

5. Wood-glue peg into peg hole.

6. To indicate position of tail hole, measure and mark 2⅜″ from peg hole.

7. Using a ³⁄₃₂″ bit, drill a ⅛″-deep tail hole.

8. For legs, cut four 1⁷⁄₁₆″ lengths of ¾″ dowelling.

9. For each leg, sand one cut edge to round it (top).

10. On upper inside of each leg, whittle a ½″ × ½″ area flat.

11. Wood-glue flattened side of front legs to each side of body 2⅝″ from tip of trunk. Wood-glue flattened side of back legs to each side of body 1¹⁄₁₆″ from front legs.

12. For feet, cut four ¹⁵⁄₁₆″ lengths from the handle end of four flat wooden ice-cream spoons. Sand cut edges (heels) to round them.

13. Wood-glue feet to bottom of legs so heels are flush with back of ankles, toes point slightly out, and Colossus stands upright.

14. For tusks, cut a 3¼″ length of ¼″ dowelling.

15. To indicate angle of tusk cut, measure and mark 1½″ from right end. Rotate dowelling so mark is away from you, then measure and mark 1½″ from left end. Cut angle.

16. At flat end of each tusk, whittle lower ¾″ to a point.

17. Wood-glue angled end of each tusk to dots on body so tusks point out and slightly down.

18. Paint body, legs, and feet pale blue-grey.

19. Paint tusks and three toenails on each foot white.

20. Referring to 12–11, paint eyes black and cheeks dark pink.

21. At tip of trunk, use black to paint a ⅛″ × ⁷⁄₁₆″ trunk opening.

22. Following 12–12, cut two ears from tagboard.

23. Paint ears pale blue-grey.

24. Referring to 12–11, tacky-glue ears to each side of head.

25. Following 12–13, cut tail from grey synthetic suede.

26. Tacky-glue end of tail into tail hole.

PEEWEE

1. For head, cover one hole of a 25mm bead with a tagboard circle.

2. For nose, cut an 8mm bead in half. (Reserve one half for hat pompon.)

3. With half-holes of bead horizontal, position nose on front of Peewee's head so it is centered horizontally and vertically. Trace outline of nose. Sand nose area flat.

4. Wood-glue nose to head.

5. Fill half-bead holes with paste wood filler. Allow to dry and sand smooth.

6. For ears, cut two ¼″ lengths from the rounded ends of an ice-cream stick. Sand cut edges to contour

them so they will lie close to the head. Sand sides of head to expose raw wood.

7. Wood-glue ears to each side of head, making sure they are centered from top to bottom.

8. Paint head flesh.

9. Referring to 12–14, paint eyes black and nose bright red. Paint mouth and cheeks dark pink.

10. For body, cover both holes of a 44mm × 28mm bead with tagboard circles.

11. Draw a line down length of body to indicate center front.

12. Measure and mark position of left and right arms ⅜″ from top of body and ⅞″ from center line. At each mark, whittle a ⅜″ × ⅜″ area flat.

13. Tacky-glue head to top of body so head faces forward.

14. For shoes, cut two 1¹⁄₁₆″ lengths from the handle end of two flat wooden ice-cream spoons. Sand cut edges (heels) to round them.

15. Tacky-glue shoes to bottom of body, making sure toes point out, back inner edges of heels butt, and Peewee stands upright.

16. For shoe pompons, cut an 8mm bead in half. With half-holes of beads vertical, wood-glue one to center top of each shoe, ⅛″ from tip of toe.

17. For arms, cut two 1¹⁄₁₆″ lengths of ⅜″ dowelling.

18. To indicate angle of elbow cuts, measure and mark ⁷⁄₁₆″ from right end. Rotate dowelling so mark is away from you, then measure and mark ½″ from left end. Cut angle.

19. At flat end of two lower (shorter) arms, attach 10mm-bead hands.

20. For each arm, whittle inside area of upper arm flat.

21. With shoulders even with top of body, wood-glue arms to body so left hand is at waist level and right hand is below left.

12–14. *Peewee.*   12–15. *Giggles.*

22. Paint hands flesh.

23. Paint shoes medium yellow.

24. Paint shoe pompons, arms, and torso medium orange.

25. For collar, use the 11″ length of yellow satin ribbon.

26. Taking care not to twist ribbon, overlap short edges ¼″ to form a circle. Tacky-glue overlap to secure. With matching sewing thread used double in needle, run small gathering stitches along one edge. Draw threads to gather.

27. Place collar over head and tie thread ends securely at center back of neck. Dot knot with tacky glue and trim thread ends close to knot.

28. For hair, cut two ½″ lengths of pink chenille hair. Tacky-glue a length of hair horizontally over each ear.

29. For hat, use a pencil compass to describe a 1¾″-diameter circle on tagboard. Cut circle in half. (Reserve one half for Chucky Chuckles.) Roll half-circle into a cone with a ¹³⁄₁₆″-diameter bottom opening. Tacky-glue overlap.

30. Paint hat medium orange.

31. For pompon at top of hat, cut a toothpick in half. Discard one half. Cut ⅜″ off the tapered end. Wood-glue the tapered end of toothpick into an 8mm bead.

32. Trim toothpick end so only ½″ extends beyond hole.

33. Using medium yellow, paint top pompon and half-bead pompon reserved from nose.

34. Tacky-glue end of toothpick into hole at top of hat.

35. With half-holes of bead vertical, tacky-glue half-bead pompon to center front of hat.

36. Tacky-glue hat to top of head.

GIGGLES

1. For head, cover one hole of a 25mm bead with a tagboard circle.

2. For head platform that will allow Giggles to stand on his head, cut a ⅜″ length from an ice-cream stick. Sand corners to round them.

3. Tacky-glue platform to center top of head.

4. For nose, cut an 8mm bead in half. (Reserve one half for Flowers.)

5. With half-holes of bead horizontal, position nose on front of Giggles's head so it is centered horizontally and vertically. Trace outline of nose. Sand nose area flat.

6. Wood-glue nose to head.

7. Fill half-holes with paste wood filler. Allow to dry and sand smooth.

8. Paint head flesh.

9. Referring to 12–15, paint eyes black, nose bright red, and cheeks dark pink.

10. For body, cover both holes of a 44mm × 28mm bead with tagboard circles.

11. Draw a line down length of body to indicate center front.

12. Measure and mark position of left and right arms ¼″ from top of body and 1″ from center line. At each mark, whittle a ⅜″ × ⅜″ area flat.

13. Tacky-glue head to top of body so head faces forward.

14. For arms, cut a 3¼″ length of ⅜″ dowelling.

15. To indicate angle of each shoulder cut, measure and mark 1⁹⁄₁₆″ from right end. Rotate dowelling so mark is away from you, then measure and mark 1⁹⁄₁₆″ from left end. Cut angle.

16. To indicate angle of each wrist cut, place arm on work surface so the shoulder end is at top. Rotate arm so the face of the shoulder angle cut is facing up. At opposite end, measure and mark ⅛″ from flat end. Cut angle.

17. With shoulders ⅛″ from top of body, wood-glue arms to body so arms are raised.

18. For hands, cut two ¾″ lengths from the rounded ends of an ice-cream stick. Sand corners at cut ends (wrist ends) to round them.

19. Wood-glue hands to ends of arms so wrist ends are flush with inside edge of arms, fingers point out and back, and Giggles stands on his head.

20. For legs, cut two 1¼″ lengths of ⅜″ dowelling.

21. To indicate angle of each knee cut, measure and mark ⁹⁄₁₆″ from right end. Rotate dowelling so mark is away from you, then measure and mark ⁹⁄₁₆″ from left end. Cut angle.

22. To complete the legs, reverse the knee cuts and wood-glue upper and lower legs together so knee joints are crooked.

23. Tacky-glue legs to bottom of body so sides of legs are flush with sides of body, centered from front to back, and ankles jut back and out.

24. For shoes, cut two ¹¹⁄₁₆″ lengths from the rounded

ends of an ice-cream stick. Sand cut edges to round them.

25. Wood-glue shoes to bottom of legs making sure toes point forward.

26. Paint hands flesh.

27. Paint shoes medium purple.

28. Paint legs, arms, bottom edge of torso, and torso white.

29. For collar, cut an 11″ length of blue satin ribbon.

30. Repeat step 26 of Peewee.

31. Place collar over head and tie thread ends securely at center back of neck. Dot knot with tacky glue and trim thread ends close to knot.

32. For sleeve and leg ruffles, cut four 5½″ lengths of blue satin ribbon.

33. Repeat step 26 of Peewee.

34. For each, place ruffle over hand (or foot) and tie thread ends securely at underside of wrist (or foot). Dot knot with tacky glue and trim thread ends close to knot.

35. Referring to 12–15, tacky-glue three 5mm light blue pompons to upper center front of torso, placing the first under collar and the next two spaced ⅜″ apart.

36. For each shoe pompon, tacky-glue a 5mm light blue pompon to center top of shoe, ¹⁄₁₆″ from tip of toe.

37. For bangs, cut a ½″ length of orange chenille hair. Tacky-glue bangs horizontally to center front of head, butting top edge with edge of platform. Cut a 5″ length of hair. Starting at one side of bangs, tacky-glue hair around head forming hair into short loops. Butt tops of loops and ends to platform.

CHUCKY CHUCKLES

1. For head, cover one hole of a 25mm bead with a tagboard circle.

2. For nose, use an 8mm bead.

3. Fill bead holes with paste wood filler. Allow to dry and sand smooth.

4. With bead holes horizontal, sand one side of nose so it will lie close to head.

5. Position nose on front of Chucky Chuckles's head so it is centered horizontally and vertically. Trace outline of nose. Sand nose area of head flat.

6. Wood-glue nose to head.

7. For ears, cut two ¼″ lengths from the rounded ends of an ice-cream stick. Sand cut edges to contour

them so they will lie close to the head. Sand sides of head to expose raw wood.

8. Wood-glue ears to each side of head, making sure they are centered from top to bottom.

9. Paint head flesh.

10. Referring to 12–16, paint eyes black, nose bright red, and cheeks dark pink. Paint mouth and chin black.

11. For body, cover both holes of a 44mm × 28mm bead with tagboard circles.

12. Draw a line down length of body to indicate center front.

13. Measure and mark position of left and right arms ¼″ from top of body and ¹⁵⁄₁₆″ from center line. At each mark, whittle a ⅜″ × ⅜″ area flat.

14. Tacky-glue head to top of body so head faces forward.

15. For legs, cut two 1″ lengths of ⅜″ dowelling.

16. Tacky-glue legs to bottom of body so sides of legs are flush with sides of body and centered from front to back.

17. For shoes, cut two 1⅛″ lengths from the handle end of two flat wooden ice-cream spoons. Sand cut edges (heels) to round them.

18. Wood-glue shoes to bottom of legs, making sure toes point out, back inner edges of heels butt, and Chucky Chuckles stands upright.

19. For shoe pompons, cut a 10mm bead in half. With half-holes of beads vertical, wood-glue a pompon to center top of each shoe, ⅛″ from tip of toe.

20. For arms, cut two 1⅛″ lengths of ⅜″ dowelling.

21. To indicate angle of each elbow cut, measure and mark ⁹⁄₁₆″ from right end. Rotate dowelling so mark is away from you, then measure and mark ½″ from left end. Cut angle.

22. At flat end of two lower (shorter) arms, attach 10mm-bead hands.

23. With shoulders ⅛″ from top of body, wood-glue

12–16. *Chucky Chuckles.*

arms to body so hands are raised and slightly forward.

24. Paint hands flesh.

25. Paint shoes black.

26. Paint shoe pompons, legs, arms, bottom edge of torso, and torso bright red.

27. For collar, cut an 11″ length of white satin ribbon.

28. Repeat step 26 of Peewee.

29. Place collar over head and tie thread ends securely at center back of neck. Dot knot with tacky glue and trim thread ends close to knot.

30. For sleeve ruffles, cut two 5½″ lengths of white satin ribbon.

31. Repeat step 26 of Peewee.

32. For each, place ruffle over hand and tie thread ends securely at underside of wrist. Dot knot with tacky glue and trim thread ends close to knot.

33. For pants ruffle cut a 13″ length of white satin ribbon.

34. Repeat step 26 of Peewee.

35. Place ruffle over feet and tie thread ends securely at center back of ankles. Dot knot with tacky glue and trim thread ends close to knot.

36. Referring to 12–16, tacky-glue two 5mm white pompons to upper center front of torso, placing the first below collar and the next ½″ below it.

37. For hat, use the half-circle reserved from Peewee's hat. Roll into a cone with a $^{13}/_{16}$″-diameter bottom opening. Tacky-glue overlap.

38. Paint hat bright red.

39. Tacky-glue the ¾″ white pompon to tip of hat.

40. Tacky-glue hat to top of head, tilting it slightly towards Chucky Chuckles's right.

41. For bangs, cut three ½″ lengths of white chenille hair. Tacky-glue bangs vertically and side by side to center front of head so top ends butt bottom of hat. Cut seven ¾″ lengths of hair. Tacky-glue vertically and side by side around head, butting top ends with bottom of hat.

BIG TOP

1. For base, cut a 16¼″ length of ¼ × 5¼ lattice.

2. Following 12–17, 12–18, and 12–19, cut yellow, blue, and purple tent tops from ¼ × 5¼ lattice.

3. For yellow tent top, transfer front rigging holes indicated by dots on pattern. Transfer side rigging holes, indicated by arrow on pattern, to cut edge of tent.

4. Using a $^1/_{16}$″ bit, drill ⅛″-deep rigging holes.

5. Cut tent bottoms from ½ × 5½ lattice. Cut yellow tent bottom 7″ wide × 4½″ high, blue 5½″ wide × 5⅝″ high, and purple 4¼″ wide × 6¼″ high.

6. For each tent bottom, whittle off both top back corners, angling the cut from the back to the top front corners.

7. Wood-glue tent tops to front of tent bottoms. Overlap yellow tent top ½″ over tent bottom. Overlap blue and purple tops ¾″ over their tent bottoms.

8. Leaving bottom edge of tent bottom unpainted, paint yellow tent top medium yellow and bottom white. Paint blue tent top light blue and bottom white. Paint purple tent top medium purple and bottom pale blue-grey.

9. For opening in yellow tent, cut a triangle with 2$^1/_{16}$″ × 3¾″ right-angle sides from navy synthetic suede. Tacky-glue to tent, butting short side with bottom edge and positioning vertical side 2″ from right edge.

10. Following 12–20, cut tent flap from grey synthetic suede.

11. Run a bead of tacky glue on wrong side of long edge of tent flap. Butt long edge of tent flap to diagonal edge of opening.

12. Apply a dot of tacky glue to wrong side of tent corner. Adhere corner to front of tent, allowing center of flap to drape in a loose fold.

13. On base, draw a line parallel with and 2⅜″ from one long edge (front). To indicate yellow tent pilot holes, measure and mark on the line 3¾″, 7¼″, and 10¼″ from right edge of base.

14. To indicate blue tent pilot holes, draw a line parallel with and 3⅞″ from front of base. Measure and mark on the line 3″, 5¼″, and 7½″ from left edge of base.

15. To indicate purple tent pilot holes, draw a line parallel with and 4⅜″ from front edge of base. Measure and mark on the line 3½″, 5⅛″, and 6¾″ from right edge of base.

16. Using a $^1/_{16}$″ bit, drill pilot holes through base.

17. To indicate pilot holes for each tent, draw a line along center of bottom edge. Measure and mark on line ½″ from each end and at middle.

18. Using a $^1/_{16}$″ bit, drill ½″-deep pilot holes.

19. To indicate front rigging postholes, draw a line

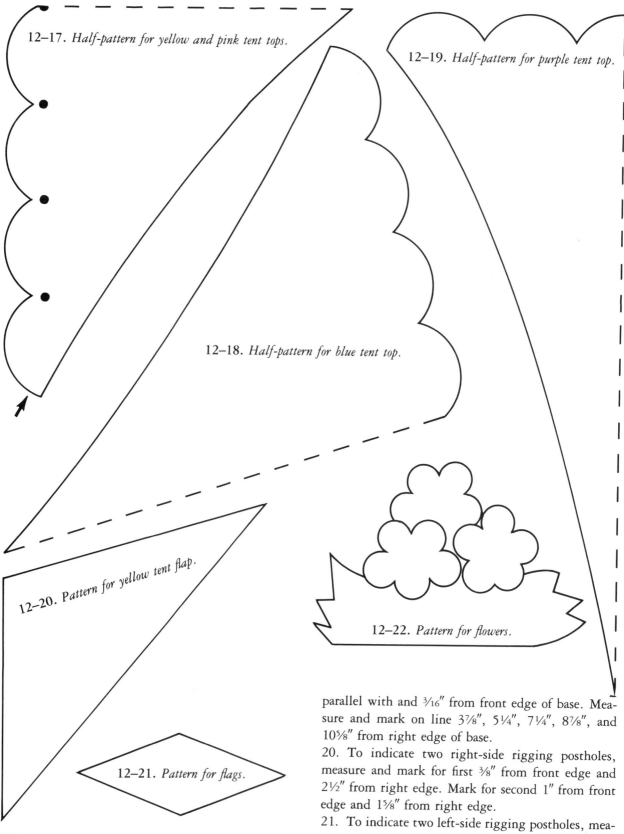

12–17. *Half-pattern for yellow and pink tent tops.*

12–19. *Half-pattern for purple tent top.*

12–18. *Half-pattern for blue tent top.*

12–20. *Pattern for yellow tent flap.*

12–22. *Pattern for flowers.*

12–21. *Pattern for flags.*

parallel with and ³⁄₁₆″ from front edge of base. Measure and mark on line 3⅞″, 5¼″, 7¼″, 8⅞″, and 10⅝″ from right edge of base.

20. To indicate two right-side rigging postholes, measure and mark for first ⅜″ from front edge and 2½″ from right edge. Mark for second 1″ from front edge and 1⅝″ from right edge.

21. To indicate two left-side rigging postholes, mea-

sure and mark for first ⅜″ from front edge and 3⅞″ from left edge. Mark for second 1″ from front edge and 3″ from left edge.

22. Using a 3/32″ bit, drill ⅛″-deep postholes.

23. Matching pilot holes in base to pilot holes in tent bottoms, wood-glue and screw tents to base.

24. Paint base very dark green.

25. For rigging posts, cut nine 9/16″ lengths from the thickest part of toothpicks.

26. Wood-glue rigging posts into postholes.

27. For yellow tent rigging, cut nine 6″ lengths of gold elastic cord. For each rigging, tie a knot close to one end and tacky-glue knot into rigging hole in tent. Tie other end around rigging post. Tacky-glue knot to post and trim end to ½″.

28. Use four red-bead-head straight pins for flagpoles.

29. Following 12–21, cut two flags from yellow, one from blue, and one from red adhesive vinyl. To assemble each flag, remove protective paper, place flagpole (below bead) across center, and adhere the two sides together. (Use one yellow flag for pink tent.)

30. Referring to 12–1, insert flagpoles into center top of tents and tacky-glue to secure.

PINK TENT

1. Following 12–17, cut two tent top halves from ¼ × 5¼ lattice. Flop one over to reverse it.

2. For corner angles, trim long straight edge of each, from base to tip to 55°, angled from front of tent to back.

3. For tent bottom, cut two 3⅜″ wide × 4″ high rectangles from ½ × 5½ lattice.

4. For corner angles, trim one long straight edge of each to 55°.

5. Wood-glue tent bottom corner angles together.

6. Whittle off both top back corners, angling the cut from the back to the top front corners.

7. Wood-glue tent top corner angles together.

8. Wood-glue tent top to front of tent bottom overlapping ½″.

9. For tent bottom seam detail, use the 3¾″ length of ⅛″ dowelling.

10. Whittle one end to fit into contour of tent top.

11. Wood-glue seam detail to tent bottom seam.

12. Paint tent top medium pink and tent bottom white.

13. Referring to 12–1, insert flagpole into center top of tent and tacky-glue to secure.

FLOWERS

1. Following 12–22, cut flowers from ¼ × 5¼ lattice. Transfer outline of each flower onto cut-out.

2. Paint top flower light blue, right flower dark pink, and left flower medium yellow. Paint leaves and back of flowers very dark green.

3. For flower centers, cut a 10mm bead in half and use the 8mm half-bead reserved from Giggles's nose.

4. Paint flower centers medium orange.

5. Tacky-glue the 8mm flower center to center of top flower and the two 10mm flower centers to centers of right and left flowers.

SHRUBS (MAKE 2)

See Project 5 for large shrub directions.

13 · A Night at the Ballet

MATERIALS

Beads

seven white 25mm large-hole wood beads
one white 20mm large-hole wood bead
fourteen white 8mm regular-hole wood beads
twenty-nine 3mm silver-plated beads

Wood

36″ length of ¼″ dowelling

13–1.

1⅜" length of ⁷⁄₁₆" dowelling
10" length of ⅝" dowelling
36" length of ¼ × 5¼ clear pine lattice
one 1¹¹⁄₁₆" wooden egg
seven ice-cream sticks
two flat wooden ice-cream spoons
seven round toothpicks

Paints (Acrylic)

Flesh, black, white, dark pink, dark orange, medium yellow, pale blue-grey, dark blue-grey, and medium purple

Fabric and Trims

white, black, and orange curly chenille hair
2¼ yards of ¹⁄₁₆"-wide white satin ribbon
24" of ⅛"-wide white grosgrain ribbon
2⅜" length of ¾"-wide white lace
13" × 13" square of white tulle
four 1¼"-long white down feathers

Miscellaneous

small amount of white tagboard
sewing needle
white sewing thread

DAME JOSEPHINE

1. For head, cover one hole of a 25mm bead with a tagboard circle. Paint head flesh.

2. Referring to 13–2, paint eyes black, hair white, and cheeks dark pink.

3. For body, cut a 1" length of ⅝" dowelling.

4. Draw a line down length of body to indicate center front.

5. Measure and mark position of left and right arms ⅛" from top of body and ⁹⁄₁₆" from center line. At each mark, whittle a ¼" × ¼" area flat.

6. Sand bottom edge of head to expose raw wood.

7. Wood-glue head to top of body so head faces forward.

8. For legs, cut a 2⅝" length of ¼" dowelling.

9. To indicate angle of ankle cut, measure and mark 1¼" from right end. Rotate dowelling so mark is away from you, then measure and mark 1¼" from left end. Cut angle.

10. To indicate angle of each hip cut, place leg on work surface so the ankle end is at top. Rotate leg so the face of the ankle angle cut is facing down. At opposite end, measure and mark ⅛" from flat end. Cut angle.

11. With side of right leg flush with side of body and positioned ¹⁄₁₆" closer to front of the body than the back, wood-glue right hip to bottom of body so ankle juts forward.

12. With side of left leg flush with side of body and centered from front to back, wood-glue left hip to bottom of body so ankle juts back and crosses over back of right leg.

13. For ballet slippers, cut two ¹¹⁄₁₆" lengths from the rounded ends of an ice-cream stick. Sand corners to round them.

14. Wood-glue ballet slippers to bottom of legs so heels are flush with back of ankles, right toe points towards her right, left toe points towards her left, side of left slipper is ⅛" from heel of right slipper, and Dame Josephine stands upright.

15. For arms, cut two 1⅛" lengths of ¼" dowelling.

16. To indicate angle of each elbow cut, measure and mark ⁹⁄₁₆" from right end. Rotate dowelling so mark is away from you, then measure and mark ½" from left end. Cut angle.

17. At flat end of two lower (shorter) arms, attach 8mm-bead hands.

18. To complete the arms, reverse the elbow cuts and wood-glue upper and lower arms together so elbow joints are crooked.

19. For each arm, whittle inside area of shoulder flat.

20. With shoulders even with top of body, wood-glue tops of arms to body so hands are raised up.

21. Paint hands, arms, top edge of torso, and top ⁵⁄₁₆" of torso flesh.

22. Paint ballet slippers, legs (tights), bottom edge of torso, and bottom ¹¹⁄₁₆" of torso (leotard) white.

23. Paint two ⅛"-wide white leotard straps on each side of front and back.

24. For topknot, cut a 1½" length of white hair. Beginning at center back of head, coil and tacky-glue hair into a ¾"-diameter circle on center top of head, piling end of hair on top of circle.

25. For ballet slipper ties, cut two 6½" lengths of white satin ribbon.

26. For each tie, tacky-glue center of ribbon to center back of leg, ¾" from bottom of slipper.

27. Crisscross twice down front of leg and end at back of ankle.

13–2. *Dame Josephine.*

13–3. *Jacques.*

28. Trim ends so they overlap ⅛″ and tacky-glue in place.

29. For fancy leotard, tacky-glue the 2⅜″ length of ¾″-wide white lace around body, overlapping short edges at center back.

30. For tutu, cut a 1½″ × 13″ rectangle from white tulle. Fold in half lengthwise. With white sewing thread used double in needle, run small gathering stitches along the fold. Draw threads at each end to gather.

31. Place tutu around waist and tie thread ends securely at center back. Dot knot with tacky glue and trim thread ends close to knot.

32. For bow accent at back of leotard, cut a 4″ length of white grosgrain ribbon.

33. Tie ribbon into a ⅞″-wide bow. Secure knot with tacky glue. Trim ends at an angle. Tacky-glue to upper center back of leotard.

34. For tiara, string eighteen 3mm silver-plated beads onto a 10″ length of white thread.

35. Place tiara around base of topknot and tie ends securely at center back of head. Dot knot with tacky glue and trim thread ends close to knot.

36. Tacky-glue two white down feathers to center back of topknot.

JACQUES

1. For head, cover one hole of a 25mm bead with a tagboard circle. Paint head flesh.

2. Referring to 13–3, paint eyes black and cheeks dark pink.

3. For body, cut a ¹⁵⁄₁₆″ length of ⅝″ dowelling.

4. Draw a line down length of body to indicate center front.

5. Measure and mark position of left and right arms ⅛″ from top of body and ⁹⁄₁₆″ from center line. At each mark, whittle a ¼″ × ¼″ area flat.

6. Sand bottom edge of head to expose raw wood.

7. Wood-glue head to top of body so head faces forward.

8. For legs, cut two 1⅜″ lengths of ¼″ dowelling.

9. Wood-glue legs to bottom of body so sides of legs are ¹⁄₁₆″ from sides of body and centered from front to back.

10. For ballet slippers, cut two ¹¹⁄₁₆″ lengths from the rounded ends of an ice-cream stick. Sand corners to round them.

11. Wood-glue ballet slippers to bottom of legs so heels butt each other, toes point out, and Jacques stands upright.

12. For arms, cut two 1⅛″ lengths of ¼″ dowelling.

13. To indicate angle of each shoulder/elbow cut, measure and mark ½″ from right end. Rotate dowelling so mark is away from you, then measure and mark ⁹⁄₁₆″ from left end. Cut angle.

14. At flat end of two lower (shorter) arms, attach 8mm-bead hands.

15. To complete each arm, wood-glue angled end of lower arm to flat end of upper arm, making sure elbow is crooked and the shoulder angle of upper arm is parallel with the angled end of lower arm.

16. With shoulders even with top of body, wood-glue arms to body so hands are raised and slightly forward.

17. Paint hands flesh.

18. For V-neck opening in shirt, measure and mark a ⅜″-wide × ⅜″-long triangle at center front of body. Paint triangle flesh.

19. Paint ballet slippers, legs (tights), rest of body, and arms (shirt) black.

20. For hair, cut sufficient ⅛″ lengths of black hair to cover head. Tacky-glue hair to head.

CHRISTINE

1. For head, cover one hole of a 25mm bead with a tagboard circle. Paint head flesh.

2. Referring to 13–4, paint eyes and hair black, and cheeks dark pink.

3. For body, cut a 1″ length of ⅝″ dowelling.

4. Draw a line down length of body to indicate center front.

5. Measure and mark position of left and right arms ⅛″ from top of body and ⁹⁄₁₆″ from center line. At each mark, whittle a ¼″ × ¼″ area flat.

6. Sand bottom edge of head to expose raw wood.

7. Wood-glue head to top of body so head faces forward.

8. For legs, cut two 1⁵⁄₁₆″ lengths of ¼″ dowelling.

9. Wood-glue legs to bottom of body so sides of legs are flush with sides of body and centered from front to back.

10. For ballet slippers, cut two ¹¹⁄₁₆″ lengths from the rounded ends of an ice-cream stick. Sand corners to round them.

11. Wood-glue ballet slippers to bottom of legs so heels extend ⅛″ behind ankles, toes point out, and Christine stands upright.

12. For arms, cut two 1⁵⁄₁₆″ lengths of ¼″ dowelling.

13. At flat end of each arm, attach an 8mm-bead hand.

14. With shoulders even with top of body, wood-glue tops of arms to body so hands are at shoulder level.

15. For topknot, cut a 1″ length of black hair. Tacky-glue ends together to form a circle. Tacky-glue topknot to center top of head.

16. Paint hands, arms, top edge of torso, and top ⁵⁄₁₆″ of torso flesh.

17. Paint ballet slippers, legs (tights), bottom edge of torso, and bottom ¹¹⁄₁₆″ of torso (leotard) white.

18. Paint two ⅛″-wide white leotard straps on each side of front and back.

19. For ballet slipper ties, cut two 6½″ lengths of white satin ribbon.

20. For each tie, tacky-glue center of ribbon to center back of leg, ¾″ from bottom of slipper.

21. Crisscross twice down front of leg and end at back of ankle.

22. Trim ends so they overlap ⅛″ and tacky-glue in place.

23. For tutu, cut a 1½″ × 13″ rectangle from white tulle. Fold in half lengthwise. With white sewing thread used double in needle, run small gathering stitches along the fold. Draw threads at each end to gather.

24. Place tutu around waist and tie thread ends securely at center back. Dot knot with tacky glue and trim thread ends close to knot.

25. For bow accent at back of leotard, cut a 4″ length of white grosgrain ribbon.

26. Tie ribbon into a ⅞″-wide bow. Secure knot with tacky glue. Trim ends at an angle.

27. Tacky-glue bow to upper center back of leotard.

JOANNA

1. For head, cover one hole of a 25mm bead with a tagboard circle. Paint head flesh.

2. Referring to 13–5, paint eyes and hair black, and cheeks dark pink.

3. For body, cut a 1″ length of ⅝″ dowelling.

4. Draw a line down length of body to indicate center front.

5. Measure and mark position of left and right arms ⅛″ from top of body and ⁹⁄₁₆″ from center line. At each mark, whittle a ¼″ × ¼″ area flat.

6. Sand bottom edge of head to expose raw wood.

7. Wood-glue head to top of body so head faces forward.

8. For legs, cut two 1⁵⁄₁₆″ lengths of ¼″ dowelling.

9. Wood-glue legs to bottom of body so sides of legs are ¹⁄₁₆″ from sides of body and centered from front to back.

10. For ballet slippers, cut two ¹¹⁄₁₆″ lengths from the rounded ends of an ice-cream stick. Sand corners to round them.

11. Wood-glue ballet slippers to bottom of legs so heels butt each other, toes point out, and Joanna stands upright.

12. For arms, cut two 1″ lengths of ¼″ dowelling.

13. To indicate angle of each elbow cut, measure and mark ½″ from right end. Rotate dowelling so mark is away from you, then measure and mark ⁷⁄₁₆″ from left end. Cut angle.

14. At flat end of two lower (shorter) arms, attach 8mm-bead hands.

15. To complete the arms, reverse the elbow cuts and wood-glue upper and lower arms together so elbow joints are crooked.

16. For each arm, whittle inside area of shoulder flat.

17. With shoulders even with top of body, wood-

13–4. *Christine.*

13–5. *Joanna.*

13–6. *Lisa.*

13–7. *Frances.*

glue top of arms to body so hands hang down.

18. For topknot, cut a 1″ length of black hair. Tacky-glue ends together to form a circle. Tacky-glue top-knot to center top of head.

19. Repeat steps 16 to 27 of Christine.

LISA

1. For head, cover one bead hole of a 25mm bead with a tagboard circle. Paint head flesh.

2. Referring to 13–6, paint eyes and hair black, and cheeks dark pink.

3. For body, cut a 1″ length of ⅝″ dowelling.

4. Draw a line down length of body to indicate center front.

5. Measure and mark position of left and right arms ⅛″ from top of body and ⁹⁄₁₆″ from center line. At each mark, whittle a ¼″ × ¼″ area flat.

6. Sand bottom edge of head to expose raw wood.

7. Wood-glue head to top of body so head faces forward.

8. For legs, cut a 2⅝″ length of ¼″ dowelling.

9. To indicate angle of ankle cut, measure and mark 1¼″ from right end. Rotate dowelling so mark is away from you, then measure and mark 1¼″ from left end. Cut angle.

10. To indicate angle of each hip cut, place leg on work surface so the ankle end is at top. Rotate leg so the face of the ankle angle cut is facing down. At opposite end, measure and mark ⅛″ from flat end. Cut angle.

11. With side of right leg flush with side of body and positioned ¹⁄₁₆″ closer to the front of the body than the back, wood-glue right hip to bottom of body so ankle juts forward.

12. With side of left leg flush with side of body and centered from front to back, wood-glue left hip to bottom of body so ankle juts back and crosses over back of right leg.

13. For ballet slippers, cut two ⅝″ lengths from the rounded ends of an ice-cream stick. Sand corners to round them.

14. Wood-glue ballet slippers to bottom of legs so heels are flush with back of ankles, right toe points forward, left toe points towards her left and butts heel of right slipper, and Lisa stands upright.

15. For left arm, cut a 1″ length of ¼″ dowelling.

16. To indicate angle of left elbow cut, measure and mark ½″ from right end. Rotate dowelling so mark is away from you, then measure and mark ⁷⁄₁₆″ from left end. Cut angle.

17. For right arm, cut a 1¹⁄₁₆″ length of ¼″ dowelling.

18. At flat end of left lower (shorter) arm and one end of right arm, attach an 8mm-bead hand.

19. To complete the left arm, reverse the elbow cuts and wood-glue upper and lower arms together so elbow joint is crooked.

20. For left arm, whittle inside area of shoulder flat.

21. With shoulders even with top of body, wood-glue right arm to body so hand is at shoulder level. Wood-glue left arm to body so hand is raised up.

22. For chignon, cut a 1″ length of black hair. Tacky-glue ends together to form a circle. Tacky-glue to center back of head.

23. Repeat steps 16 to 27 of Christine.

FRANCES

1. For head, cover one hole of a 25mm bead with a tagboard circle. Paint head flesh.

2. Referring to 13–7, paint eyes and hair black, and cheeks dark pink.

3. For body, cut a 1″ length of ⅝″ dowelling.

4. Draw a line down length of body to indicate center front.

5. Measure and mark position of left and right arms ⅛″ from top of body and ⁹⁄₁₆″ from center line. At each mark, whittle a ¼″ × ¼″ area flat.

6. Measure and mark position of right leg ⅛″ from bottom of body and ⁹⁄₁₆″ from center line. At mark, whittle a ¼″ × ¼″ area flat.

7. Sand bottom edge of head to expose raw wood.

8. Wood-glue head to top of body so head faces forward.

9. For legs, cut a 2⅝″ length of ¼″ dowelling.

115

10. To indicate angle of left ankle/right hip cut, measure and mark 1¼″ from right end. Rotate dowelling so mark is away from you, then measure and mark 1¼″ from left end. Cut angle.
11. With side of left leg ⅛″ from side of body and centered from front to back, wood-glue flat end of left leg to bottom of body so the point of ankle angle is at inside of leg.
12. With point of right hip angle flush with bottom of body, wood-glue leg to side of body so ankle points up.
13. For left ballet slipper, cut a ¾″ length from the rounded end of an ice-cream stick. For right ballet slipper, cut a 9/16″ length from the other rounded end of the ice-cream stick. Sand corners to round them.
14. Wood-glue left ballet slipper to bottom of left leg so heel extends ⅛″ behind ankle, toe points towards her left, and Frances stands upright.
15. Wood-glue right ballet slipper to bottom of right leg so heel of slipper is flush with back of ankle and toe points up.
16. For right arm, cut a 1 3/16″ length of ¼″ dowelling.
17. To indicate angle of right elbow cut, measure and mark ⅝″ from right end. Rotate dowelling so mark is away from you, then measure and mark ½″ from left end. Cut angle.
18. For left arm, cut a 1″ length of ¼″ dowelling.
19. At flat end of lower (shorter) right arm and one end of left arm, attach an 8mm-bead hand.
20. To complete the right arm, reverse the elbow cuts and wood-glue upper and lower arms together so elbow joint is crooked.
21. For right arm, whittle inside area of shoulder flat.
22. With shoulders even with top of body, wood-glue top of left arm to body so the hand is at shoulder level. Wood-glue right arm to body so hand is raised up.

13–8. *Patricia.*

23. For topknot, cut a 1″ length of black hair. Tacky-glue ends together to form a circle. Tacky-glue topknot to center top of head.
24. Repeat steps 16 to 27 of Christine.

PATRICIA

1. For head, cover one hole of a 25mm bead with a tagboard circle. Paint head flesh.
2. Referring to 13–8, paint eyes black, hair dark orange, and cheeks dark pink.
3. For body, cut a 1″ length of ⅝″ dowelling.
4. Draw a line down length of body to indicate center front.
5. Measure and mark position of left and right arms ⅛″ from top of body and 9/16″ from center line. At each mark, whittle a ¼″ × ¼″ area flat.
6. Sand bottom edge of head to expose raw wood.
7. Wood-glue head to top of body so head faces forward.
8. For legs, cut a 2⅝″ length of ¼″ dowelling.
9. To indicate angle of ankle cut, measure and mark 1¼″ from right end. Rotate dowelling so mark is away from you, then measure and mark 1¼″ from left end. Cut angle.
10. To indicate angle of each hip cut, place leg on work surface so the ankle end is at top. Rotate leg so the face of the ankle angle cut is facing down. At opposite end, measure and mark ⅛″ from flat end. Cut angle.
11. With side of right leg flush with side of body and positioned 1/16″ closer to the front of the body than the back, wood-glue right hip to bottom of body so ankle juts forward.
12. With side of left leg flush with side of body and centered from front to back, wood-glue left hip to bottom of body so ankle juts back and crosses over back of right leg.
13. For ballet slippers, cut two 11/16″ lengths from the rounded ends of an ice-cream stick. Sand corners to round them.
14. Wood-glue ballet slippers to bottom of legs so heels are flush with back of ankles, right toe points towards her right, left toe points towards her left, side of left slipper is ⅛″ from heel of right slipper, and Patricia stands upright.
15. For left arm, cut a 1″ length of ¼″ dowelling.
16. To indicate angle of left elbow cut, measure and

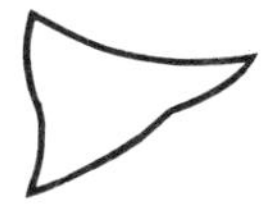

13–9. *Pattern for swan's beak.*

13–10. *Swan.*

mark 3/8″ from right end. Rotate dowelling so mark is away from you, then measure and mark 1/2″ from left end. Cut angle.

17. For right arm, cut a 1 1/16″ length of 1/4″ dowelling.

18. To indicate angle of right elbow cut, measure and mark 1/2″ from right end. Rotate dowelling so mark is away from you, then measure and mark 1/2″ from left end. Cut angle.

19. At flat end of left lower (shorter) arm and one right arm half, attach an 8mm-bead hand.

20. To complete the left arm, reverse the elbow cuts and wood-glue upper and lower arms together so elbow joint is crooked.

21. To complete the right arm, wood-glue angled end of lower arm to flat end of upper arm, making sure the elbow is crooked and the shoulder angle of the upper arm is parallel with the angled end of the lower arm.

22. For left arm, whittle inside area of shoulder flat.

23. With shoulders even with top of body, wood-glue left arm to body so hand hangs down. Wood-glue top of right arm to body so hand points out to the right and is at waist level.

24. For topknot, cut a 1″ length of orange hair. Tacky-glue ends together to form a circle. Tacky-glue topknot to center top of head.

25. Repeat steps 16 to 27 of Christine.

SWAN

1. For head, cover one hole of the 20mm bead with a tagboard circle.
2. Following 13–9, cut beak from 1/4 × 5 1/4 lattice.
3. With bottom edge of beak 1/8″ from bottom edge of head, tacky-glue beak to head.
4. Paint head white.
5. Referring to 13–10, paint eyes and lower beak black. Paint cheeks dark pink and upper beak and nostrils medium yellow.
6. For body, use the 1 11/16″ wooden egg.
7. To indicate position of bottom, neck, wings, and tail, draw a horizontal line around the equator parallel with the flat end (front) of body. Draw one vertical line around the meridian bisecting the flat end. Draw another line around the meridian at right angles to the first, dividing the flat end into four equal parts.
8. Where one meridian line crosses the equator, whittle a 1/2″ × 3/4″ oval area (bottom) flat so body will sit flat on work surface.
9. To indicate position of neck, place bottom of body on work surface. Measure and mark 1/8″ from front of body along top meridian line, then measure and mark again 11/16″ from front of body along same line. Whittle a 3/8″-wide area between these two marks flat.
10. To indicate position of each wing, measure and mark 1/2″ from front of body along both sides of meridian lines. Then measure and mark again 13/16″ from front of body along same lines. Whittle a 3/8″-wide area between these two marks flat.
11. For neck, use the 1 3/8″ length of 7/16″ dowelling.
12. To indicate neck/body angle, measure and mark 1/4″ from one cut end. Cut angle.
13. To indicate neck/head angle, place neck on work surface so neck/body angle end is at top. Rotate neck so the face of the neck/body angle cut is facing down. At opposite end, measure and mark 1/8″ from flat end. Cut angle.
14. Wood-glue neck to body so neck angles towards back of body.
15. Sand bottom edge of head to expose raw wood.
16. Wood-glue head to neck so head faces forward.
17. Following 13–11, cut tail from 1/4 × 5 1/4 lattice.
18. Wood-glue tail to center back of body so bottom end of tail is 1/8″ above narrow end of body and tail angles up.
19. Following 13–12, cut two wings from two flat wooden ice-cream spoons. Flop one over to reverse it.
20. With wing tips pointing up, wood-glue wings to each side of body.
21. Paint body white.
22. For tiara, string eleven 3mm silver-plated beads onto a 10″ length of white thread. Tie ends securely. Dot knot with tacky glue and trim thread ends close to knot.

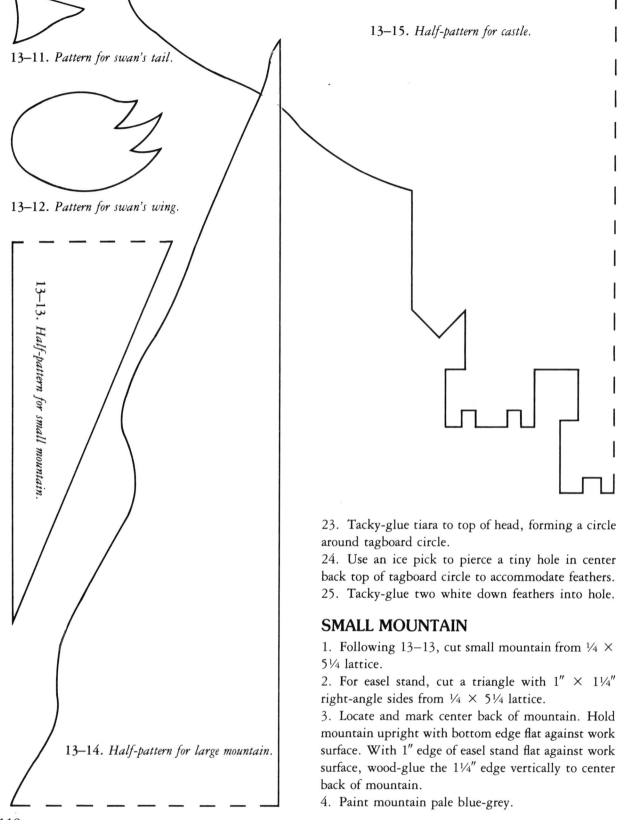

13–11. *Pattern for swan's tail.*

13–12. *Pattern for swan's wing.*

13–13. *Half-pattern for small mountain.*

13–15. *Half-pattern for castle.*

13–14. *Half-pattern for large mountain.*

23. Tacky-glue tiara to top of head, forming a circle around tagboard circle.

24. Use an ice pick to pierce a tiny hole in center back top of tagboard circle to accommodate feathers.

25. Tacky-glue two white down feathers into hole.

SMALL MOUNTAIN

1. Following 13–13, cut small mountain from ¼ × 5¼ lattice.

2. For easel stand, cut a triangle with 1″ × 1¼″ right-angle sides from ¼ × 5¼ lattice.

3. Locate and mark center back of mountain. Hold mountain upright with bottom edge flat against work surface. With 1″ edge of easel stand flat against work surface, wood-glue the 1¼″ edge vertically to center back of mountain.

4. Paint mountain pale blue-grey.

LARGE MOUNTAIN

1. Following 13–14, cut large mountain from ¼ × 5¼ lattice.
2. For easel stand, cut a triangle with 1¼″ × 1¾″ right-angle sides from ¼ × 5¼ lattice.
3. Locate and mark center back of mountain. Hold mountain upright with bottom edge flat against work surface. With 1¼″ edge of easel stand flat against work surface, wood-glue the 1¾″ edge vertically to center back of mountain.
4. Paint mountain dark blue-grey.

CASTLE

1. Following 13–15, cut castle from ¼ × 5¼ lattice.
2. For easel stand, cut a triangle with 1⅜″ × 3¼″ right-angle sides from ¼ × 5¼ lattice.
3. Locate and mark center back of castle. Hold castle upright with bottom edge flat against work surface. With 1⅜″ edge of easel stand flat against work surface, wood-glue the 3¼″ edge vertically to center back of castle.
4. Paint castle medium purple.

14 · Up at the North Pole

MATERIALS

Beads

one white 44mm × 28mm large-hole wood bead
one white 32mm × 22mm large-hole wood bead
five white 20mm large-hole wood beads
one white 16mm × 15mm large-hole wood bead
five white 10mm regular-hole wood beads
fourteen white 8mm regular-hole wood beads
two white 3mm regular-hole wood beads

Wood

26″ length of ³⁄₁₆″ dowelling
6″ length of ¼″ dowelling
10″ length of ⁵⁄₁₆″ dowelling
15″ length of ⅜″ dowelling
6″ length of ½″ dowelling
9″ length of ⅝″ dowelling
1¾″ length of ⅞″ dowelling
12″ length of ¼ × 5¼ clear pine lattice
10″ × 14″ rectangle of ¾″ plywood
one 2½″ wooden egg
fourteen ice-cream sticks
twenty-eight round toothpicks
three square toothpicks

Paints (Acrylic)

Flesh, black, bright red, dark pink, medium pink, dark red brown, medium yellow-green, medium grey-

14–1.

green, ochre, white, dark ultramarine, medium yellow, dark yellow, medium orange, off-white and very dark blue-grey

Fabric and Trims

9″ × 12″ pieces of white, red, and green felt
small amount of white fake fur
one 1″ white pompon
white, orange, and yellow curly chenille hair

Hardware

four ⅝ × 18 wire brads
two 6 × 24 flathead wood screws

Miscellaneous

small amount of white tagboard
small amount of black and brass adhesive vinyl
3⅜″ length of 22-gauge galvanized steel wire
3½″ × 3½″ square of medium-weight cardboard
small amount of heavyweight aluminum foil
yellow and red permanent markers
charcoal

SANTA

1. For head, cover one hole of the 44mm × 28mm bead with a tagboard circle. Paint head flesh.

2. Referring to 14–2, paint eyes black, nose and mouth bright red, and cheeks dark pink.

3. For body, whittle the pointed end of the 2½″ wooden egg to flatten (top).

4. Draw a line down length of body to indicate center front.

5. Measure and mark position of left and right arms ⅜″ from top of body and 1⁵⁄₁₆″ from center line. At each mark, whittle a ⅜″ × ⅜″ area flat.

6. Sand bottom edge of head to expose raw wood.

7. Wood-glue head to top of body so head faces forward.

8. For boots, cut two 1″ lengths from the rounded ends of an ice-cream stick.

9. Wood-glue boots to bottom of body, making sure toes point slightly out and Santa stands upright.

10. For arms, cut a 1¹³⁄₁₆″ length of ⅜″ dowelling.

11. To indicate angle of shoulder cut, measure and mark ¾″ from right end. Rotate dowelling so mark is away from you, the measure and mark ¾″ from left end. Cut angle.

12. At flat end of each arm, attach a 10mm-bead hand.

13. Wood-glue arms to body so hands are slightly above waist level.

14. Paint hands black.

15. Paint boots black.

16. Paint body and arms bright red.

17. For collar, cut a ⁵⁄₁₆″ × 3″ strip from white felt. Tacky-glue around bottom of body, trimming short edges to butt at center back.

18. For hem, cut a ⁵⁄₁₆″ × 6″ strip from white felt. Tacky-glue around bottom of body, trimming short edges to butt at center back.

19. For cuffs, cut two ⁵⁄₁₆″ × 1½″ strips from white felt. Tacky-glue around wrists, trimming short edges to butt at underside of arms.

20. For belt, cut a ¼″ × 6″ strip of black adhesive vinyl. Adhere around waist, overlapping short edges at center back.

21. For buckle, cut a ⅜″ × ½″ rectangle of brass adhesive vinyl. Trim corners to round them. Adhere to center front of belt.

22. For buttons, cut two ¼″-diameter circles from white felt. Tacky-glue down center front with the first button ⅛″ below collar and the second ⅛″ above belt.

23. For eyebrows, cut two tiny one-quarter-moon shapes from white felt. Tacky-glue above eyes.

24. Following 14–3, cut beard from white fake fur. Tacky-glue to face, placing opening in beard over mouth.

25. Following 14–4, cut hat from red felt. Overlap long edges ³⁄₁₆″ and tacky-glue together to form hat.

26. For hair, cut a ⁵⁄₁₆″ × 3″ strip from white fake fur.

14–4. *Pattern for Santa's hat.*

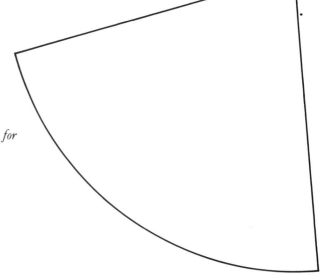

14–3. *Pattern for Santa's beard.*

14–2. *Santa.*

27. With hat seam at center back of head, tacky-glue hat to head, and at the same time, tacky-glue hair around head, tucking the hair under the edge of the hat.

28. For hatband, cut a 5/16″ × 4¼″ strip from white felt. Tacky-glue around edge of hat, trimming short edges to butt at center back.

29. Glue white pompon to tip of hat.

30. Fold hat in half towards Santa's left and tacky-glue to secure.

MRS. CLAUS

1. For head, cover one hole of the 32mm × 22mm bead with a tagboard circle. Paint head flesh.

2. Referring to 14–5, paint eyes black and cheeks medium pink.

3. For body, cut a 1¾″ length of 7/8″ dowelling.

4. Draw a line down length of body to indicate center front.

5. Measure and mark position of left and right arms 3/16″ from top of body and 11/16″ from center line. At each mark, whittle a 3/8″ × 3/8″ area flat.

6. Sand bottom edge of head to expose raw wood.

7. Wood-glue head to top of body so head faces forward.

8. For shoes, cut two 7/8″ lengths from the rounded ends of an ice-cream stick.

9. Wood-glue shoes to bottom of body, making sure toes point slightly out and Mrs. Claus stands upright.

10. For arms, cut a 1⅛″ length of 3/8″ dowelling.

11. To indicate angle of shoulder cut, measure and mark ½″ from right end. Rotate dowelling so mark is away from you, then measure and mark ½″ from left end. Cut angle.

12. At flat end of each arm, attach a 10mm-bead hand.

13. With shoulders even with top edge of body, wood-glue arms to body so hands are at waist level.

14. Paint hands flesh.

15. Paint shoes black.

16. Paint body and arms bright red.

17. For collar, cut a 3/16″ × 3″ strip from white felt. Tacky-glue around neck, trimming short edges to butt at center back.

18. For hem, cut a 3/16″ × 3″ strip from white felt. Tacky-glue around bottom of body, trimming short edges to butt at center back.

19. For cuffs, cut two 3/16″ × 1½″ strips from white felt. Tacky-glue around wrists, trimming short edges to butt at underside of arms.

20. For buttons, cut three ¼″-diameter circles from white felt. Tacky-glue down center front with the first button at top of body edge and the other two spaced ⅛″ apart.

21. Cut three 1″ lengths of white hair. Fold each with slightly uneven ends. Working from her left to right and with folds at top, tacky-glue around front of head, beginning just above Mrs. Claus's left eye. Cut three 1½″ lengths of hair. Fold each with uneven ends. Continuing to work from her left to right, tacky-glue around back of head, leaving a one-curl-width space between first and last curl. Cut a 6½″ length of hair. Tacky-glue one end between the first and last curl, then fill in the empty space at top of head by coiling the hair into a topknot.

ARTISTIC ARTIE

1. For head, cover one hole of a 20mm bead with a tagboard circle. Paint head flesh.

2. Referring to 14–6, paint eyes black and cheeks dark pink.

14–5. *Mrs. Claus.*

14–6. *Artistic Artie.*

14–7. *Artistic Artie's and Helping Hannah's feet.*

14–8. *Pattern for Artistic Artie's and Helping Hannah's hats.*

121

3. For body, cut a 2¹⁄₁₆″ length of ⁵⁄₈″ dowelling.

4. Draw a line down length of body to indicate center front.

5. Measure and mark position of left and right arms ⅛″ from top of body and ½″ from center line. At each mark, whittle a ³⁄₁₆″ × ³⁄₁₆″ area flat.

6. Sand bottom edge of head to expose raw wood.

7. Wood-glue head to top of body so head faces forward.

8. For shoes, cut two ¹¹⁄₁₆″ lengths from the rounded ends of an ice-cream stick. Referring to 14–7, trim one back corner of each shoe so inside edges butt and toes point out.

9. Wood-glue shoes to bottom of body, making sure Artie stands upright.

10. For arms, cut a 1½″ length of ³⁄₁₆″ dowelling.

11. To indicate angle of shoulder cut, measure and mark ¹¹⁄₁₆″ from right end. Rotate dowelling so mark is away from you, then measure and mark ¹¹⁄₁₆″ from left end. Cut angle.

12. At flat end of each arm, attach an 8mm-bead hand.

13. With shoulders even with top edge of body, wood-glue arms to body so left hand is at eye level and right hand is at waist level.

14. Paint hands flesh.

15. Paint shoes dark red-brown.

16. Paint body and arms medium yellow-green.

17. Following 14–8, cut hat from green felt, using pinking shears to cut bottom edge. Overlap long edges ³⁄₁₆″ and tacky-glue together to form hat.

18. With seam at center back of head, tacky-glue hat to head. Fold hat in half towards Artie's back right and tacky-glue to secure.

19. Cut a small curl of orange hair and tacky-glue to center forehead just below edge of hat.

20. For paintbrush, cut a ⅝″ length from the thickest part of a round toothpick. Wood-glue cut end into bead hole in left hand.

21. Paint bottom ⁵⁄₁₆″ of brush handle black and bristles medium grey-green.

WORKBENCH

1. For top, cut a 1¼″ × 4⅜″ rectangle from ¼ × 5¼ lattice.

2. For legs, cut four 1⅜″ lengths of ⅜″ dowelling.

3. Using a ¹⁄₁₆″ bit, drill a ⅛″-deep pilot hole in center top of each leg.

4. On one side of each leg, measure and mark ⅜″ from top. Whittle a ⅜″-wide × ⅛″-deep notch below each mark to accommodate leg supports.

5. At each corner of workbench top, measure and mark ⅜″ from short edge and ¼″ from long edge.

6. Using a ¹⁄₁₆″ bit, drill pilot holes through top at each mark.

7. Wood-glue and nail legs to top, making sure leg notches face the long edge of both sides of workbench.

8. For each leg support, wood-glue an ice-cream stick into notches.

MALLET

1. For mallet head, cut a ⁷⁄₁₆″ length of ⁵⁄₁₆″ dowelling.

2. Using a ³⁄₁₆″ bit, drill a ⅛″-deep hole ⁵⁄₃₂″ from one end.

3. For handle, cut a 1¼″ length of ³⁄₁₆″ dowelling.

4. Wood-glue handle into hole in mallet head.

5. Paint head medium grey-green.

6. Paint bottom ⅜″ of handle black.

7. Paint rest of handle ochre.

8. Paint a ⅛″-wide bright red band on handle ¼″ from mallet head.

BABY DOLL

1. For body, cut a ½″ length of ⁵⁄₁₆″ dowelling.

2. Draw a line down length of body to indicate center front.

3. To indicate position of neck, locate center on one cut end of body.

4. Using a ³⁄₃₂″ bit, drill a ⅛″-deep neck hole.

5. To indicate position of left and right arms, measure and mark ¹⁄₁₆″ from top of body and ⁵⁄₁₆″ from center line.

6. Using a ³⁄₃₂″ bit, drill ⅛″-deep armholes.

7. To indicate position of leg holes on bottom of body, measure and mark ⅛″ from each side edge and center front to back.

8. Using a ³⁄₃₂″ bit, drill ⅛″-deep leg holes.

9. For head and neck, cut ⅜″ off one end of a round toothpick and discard. Wood-glue the cut end of toothpick into a 10mm bead.

10. Trim toothpick so only ³⁄₁₆″ extends beyond hole.

11. Wood-glue neck into neckhole.

12. For arms, cut a round toothpick in half. For hands, wood-glue a 3mm bead onto each pointed end.

13. Trim top of arms so overall length is ⁹⁄₁₆″. Wood-glue arms into armholes.

14. For shoes, cut two ⅛″ lengths of ³⁄₁₆″ dowelling. Using an ice pick, make an indentation in center of each shoe to accommodate legs.

15. For legs, cut two ¾″ lengths from the thickest part of toothpicks.

16. Wood-glue legs into leg holes.

17. Wood-glue legs into indentations in shoes.

18. Paint entire body flesh.

19. Referring to 14–9, paint eyes and eyebrows black.

20. For diaper, paint top ¹⁄₁₆″ of legs, bottom edge of torso, and bottom ³⁄₁₆″ of torso white.

21. For socks, paint bottom ⁵⁄₁₆″ of legs white.

22. Use black to outline diaper waist and legs, and to paint safety pin.

23. Paint shoes black.

24. Cut a tiny curl from orange hair and tacky-glue end into bead hole at top of head.

HELPING HANNAH

1. For head, cover one hole of a 20mm bead with a tagboard circle. Paint head flesh.

2. Referring to 14–10, paint eyes black and cheeks dark pink.

3. For body, cut a 1¹¹⁄₁₆″ length of ⅝″ dowelling.

4. Draw a line down length of body to indicate center front.

5. Measure and mark position of left and right arms ⅛″ from top of body and ⅜″ from center line. At each mark, whittle a ³⁄₁₆″ × ³⁄₁₆″ area flat.

6. Sand bottom edge of head to expose raw wood.

7. Wood-glue head to top of body so head faces forward.

8. For shoes, cut two ¹¹⁄₁₆″ lengths from the rounded ends of an ice-cream stick. Referring to 14–7, trim one back corner of each shoe so inside edges butt and toes point out.

9. Wood-glue shoes to bottom of body, making sure Hannah stands upright.

10. For arms, cut a 1½″ length of ³⁄₁₆″ dowelling.

11. To indicate angle of shoulder cut, measure and mark ¹¹⁄₁₆″ from right end. Rotate dowelling so mark is away from you, then measure and mark ¹¹⁄₁₆″ from left end. Cut angle.

12. At flat end of each arm, attach an 8mm-bead hand.

13. With shoulders even with top edge of body, wood-glue arms to body so hands are at waist level.

14. Repeat steps 14 to 17 of Artistic Artie.

15. With seam at center back of head, tacky-glue hat to head. Fold hat in half towards Hannah's right and tacky-glue to secure.

16. Cut two small curls of yellow hair and tacky-glue to each side of head just below edge of hat.

PAINT CANS (MAKE 3)

1. For each can, cut a ½″ length of ½″ dowelling.

2. In center top of can, use a ³⁄₃₂″ bit to drill a ⅛″-deep brush-handle hole at an angle.

3. Paint outside of can white.

4. Paint top of can and drips down the sides. Paint one can bright red, one dark ultramarine, and one medium yellow.

5. At each side of can, use medium grey-green to paint a small dot for wire-handle base.

6. Use an ice pick to make a shallow indentation in center of each dot to accommodate wire handles.

7. For handle, cut a 1⅛″ length of wire. Using needle-nose pliers, bend it into a handle shape.

8. Use needle-nose pliers to embed handle ends into indentations in can. Dot with tacky glue to secure.

9. For paintbrush handle, cut a ½″ length from the thickest part of a round toothpick. Paint handle black. Tacky-glue handle into brush-handle hole.

HAMMERING HANK

1. For head, cover one hole of a 20mm bead with a tagboard circle. Paint head flesh.

2. Referring to 14–11, paint eyes black and cheeks dark pink.

3. For body, cut a 1″ length of ⅝″ dowelling.

4. Draw a line down length of body to indicate center front.

5. Measure and mark position of left and right arms ³⁄₁₆″ from top of body and ⁷⁄₁₆″ from center line. At each mark, whittle a ¼″ × ¼″ area flat.

6. Measure and mark position of right and left legs ³⁄₁₆″ from bottom edge of body and ¼″ from center line. At each mark, whittle a ¼″ × ¼″ area flat.

7. Sand bottom edge of head to expose raw wood.

8. Wood-glue head to top of body so head faces forward.

9. For legs, cut two ⅞″ lengths of ⁵⁄₁₆″ dowelling.

10. Wood-glue legs to body.

11. For shoes, cut two ⁷⁄₁₆″ lengths from the rounded ends of an ice-cream stick.

12. With Hank sitting, wood-glue shoes to bottom of legs so heels are flush with back of ankles and toes point out.

13. For arms, cut a 1¹⁄₁₆″ length of ¼″ dowelling.

14. To indicate angle of shoulder cut, measure and mark ⁷⁄₁₆″ from right end. Rotate dowelling so mark is away from you, then measure and mark ⁷⁄₁₆″ from left end. Cut angle.

15. Using a ³⁄₃₂″ bit, drill a ⅛″-deep hole into flat end of each arm.

16. With shoulders even with top edge of body, wood-glue arms to body so left wrist is at eye level and right wrist is at cheek level.

17. For hammer hole in right hand, use a ³⁄₃₂″ bit to drill a ⅛″-deep hole in the side of an 8mm bead.

18. At flat end of left arm, attach an 8mm-bead hand. At flat end of right arm, attach the right-bead hand, making sure the drilled hole faces up.

19. Paint hands flesh.

20. Paint shoes dark red-brown.

21. Paint body, arms, and legs medium yellow-green.

22. Following 14–12, cut hat from green felt, using pinking shears to cut bottom edge. Overlap long edges ³⁄₁₆″ and tacky-glue together to form hat.

23. With seam at center back of head, tacky-glue hat to head.

24. Cut a small curl of yellow hair and tacky-glue to center forehead just below edge of hat.

25. For hammer head, cut a ⁵⁄₁₆″ length of ³⁄₁₆″ dowelling.

26. Using a ³⁄₃₂″ bit, drill a ⅛″-deep hole in center of hammer head.

27. For handle, cut a 1⅛″ length from the thickest part of a round toothpick.

28. Wood-glue end of toothpick into hole in hammer head.

29. Wood-glue end of handle into drilled hole in hand.

30. Paint hammer head black and handle bright red.

HAMMERING HELEN

1. For head, cover one hole of a 20mm bead with a tagboard circle. Paint head flesh.

2. Referring to 14–13, paint eyes black and cheeks dark pink.

3. For body, cut a ¹³⁄₁₆″ length of ⅝″ dowelling.

4. Repeat steps 4 to 8 of Hammering Hank.

5. Wood-glue head to top of body so head faces forward.

6. For legs, cut two ¹³⁄₁₆″ lengths of ⁵⁄₁₆″ dowelling.

7. Wood-glue legs to body.

8. For shoes, cut two ⁷⁄₁₆″ lengths from the rounded ends of an ice-cream stick.

9. With Helen sitting, wood-glue shoes to bottom of legs so heels are flush with work surface.

10. For arms, cut two ⅝″ lengths of ¼″ dowelling.

11. Using a ³⁄₃₂″ bit, drill a ⅛″-deep hole into one end of each arm to accommodate hands.

12. With shoulders ¹⁄₁₆″ from top edge of body, wood-glue arms to body so they are parallel with legs.

13. Repeat step 17 of Hammering Hank.

14–9. *Baby doll.*

14–10. *Helping Hannah.*

14–11. *Hammering Hank.*

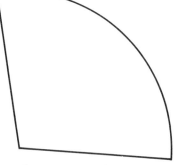

14–12. *Pattern for Hammering Hank's and Helen's hats.*

14–13. *Hammering Helen.*

124

14. At flat end of left arm, attach an 8mm-bead hand. At flat end of right arm, attach the right-bead hand, making sure the drilled hole is facing forward and slightly up.

15. Repeat steps 19 to 30 of Hammering Hank. Substitute orange hair for yellow hair.

DOLLHOUSE

1. Following 14–14, cut dollhouse from ¾″ plywood.

2. For roof, cut four ¹⁵⁄₁₆″ lengths of ice-cream stick.

3. For each side of roof, butt two roof pieces together. At peak, sand underside edges of each roof piece at an angle so they butt tightly together.

4. Wood-glue roof pieces to dollhouse.

5. For chimney, cut a ⅝″ length of ³⁄₁₆″ dowelling.

6. For chimney hole, on left side of roof, measure and mark ⅜″ from roof peak and center front to back.

7. Using a ³⁄₁₆″ bit, drill a ⅛″-deep chimney hole.

8. Wood-glue chimney into hole.

9. Paint house white.

10. Referring to 14–1, paint windows medium yellow.

11. Paint door, window frames, and shutters black.

12. Paint roof bright red.

13. Paint chimney and outline of roof shingles black.

HANDSAW

1. For handle, cut a ⁹⁄₁₆″ length of ¼″ dowelling.

2. To accommodate saw blade, rout out a ¹⁄₁₆″-deep groove down length of handle.

3. Following 14–16, cut saw blade from an ice-cream stick.

4. Wood-glue blade into groove in handle with top of blade flush with one end of handle.

5. Paint blade medium grey-green and handle ochre.

TOPSY-TURVY TINA

1. For head, cover one hole of a 20mm bead with a tagboard circle. Paint head flesh.

2. Referring to 14–15, paint eyes black and cheeks dark pink.

3. For body, cut a ⅞″ length of ⅝″ dowelling.

4. Draw a line down length of body to indicate center front.

5. Measure and mark position of left and right arms

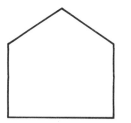

14–14. *Pattern for dollhouse.*

14–15. *Topsy-Turvy Tina.*

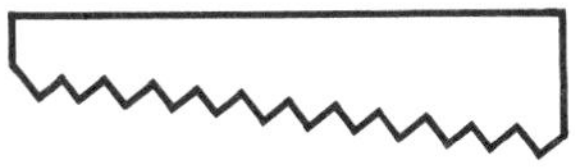

14–16. *Pattern for handsaw blade.*

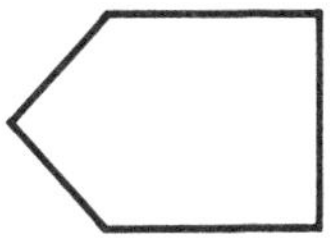

14–18. *School bus.*

14–17. *Pattern for train.*

³⁄₁₆″ from top of body and ⁷⁄₁₆″ from center line. At each mark, whittle a ¼″ × ¼″ area flat.

6. Measure and mark position of right and left legs ³⁄₁₆″ from bottom edge of body and ¼″ from center line. At each mark, whittle a ¼″ × ¼″ area flat.

7. Sand bottom edge of head to expose raw wood.

8. Wood-glue head to top of body so head faces forward.

9. For upper legs, cut two ⅝″ lengths of ⁵⁄₁₆″ dowelling.

10. At one end of each upper leg, whittle a ⅛″-deep × ¼″-long notch to accommodate lower legs.

11. For lower legs, cut two ⅝″ lengths of ⁵⁄₁₆″ dowelling.

12. Wood-glue tops of lower legs to notches at bottom of upper legs.

13. With Tina standing on her head, wood-glue tops of upper legs to body, making sure ankles point up.

14. For shoes, cut two ⁷⁄₁₆″ lengths from the rounded ends of an ice-cream stick.

15. Wood-glue shoes to bottom of legs so shoe heels are flush with back of ankles and sides of shoes are parallel with upper legs.

16. For arms, cut two ⅝″ lengths of ¼″ dowelling.

17. At one end of each arm, attach an 8mm-bead hand.

18. With shoulders ¹⁄₁₆″ from top edge of body, wood-glue arms to body.

19. Paint hands flesh.

20. Paint shoes dark red-brown.

21. Paint body, arms, and legs medium yellow-green.

22. For hat, use pinking shears to cut a 1″-diameter circle from green felt. Tacky-glue hat to top of head.

23. Cut five ⅜″ and five ⅝″ lengths of yellow hair. Placing them vertically and just below edge of hat, tacky-glue the five shorter curls around front of head and the five longer curls around back of head.

TRAIN

1. For engine compartment, cut two ⅝″ × ⅞″ rectangles from ¼ × 5¼ lattice. Wood-glue broad faces together.

2. Following 14–17, cut engine from ¼ × 5¼ lattice.

3. With bottom edges even, wood-glue back edge of engine to compartment.

4. For smokestack, cut a ½″ length of ½″ dowelling. Wood-glue to top of engine.

5. For roof, cut two 1⅛″ lengths of ice-cream stick. Placing them side by side and centered, wood-glue to roof.

6. For back wheels, cut four ⅛″ lengths of ½″ dowelling. Wood-glue two wheels to each side of engine compartment.

7. For front wheels, cut two ⅛″ lengths of ⅜″ dowelling. Wood-glue wheels to each side of engine.

8. Paint engine and compartment black.

9. Referring to 14–1, paint one window on each side of compartment white.

10. Paint roof bright red, wheels medium grey-green, and wheel centers black.

11. For water car base, cut a ⅝″ × ⅞″ rectangle from ¼ × 5¼ lattice.

12. For wheels, cut four ⅛″ lengths of ⅜″ dowelling. Wood-glue two wheels to each side of base.

13. For water tank, whittle one side of the 16mm × 15mm bead to flatten. Cover holes with tagboard circles.

14. Wood-glue whittled area of water tank to center of base.

15. Referring to 14–1, paint base dark ultramarine, tank white, wheels medium grey-green, and wheel centers black.

16. For logger base, cut a ½″ × ⅞″ rectangle from ¼ × 5¼ lattice.

17. For wheels, cut four ⅛″ lengths of ⅜″ dowelling. Wood-glue two wheels to each side of base.

18. Referring to 14–1, paint base black, wheels medium grey-green and wheel centers black.

19. For logs, cut twelve 1¹⁄₁₆″ lengths from the thickest part of round toothpicks.

20. Paint logs dark red-brown.

21. Tacky-glue logs to base, stacking them in a pyramid.

22. For caboose, cut two ⁹⁄₁₆″ × ⅞″ rectangles from ¼ × 5¼ lattice. Wood-glue broad faces together.

23. For roof, cut two 1⅛″ lengths of ice-cream stick. Placing them side by side and centered, wood-glue to roof.

24. For wheels, cut four ⅛″ lengths of ⅜″ dowelling. Wood-glue two wheels to each side of caboose.

25. Paint caboose bright red.

26. Referring to 14–1, use white to paint a small window at each side and a wide window at front of caboose. On left side of caboose back, paint a door opening white.

27. Outline window and door frames black.

28. Paint roof black, wheels medium grey-green, and wheel centers black.

SCHOOL BUS

1. For body, cut a ¾″ × 1⅜″ rectangle from ¾″ plywood.

2. For hood, cut away a ⁵⁄₁₆″-high × ⅛″-deep rectangle from one short end of body.

3. For wheels, cut four ⅛″ lengths of ⅜″ dowelling. Wood-glue two wheels to each side of bus.

4. Paint bus and wheels dark yellow.

5. Referring to 14–1, paint front windshield, headlights, and left side windows white.

6. Referring to 14–18, paint back windows, door window, right-side windows, and side-door opening white.

7. Use black to outline front and back windshields, headlights, windows, door opening, and bottom edge of bus.

8. Paint grille, hood ornament, windshield wipers, side-door steps, and double stripes black.

9. For pairs of front and back flashers, paint one bright red and one medium orange.

10. Paint four taillights bright red.

11. Outline flashers and taillights with black.

12. Using black, paint "SCHOOL" above both front and back windshields.

13. Paint tires, hubcaps, and wheel spokes black.

14. For front and rear bumpers, cut two ¾″ lengths from the thickest part of square toothpicks. Paint bumpers black.

15. With bottom edges of bumpers flush with bottom edge of bus, tacky-glue bumpers to front and rear.

FIREPLACE

1. For base, cut a 2½″ × 7⅜″ rectangle from ¼ × 5¼ lattice.

2. Following 14–19, cut fireplace from ¾″ plywood.

3. Wood-glue bottom of fireplace to base, with back edge of fireplace ½″ from back edge of base and centered side to side.

4. To reinforce, measure and mark on bottom of base 1⁹⁄₁₆″ from each side and ¹³⁄₁₆″ from back.

5. Using a ³⁄₃₂″ bit, drill two ½″-deep pilot holes. Insert wood screws.

6. Paint fireplace off-white. Referring to 14–1, paint stonework very dark blue-grey.

7. For opening in chimney stack, measure and mark a ⁵⁄₁₆″ × 1¾″ rectangle at center top and paint black.

8. Paint base medium grey-green.

9. For back wall, use the 3½″ × 3½″ square of cardboard. Paint one side black.

10. Tacky-glue back wall to back of fireplace.

GRATE

1. For base, cut a ⅞″ × 2″ rectangle from ¼ × 5¼ lattice.

2. At each corner, measure and mark ¼″ from short edge and ⅛″ from long edge.

3. Using a ³⁄₃₂″ bit, drill ⅛″-deep holes.

4. Cut the ends off four round toothpicks. Wood-glue cut end of each into an 8mm bead.

5. Trim toothpicks so overall length is ¾″.

6. Wood-glue toothpick ends into holes in base.

7. For legs, cut two ⅞″ lengths of ³⁄₁₆″ dowelling. Whittle one long side of each to flatten.

8. Wood-glue whittled area of legs to right and left side of base bottom with legs parallel to and ¼″ from short edges.

9. Paint grate black.

10. Following 14–20, cut two flames from heavyweight aluminum foil. Flop one over to reverse it. Outline both sides of each with yellow permanent

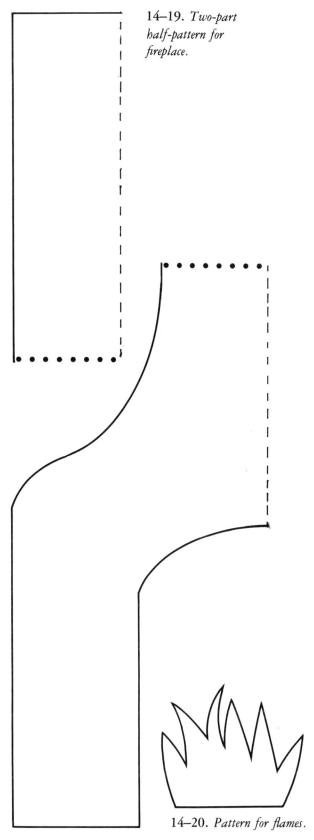

14–19. *Two-part half-pattern for fireplace.*

14–20. *Pattern for flames.*

marker, then color center using red permanent marker.

11. For logs, cut three 1⅜" and five 2" lengths of ³⁄₁₆" dowelling. "Dirty" logs by rubbing with charcoal.

12. Stack and tacky-glue logs together into grate, and, at the same time, insert and tacky-glue flames in place.

MILK TRUCK

1. For body, cut a ½" × ⅞" rectangle from ½ × 5½ lattice.

2. For hood, cut away a ¼"-high × ⅛"-deep rectangle from one short end of body.

3. For wheels, cut four ⅛" lengths of ⅜" dowelling. Wood-glue two wheels to each side of truck.

4. Paint truck dark ultramarine.

5. Referring to 14–1, paint front windshield white.

6. Paint two small back-door windows white.

7. Outline front windshield and back-door windows with black.

8. Paint windshield wiper and define double doors at back, using black.

9. Paint grille medium grey-green.

10. Outline grille and paint vertical lines black.

11. Paint headlights medium yellow.

12. Paint four taillights bright red.

13. Paint wheels white.

14. Paint tires and wheel spokes black.

15. Paint wheel centers bright red.

16. Using white, paint "MILK" along each side.

17. For front bumper, cut one ¾" length from the thickest part of a square toothpick. Paint bumper medium grey-green.

18. With bottom edge of bumper flush with front bottom edge of truck, tacky-glue bumper to front.

INDEX